Money, Interest, and the Structure of Production

Capitalist Thought: Studies in Philosophy, Politics, and Economics

Series Editor: Edward W. Younkins, Wheeling Jesuit University

Mission Statement

This book series is devoted to studying the foundations of capitalism from a number of academic disciplines including, but not limited to, philosophy, political science, economics, law, literature, and history. Recognizing the expansion of the boundaries of economics, this series particularly welcomes proposals for monographs and edited collections that focus on topics from transdisciplinary, interdisciplinary, and multidisciplinary perspectives. Lexington Books will consider a wide range of conceptual, empirical, and methodological submissions, Works in this series will tend to synthesize and integrate knowledge and to build bridges within and between disciplines. They will be of vital concern to academicians, business people, and others in the debate about the proper role of capitalism, business, and business people in economic society.

Advisory Board

Books in Series

The Ontology and Function of Money: The Philosophical Fundamentals of Monetary Institutions by Leonidas Zelmanovitz

Andrew Carnegie: An Economic Biography by Samuel Bostaph

Water Capitalism: Privatize Oceans, Rivers, Lakes, and Aquifers Too by Walter E. Block and Peter Lothian Nelson

Capitalism and Commerce in Imaginative Literature: Perspectives on Business from Novels and Plays edited by Edward W. Younkins

Pride and Profit: The Intersection of Jane Austen and Adam Smith by Cecil E. Bohanon and Michelle Albert Vachris

The Seen, the Unseen, and the Unrealized: How Regulations Affect Our Everyday Lives by Per L. Bylund

Money, Interest, and the Structure of Production: Resolving Some Puzzles in the Theory of Capital by Mateusz Machaj

Money, Interest, and the Structure of Production

Resolving Some Puzzles in the Theory of Capital

Mateusz Machaj

LEXINGTON BOOKS
Lanham • Boulder • New York • London

Published by Lexington Books
An imprint of The Rowman & Littlefield Publishing Group, Inc.
4501 Forbes Boulevard, Suite 200, Lanham, Maryland 20706
www.rowman.com

Unit A, Whitacre Mews, 26-34 Stannary Street, London SE11 4AB

British Library Cataloguing in Publication Information Available

Library of Congress Cataloging-in-Publication Data Available

ISBN 978-1-4985-5754-2 (cloth : alk. paper)
ISBN 978-1-4985-5755-9 (electronic)

∞™ The paper used in this publication meets the minimum requirements of American National Standard for Information Sciences—Permanence of Paper for Printed Library Materials, ANSI/NISO Z39.48-1992.

Printed in the United States of America

To Paulina and Tomasz

Contents

Acknowledgments

I would like to thank Witold Kwaśnicki, Arkadiusz Sieroń, and Mateusz Benedyk for insightful and critical comments on an earlier version of the draft. Special thanks go to Harry David, who helped me to polish (or perhaps de-Polish!) my English.

I owe a great debt to my beloved parents, and to my dear brother Łukasz for continuing academic inspiration. Last but not least I thank my dear wife for her continuous support.

Introduction

This book contributes to the discipline that decades ago would have been called capital theory. Since, in the current era, considerations of what we now refer to as capital are usually placed in financial and monetary economics, the safer way to speak of the discipline is to call it production-structure theory.[1] Increased specialization and improved capital equipment in an overall production process divided into more stages are making the modern capitalist economy more and more sophisticated. One of the first economists to deliberate on successive stages of production was William Stanley Jevons, with his investment figures. After some developments in the 1930s, Jevons's legacy was lost, only to reappear in some of the works by heterodox economists. The aim of the book is to study developments in the field of production-structure theory—especially and importantly regarding the nature of capital—and demonstrate that they can add significant value to crucial economic issues.

The central proposition concerns the decisive role of the production structure, which unfortunately has been forgotten in the state of contemporary economics. I argue that models of interest and monetary markets will necessarily be deficient in portraying the market process if they do not refer to the production structure. I plan to show that the notion of the production structure applies to various fields of economic theory: starting from purely theoretical models (such as models discussed in the reswitching debate), through more empirical yet still largely theoretical generalizations (such as Say's law), and ending with empirical works on potential output and "optimal" monetary policies. Each section is devoted to major puzzles in capital theory that could potentially be resolved by reviving the concept of the production structure.

The first chapter examines the interest rate theories that clashed at the turn of the twentieth century: neoclassical productivity theories versus time-preference theories. Despite heated debates, they shared a common goal: to establish the underlying, nonmonetary variables that determine the interest rate (a microeconomic relationship with macroeconomic consequences). I argue that the productivity side of the debate can be defended only when placing the related investment figures in the context of monetary calculation and other monetary considerations. If true, then no inherent conflict exists between the real-preferences approach and the productivity approach. And the distinction between monetary and real becomes more nuanced than it appears at first sight.

The second chapter revisits probably the most relevant capital debate in the history of economic theory, the so-called reswitching debate, which started in the 1950s and in recent decades has recaptured attention. The reswitching debate sheds light on such a broad range of issues as quantity, allocation, and return on capital. To fully incorporate the best of the theses on capital reversals (and in a way to respond to all of them), we need to complement capital models with an additional variable aside from quantity of capital and the interest rate: the production structure. As I plan to show, it is helpful to find the proper relationship between the length of production and the height of the interest rate. The conclusions from those capital challenges prove valuable in the inquiry into potential output in the fourth chapter.

The third chapter considers capital and consumer spending in the production structure to analyze versions of Say's law. Most of the chapter concerns discussions of the controversial issues raised by Jean-Baptiste Say. I infer that the clash of ideas arose because of unclear definitions (including Say's own definitions) and murky interpretations by both proponents and opponents of Say. Problems appeared especially in not properly differentiating between savings and money balances. Yet even very formalized models of Say's law did not situate it in the context of the production structure—which perhaps is one of the reasons why some of the underconsumption theorists neglected to count capitalists' productive spending as a part of aggregate demand. In the last section, I try to combine Michal Kalecki's theory of profits and investment spending with the general concept of Say's law. I conclude that Say's law appears to hold when the money market is in a sort of equilibrium, or more specifically, an unaltered steady state.

The fourth chapter takes on an error regarding potential output which is very widespread in the macroeconomic profession. I dehomogenize the concept of fully utilizing resources into a purely theoretical, common sense approach and a policy approach that attempts to make it measurable. After making the distinction, the chapter sketches all the various ways to measure potential output using real-world data on production, employment, and capital. As I argue in the last section of the chapter, the shortcomings of using measured potential output go well beyond the ones recognized in most of the literature (shortcomings associated with technical assessment). Since macroeconomic stability is related to the (Jevonsian) structure of production, one aggregated index of production cannot properly capture policy challenges associated with equilibrium.

The fifth chapter restates the quantity theory of money and neutrality of money. I briefly explain why money can virtually never be neutral and why it always causes people to change their allocation decisions, naturally leading to the reshaping of the production structure. The point covers both changes in the money supply and in the demand to hold money. I briefly summarize alternative monetary regimes.

The sixth chapter reevaluates recent literature about monetary policy, especially the modern restatements of the money transmission mechanism. By not extensively considering capital goods, durables, and assets, contemporary monetary policy fails to address the possibility to create economic bubbles in the asset market and distortions in the production structure. As I argue, the so-called microfoundations established in the last decades of the development of macroeconomics do not properly capture the importance of the interest rate for arriving at a balanced production structure. The flaw appears in the growing body of literature reevaluating the channels of monetary policy.

The main attempt of the book is to offer a new theoretical perspective on stages of production and to prove it can enrich our understanding of a few vital economic concepts such as capital spending, return on capital, length of production, equilibrium, potential output, credit expansion, and finally macroeconomic bubbles. As I plan to prove, inquiry into those concepts requires a well-articulated theory of the structure of production.

NOTE

1. An excellent example of the confusion is demonstrated by Thomas Piketty's book, entitled *Capital in the Twenty-First Century* (emphasis added). General economic theory suggests the title should be different: *Wealth in the Twenty-First Century*, or even better, *Gross Wealth in the Twenty-First Century* (since his book does not properly account for depreciation).

Part I

MICROECONOMIC ASPECTS OF THE CAPITAL STRUCTURE

Chapter 1

Interest as a Factorial Payment

Neoclassical Roots of the Theory of Interest and Capital: Clark, Knight, Fisher

The neoclassical approach to the interest premium emerged in the marginalist works of John Bates Clark and was later developed by Frank Knight and Irving Fisher. In searching for the roots of interest, those economists had two things in common. First, to a large extent they based their reasoning on a stationary economy with repeatable processes of production. This kept their focus away from the challenges of how capital gets restructured. Second, since their other works lay in the marginalist tradition, they stayed faithful to it and looked for a truly marginal approach to explain interest. Naturally they did not accept land and labor as candidates for the driving force of interest. The exclusive candidate was capital itself.

CLARK

John Bates Clark started his analysis by contrasting capital with capital goods. First, he noted his general understanding of capital as a material factor of production, much different from labor. He considered materiality a "fundamental" aspect of capital goods. From this introductory note, Clark became unclear and stated first that capital is "permanent" because it "lasts." Then in the next sentence he said that "it must" last and despite being permanent can easily be consumed and destroyed. In fact, complete usage of capital, which would lead to a labor-intensive economy, is similar to not using it at all, such that machines would just stay in warehouses without being employed. In a way then, capital must be destroyed, but at a reasonable pace (Clark 1908, p. 117).

In interpreting this unclear passage, we get a vibrant picture of the nowadays obvious message from the author. Capital goods are being produced to perish, but capital is something different. Capital is perfectly mobile and can easily be transferred from one industry to the other, which is not true of capital goods (Clark 1908, p. 118). In describing things this way, Clark was not so much different from Eugen von Böhm-Bawerk. He diverged from Böhm-Bawerk by more realistically seeing capital in terms of monetary values. Even in everyday business life a merchant asks about the amount of "capital" he has in possession and answers in terms of monetary appraisement and nothing else. Only the secondary question "What is capital invested in?" leads to a discussion of capital goods (Clark 1888, p. 9). Capital can therefore be seen as money, existing wealth, a value that is to some extent abstract. Yet it is not fully abstract because it is necessarily linked to real, physical, tangible things such as capital goods (Clark 1908, p. 119).

From this true description, Clark started to become mystical by seeing capital as "productive wealth," wealth that, although it is invested in material things, perpetually shifts from one place to another. Capital "lives" by migrating from body to body, by moving again and again—almost like a soul of the capitalist economy. It is like a highly advanced animal that renews its tissues in very short cycles (tissues being capital goods that wear out), or so the story goes (Clark 1908, p. 120).

Another analogy Clark thought of concern water power and life. Water power is an abstraction, but concrete water movements involve actual molecules of water. In this sense it is similar to life. It goes on and on (forever?) and is bequeathed from generation to generation, but its form is always concrete and perishable. Clark tried to convince us that the same could be said about capital, which is something abstract and permanent, whereas capital goods are perishable and represent a real embodiment of capital (Clark 1908, p. 121). Clark also mentioned a sensible difference between rent and interest. Rent is a price we pay for hiring basically anything, while interest is a return on money capital (Clark 1908, p. 124).

There is a certain role for abstinence in the theory of capital. Clark had, however, a distinctive approach to abstinence, one that was more consumption oriented. Keeping a capital structure intact (i.e., avoiding consuming it) does not reflect a form of abstinence. According to him no one really has to save to keep up the extensive structure of capital goods. Since capital is said to be permanent, no sacrifice is needed. Rather, true abstinence happens when capital is accumulated. Reducing one's consumption allows additional capital goods to be built. This is undoubtedly a sacrifice that has economic benefits (Clark 1908, pp. 126–127).

The above description almost paves the way for a Fisherian understanding of time preference. A decision not to consume capital is not a decision to save and accumulate. It is a decision to keep things constant. Clark's abstinence happens when consumption is further reduced. For this reason the term "abstinence" is definitely preferable to "waiting." Abstinence refers to reducing current consumption. Waiting suggests a saver has to wait until already-started processes of production can yield benefits. "Waiting" is not precise because the benefits of additional savings can be enjoyed earlier or later (Clark 1908, p. 130; Clark 1895a, p. 260).

Time plays an important role in production. Clark had no doubts about the fact that production can be divided into different stages, within some of which the intermediate products are systematically used up. Nevertheless, he went on to say that capital has no time dimension:

> Capital-goods follow one another in an endless succession, and each one has its day. Capital, on the other hand, has no periods. It works incessantly; and there is no way of dividing its continuous life, except by using arbitrary divisions, such as Capital days, months or years. There is nothing in the works without such function of it that can make a basis for such a division as we can trace in the life of capital-goods. Capital, as such, does not originate, mature and then exhaust itself, giving way place to other capital. Goods do this, but funds do not. (Clark 1908, p. 128)

Clark introduced the permanent existence of a capital fund to explain why there is no waiting involved in production. Let us imagine three production processes (A, B, and C) (see also Clark 1895a, p. 268):

A A′ A″ A‴
B B′ B″ B‴
C C′ C″ C‴

The three different processes start from left to right. Before we receive final products A‴, B‴, and C‴, previous stages have to be completed. But we are not starting from scratch. Those processes already exist, and benefits from them are being reaped constantly. Therefore, without undermining the notion of consecutive stages in the capital structure, one can argue that final goods are available to the saver and consumer without actually waiting for them (Clark 1908, pp. 130–131). The enjoyment need not be postponed. Another example Clark used concerns his famous forest metaphor. It may take over fifty years to bring a particular tree to maturity, but once a forest has grown, no one needs to wait. Moreover, consumption of a good (provided the consumption is stable) does not require an additional sacrifice to maintain a level of production (Clark 1908, pp. 131–132).

What remains to be explained in Clark is "genesis of new capital." New capital originates from abstinence. That is, it originates when people consciously reduce consumption in order to deepen the capital structure—when they divert money from consumption goods to secure production goods.

Once people have abstained, the deepened structure exists. No additional abstinence is needed. In some extraordinary way the chain of capital goods becomes "automatic" (Clark 1908, p. 134).

These considerations have led to a distinctive theory of interest. Interest is not related to savers' sacrifice. It results from a productive factor, capital. When we buy labor, we pay for it because we receive its fruits. Similarly we pay for capital because capital has the power to create products. This extraordinary power becomes a basis for interest payments (Clark 1908, p. 135).

Clark emphasized that even though capital structure could be illustrated as a geometrical figure, one has to remember that capital goods appear everywhere in the production system (Clark 1908, pp. 269–270). Some replace capital goods that have worn out. Some appear in the earlier stages of production in one sector, whereas others appear in the later stages of production in another sector (or in the same one).

The last and most controversial aspect of the Clarkian framework is Clark's concept of synchronized production. Under the influence of Böhm-Bawerk, capital theorizing in the nineteenth century started to have a lot to do with considerations of time. Clark criticized this approach. At first, he argued, it may look as if some waiting is involved in production. In the above diagram, a capitalist at stage A may have to wait or borrow goods from a capitalist at stage A‴. It looks as if one has to wait weeks or months before goods are produced and ready to be consumed (Clark 1908, p. 304). A similar problem could be described for laborers. Yet nothing of this kind really happens. The stocks of finished goods are used for consumption by all sorts of laborers and capitalists at different stages of production. They are replenished successfully, and the system works like a water pipe. At one end water flows in, at the other it flows out. No one actually has to wait for the exact particles of water to emerge that were let in on the other side (Clark 1908, p. 305; Clark 1895, pp. 99–101; Clark 1907, pp. 355–356). The whole waiting argument breaks down once we realize there is no waiting involved in production (Clark 1895, p. 259). There seems to be no real benefit associated with the burden of waiting (in production). When in modern society a coat is being made, nobody has to wait for that coat to be made. What matters is that society is organized in such a way that a coat is already available (Clark 1907, p. 367). There is no question that in the past some sheep had to be raised to produce the wool to use in making the coat. But this in Clark's view is a sort of miracle of the modern economy. No one truly has to wait because goods are available immediately.[1]

Clark credited the capitalist system with significant benefits because the capital structure allows society to use the fruits of production a lot sooner than waiting would require. In primitive society, man has only time and labor at hand. These two factors are all that can be applied to production. In those circumstances, waiting is inseparable from producing. People suffer a painful way of waiting for finished products. By adding one extra factor in production, capital, everything changes. People work simultaneously in different stages of production, and production and consumption become synchronized. The fruits of synchronicity can be enjoyed immediately by the producers even if they are involved in the very early stages. The temporal interval is not important for anybody in the whole production chain (Clark 1908, p. 308).

Clark was well aware that he was debating Böhm-Bawerk and positioning himself against capital theory as accepted by a wide range of authors. Yet he did not oppose the theory as much as many people imagine today. He agreed that building capital goods inevitably diverts labor from building consumer goods. Building an axe to chop wood makes the process of production longer, yet it leads to more production despite the initial waiting involved. Clark, however, did not stop there, but took a step forward. The established theory properly described capital goods, which can make the process longer. But it is entirely different for capital, which has a monetary side. Capital allows producers to avoid waiting (Clark 1908, p. 311).

Although Clark was very unclear in his description of the controversy in capital theory, the above remarks seem to shed light on his views. Capital goods require waiting and involve roundaboutness. But capital is not physical; it is the productive powers associated with the capitalist system itself. The true soul of the capitalist system is not in physical properties of capital goods and the waiting associated with them in physical processes. The soul of capitalism is in the monetary nature of the market process because money allows the system to create something resembling an organism. Money flows in all parts of the production structure. It allows laborers and capitalists in the earlier stages to reap benefits from the last stages without waiting for the processes to be finished. Even though Clark did not state his case in such a way, his comment on the difference between capital and capital goods may indicate such an interpretation to be valid.

Clark gave a good example. In the case of the use of iron, ships transport a lump of iron from one place to another:

> There is a long interval between the beginning of its career as a capital-good and the beginning of its service as an article of consumption. But watch capital, the entire capital of the steel-making and the cutlery making industries, and you will see this period vanish. There is always ore in the mine and in the ships, and steel in the furnaces and in the mills. If society is in a static condition, there is always the same amount of it in each department of the extended industry. (Clark 1908, p. 312)

In one of his critiques of Böhm-Bawerk Clark made it even clearer: the Austrian was theorizing about capital goods to arrive at concepts of capital.

But the capitalist never compares processes of production. He compares "sums" of money. He compares present sums with future ones. To be clearer, the capitalist compares one big present sum of money with endless future smaller sums (interest payments):

> Neither the true capitalist, who creates permanent capital, nor the quasi-capitalist, who creates a fund and then consumes it, has any occasion to compare the utility of present goods with that of future goods *of like kind and quantity*.
>
> Professor v. Böhm-Bawerk has tried to use the concept *capital goods* for scientific purposes identical with that of *capital*; and the basing of interest on goods present and future is the first result of this attempt. What men really compare is present sums with *future* ones. (Clark 1894, pp. 65–66)

Capital is about the money: present dollars and future dollars (Clark 1895a, p. 263). Somewhat paradoxically then, Clark took a sort of Misesian position against Böhm-Bawerk and argued that monetary calculation is essential to describe capital. However surprising this may sound, judging by today's standards, with his emphasis on money, Clark sounded much more "Austrian" than Böhm-Bawerk. Naturally, at the turn of the nineteenth century, things were all different in this respect. Today we are not constrained by such conditions. A reasonable synthesis of Clark and Böhm-Bawerk is possible—provided that, unlike those two, we can both separate capital goods and capital (like Clark) and emphasize the role of capital owners in non-automatically, consciously maintaining capital (like Böhm-Bawerk).[2]

KNIGHT

Most of Clark's rudimentary arguments were repeated and developed into a much more sophisticated form by Frank Knight. Building upon Clark, Knight started from a point of view that could be called "capital realism." He built his case by criticizing a theory of capital as time (contra Böhm-Bawerk). Like his forerunner he directed his attention toward the monetary side of capital, although with more of what Hayek called "mythology of capital." In his opinion, interest has a lot to do with accounting aspects of existing capital values within the production process. The discount on future monetary outlays must then come from capital itself, not anything else. In Knight's own words:

> The value of the instrument when finished at the end of the year will be $I,025. This $25 of "surplus value" over and above the direct outlay cost can only be imputed to the instrument itself, i.e. to the "capital" invested in it as this capital increases cumulative. (Knight 1934, p. 263)

It is hard to question this thesis. Since interest already appears in the accounting of capital values, one should not search for the roots of interest outside of capital. Unfortunately Knight did not stay faithful to this strict rule, and instead of focusing on capital, he switched immediately back to discussing capital goods:

> In the kind of world in which we live and think, there must be some such "bearer" (tangible or intangible) of the accumulating investment. This bearer at any stage of construction is a productive instrument, a capital good as well as a quantity of capital, and correct accounting must impute to it its rigorously definite share in the final result. (Knight 1934, p. 263)

Knight went on to describe capital as a sort of perpetual substance that grows steadily, thanks to its productive powers (money being the embodiment of the powers). "Capital" can be seen as implied economic power to employ possible new investment opportunities that lead to increased production. At the same time, capital is the equivalent of "income" but "capitalized at the rate of return" (Knight 1936, p. 433). A discount rate is the ratio of capital's power to improve production (Knight 1936, p. 434). Knight switched back and forth between a monetary view and a mythology: capital is wealth; it is money; it is a "productive property" (Knight 1916, p. 292). The accountants, business managers, and statisticians (and not the economists) have always had a proper approach and have treated capital as a money fund that produces value payments (Knight 1935b, p. 63).

Although in most works Knight attempted to focus on the "accounting" nature of capital, in simple illustrations, he used notions from the traditional "productivity" camp. He assumed a one-good economy. One good is consumed, and the good is produced with the same good as the only factor of production. Naturally the factor has to be "capital." It could be in the form of a "Crusonia plant," which grows naturally at a constant rate. It does not require cultivation, and the only role of a human being (one unit of population) is to cut a chosen quantity for consumption. If the product was consumed at the same rate as the natural rate of growth, then we would have a perfectly stationary economy (Knight 1944, p. 30).

Under those circumstances, the return on capital would equal the natural level of productivity. It would also be meaningless to discuss income, capital, and interest, since we would exist in a world with one good. Why bother with this exercise, then? Because for Knight, in the most complex economy, although the process is more complicated, the source of interest is similar. The main difference is that we have a "complex of productive agents" that maintains itself and allows for positive returns for the owner (Knight 1944, p. 31).

Capital goods wear out and therefore have to be maintained or replaced. In producing capital goods, other capital goods are used. Nevertheless, replacement of capital goods that are being used up has nothing to do with the rate of return (Knight 1936, p. 443). In this aspect of capital theory, Knight did not hesitate to criticize Böhm-Bawerk for his what he called the "nonsensical" theory of capital, which stated that capital goods could be reduced to natural primary factors; apparently the remaining surplus would be a product of time preference. This reductionist approach, Knight said, is completely ahistorical and may only be correct as an "exercise in pure logic," although even the very first, infinitesimal addition of capital at the beginning of history would not mean production under conditions of preexisting primary factors (Knight 1934, p. 262). Knight also attributed the mistake of giving primacy to primary factors to Ricardo and Jevons (Knight 1936, p. 453)—an opinion Böhm-Bawerk would undoubtedly have found surprising. For Knight, a reductionist approach to capital construction should be treated similarly to the labor theory of value—the idea that only labor is capable of producing goods and services (Knight 1936, p. 453). Knight repeated the same argument in response to Boulding (Knight 1935b, p. 45). Capital goods cannot be traced back only to increments of factors other than capital. Within all productive agents, capital is as natural a part as any other factor. No clear line between capital and other agents could legitimately be drawn (Knight 1935b, p. 46).

Having attacked the approach concerning primary factors, Knight prepared the way for a theory of capital and interest. Capital goods produce capital goods because they already have a productive power implied in them. This power is precisely the source of interest income. The durability of capital goods or the length of the processes of production is merely a technical detail. More durable factors will yield more monetary benefits in the future, which in turn will be reflected in a higher current price of the factor. What matters, however, is current income, which can be derived from those capital goods, this income being interest (or perhaps the rent earned by owning capital). Goods are traded within the market sphere because they render productive services. Capital is no different in this respect; therefore, a sale price of capital naturally arises. Anything bought and sold in the market has to offer a productive service (Knight 1936, p. 437).

As long as society does not plan to completely end its life, capital is perpetual, and so is income from it. Interest can be permanently derived from the existing capital stock. Durability of factors and roundaboutness of production are characteristic features of particular processes but do not create the potential to yield interest. Interest exists because productive powers are hidden in capital itself (Knight 1934, pp. 267–268). What makes capital different from capital goods is its homogeneous nature (Knight 1934, p. 270). Capital goods are devoted to specific uses, and it is very troublesome to liquidate them without altering the whole process of production. It is also difficult to move capital goods smoothly from one employment to another.

In this respect, capital is the opposite: it is completely mobile and can be easily adapted to any economic or technological change. Because of its mobility, capital necessarily begets an overall yield, a difference between future monetary profits and current costs (even though some owners of capital will lose). A sort of "regular" rate of return makes an accounting view of capital seem quite logical (Knight 1936, p. 444). No matter what the length of a production process or how easy it is to liquidate a particular capital good, a capital ingredient reaps benefits in the form of capital yields. Capital income is therefore independent of any particular production structure. Even if some investments will yield consumable benefits only after tens of years, interest income will be paid even after one year (Knight 1934, p. 273). Because of its homogeneous nature, capital yields the same benefits in all processes (mobility being the key reason).

Unquestionably, there is a duration between the starting point of production and the moment when the production reaches its final stage. That duration can differ from one process to another. Each production process can be divided into various phases. One could also sum up the length of each stage, including the using up of capital goods. The final result could be of interest to historians (Knight 1934, p. 275). The production period does not determine the rate of interest (Knight 1936, p. 449). Moreover, it is irrelevant. At the extremes, the production period is either zero or infinite. It is zero for current consumption, where products are consumed right away; or it is infinite for nonconsumption, where capital is being saved and invested and it constantly grows, with no net liquidation (Knight 1935, p. 625).

From the perspective of the present, production and consumption can be seen as simultaneous activities, even if we acknowledge that every act of production takes time. Time only matters at the beginning and end—that is, when economic activity starts or ends. Once the wheels start to turn, for Knight, production and consumption should not be separated analytically. A glass of milk is consumed at the same time that resources are invested in feeding a cow. Production and consumption happen at the same moment, since for every increment of production there is a corresponding level of consumption. Technologically those two activities are distinct. What is being consumed today started being produced a while ago, since everything takes time. Despite this feature of production the interval has no relevance for enjoying any particular unit of a good (Knight 1934, pp. 275–276).

Knight admitted though that matters may look different once we deal with dynamic adjustments—that is, when disinvestments or new investments happen. The key for him lay in unanticipated changes of production. Capital goods are heterogeneous and their usage under changing circumstances depends on the quantity of capital, its durability, and its immobility as the "Böhm-Bawerk school" put it. Knight went on: one of the problems of Böhm-Bawerk was his focus on objective aspects of those capital goods, as if the goods had value. The reality is that value comes from services rendered by those goods. Wealth does not consist of those "concrete things," because only services are being produced and consumed (Knight 1935c, p. 85).[3] Capitalization includes a permanent ability to satisfy human wants with a certain pool of value, no matter how fast things are physically used up (Knight 1935c, p. 86).

In addition, one cannot "minimize the importance of studies which in any way shed light on such relations or on the rationale of production control where lags are involved" (Knight 1934, p. 276). In other words, even though the time lag is of no importance in a stationary state, this perspective radically changes if conditions are different. Then such studies become of great importance.

What is essential to Knight's thinking is his view on the earning capacity of capital. Any addition to capital always induces an "accounting" change. Capital has to appear on both sides in bookkeeping, and it represents something new. An almost-magical feature of capital is that it is a hidden vehicle for interest payments. The interest rate is determined "exclusively at the margin of growth, where men are comparing large, short segments of income-flow with thinner streams reaching out to the indefinite future" (Knight 1934, p. 278). Knight was very close to the Marxian mythology of capital: capital exists for its own sake, to accumulate permanently. This unavoidable characteristic paves the way for any interest payments. He refers to the Böhm-Bawerkian "enormous fallacy" in believing capital can be consumed. "Wealth" and "capital" exist and grow as long as capitalist society exists (Knight 1936, p. 456).

What about the possibility of capital consumption? Knight mentions it but immediately adds that this poses no problem for the pure theory of capital, since a decision by one individual cannot change the fact that, overall, capital naturally grows and expands. Even if some people decide to consume all their assets, this merely leads to redistribution of ownership and it cannot change the natural course of capital accumulation (Knight 1934, p. 265). The capacity to earn will on average overpower any danger of massive net disinvestments (Knight 1934, p. 278). There are exceptions to this rule, as history teaches us, but only in societies "demoralized by crisis conditions," where markets for loanable funds have almost been destroyed. It is also questionable that enterprises could function normally under those circumstances (Knight 1936, p. 457).

The capitalization of the economy also does not have much to do with the "waiting" period (Knight 1936, p. 449). The purpose of new investment may well be shortening production. The total output produced could be achieved later if less capitalist methods were used (Knight 1934, p. 278). In other places, Knight suggested that it is better to be careful with the usage of the ceteris paribus clause when analyzing the length of production processes. Why? Because part of choosing is actually dependent upon things *not being equal* in many respects:

> In a world where "food" is scarce and where technical facts enable one to have an increased ration to-morrow or next year in exchange for any portion of today's or this year's ration, there is a presumption that, other things equal, some postponing will be done in comparison with a uniform distribution through time as a baseline or zero point. But other things are far from equal. Life is short and youth shorter, and both are uncertain as well. The permanent and cumulative saving and investment we actually and typically find in the world cannot be explained in any degree through comparison between present and future enjoyment, or "waiting" and being paid for waiting. (Knight 1934, p. 272)

Knight is concerned with a dynamic sequence of events that starts with capital accumulation, which rules out the traditional understanding of the ceteris paribus clause. When the supply of capital changes, it also changes related conditions. Therefore, one should not discuss any tendency to "equalize forces" under constant capitalist development. The capitalist economy by its very nature of change leads to constant readjustments and indefinitely generates disequilibrium. It is therefore misleading to discuss capital accumulation using stationary analysis (Knight 1936, p. 463). When capital changes, other things cannot stay in the same way (Knight 1936a, p. 628).[4]

Knight summarized his opposition to the time perspective on capital with three observations: (1) Capital is not produced by any primary means of production. Land, capital goods, and labor are all heterogeneous factors that are always used in production, and they overlap. Therefore, a strict distinction between capital and primary factors cannot be drawn. Also each of the goods in those categories is produced by other goods in other categories; hence, production and reproduction always take place through the cooperation of all factors. (2) Knight sees a second fallacy of the time perspective on capital based on his view that reproduction of goods should not be treated as genuine "economic production." Why? Because for him, under stationary conditions, consumption and production could be treated as instantaneous. Therefore, each stage of reproduction does not really matter and can be neglected right away. (3) The third fallacy of the time perspective on capital derives from the notion that the product of capital is both the product that allows for production and reproduction of an instrument itself. Knight argued that the yield of capital cannot be both the product of an instrument and the product of activity that created it (Knight 1934, p. 280). Moreover, for precisely this reason a standard demand-and-supply analysis does not apply to the capital market (Knight 1936a, p. 614).

It is also important to note that Knight's theory is different from older productivity theories of interest.[5] Productivity of capital goods is something different than the Knightian almost-metaeconomic concept of "capital productivity" in general. In production, capital goods give their marginal value, but their current price is additionally discounted by the interest rate, which represents powers of "capital" that allow production to take place (Knight 1934, p. 281). It is also evident that capital (understood as all possible capital goods along with their earning power) is always limited, and there are numerous opportunities to employ it profitably. Here lies the reason for the interest rate, which is usually higher than zero. There are always new fields to which to allocate capital, creating "demand for capital," since it is always possible to increase output by additional investments. The interest rate could only permanently reach zero under complete abundance of capital. Capital would then become a "free good" (Knight 1934, pp. 283–284) (something J. M. Keynes dreamed would happen when his policies would be introduced). As long as there are no inventions that dramatically increase the abundance of goods and services, interest could never fall to zero (Knight 1936a, pp. 623–624). In the Garden of Eden, economic values would lose their importance, and so too would capital. Knight attacked Keynes and Joseph Schumpeter, arguing that the burden of proof rested with them. They had to prove that under normal market conditions, capital as a fund could be uniformly distributed without any charge (Knight 1936a, p. 624).

Knight can be seen as a faithful follower of John Bates Clark since he treated capital as a "continuous organic whole," a value fund "measured in money units" that is used up physically only in capital goods that wear out. Yet in the entrepreneurial sense, capital is permanent; by proper allocations it saves itself from being used up. The quantity of capital is the same as the value of capital (Knight 1936, p. 460). Capital can be seen as a "wheel of wealth" in the circular-flow diagram that Knight himself invented in the modern form (see on this Patinkin 1973). Knight's works provide the building blocks of an economic "capital" theory because capital is at the center of his thinking. At one point he argued one should disregard the historical distinction between three factors of production (land, labor, and capital). Moreover, the classical doctrine of the trinity of factors is for him simply indefensible (Knight 1935d, p. 20).

While Knight's theory has been criticized by various authors, it has some interesting and valid points. First of all, he reasonably pointed out that it is challenging to separate stages of production and order them in an empirically meaningful way when capital goods produce and are produced by other capital goods. Moreover, he criticized Böhm-Bawerk on the same grounds as Böhm-Bawerk's own followers: his use of the concept of an "average period of production." To describe the concept of length of production, we can neglect the distinction between "original" and "secondary" factors of production (Hayek 1936, p. 500).

Second, he noticed and plainly illustrated the problem with treating the length of production as one of the forces determining the rate of interest, mostly in that this method seemed to generate a rate of return without reference to the investment period. As with Clark, this led him to focus more on the role of money in capital theory, rather than objective factors such as physical qualities of capital goods.

Third, Knight was at times quite keen on emphasizing dynamic aspects of capital accumulation (despite his notorious, often-repeated sentiments in favor of static analysis). This could place him in the camp of opponents of the ceteris paribus clause. When one of the factors (capital) changes, others cannot stay unaltered. Ironically he did not stay completely faithful to this dictum and he himself fell into that trap by stating that capital is always permanent (and grows).

Fourth, his emphasis on the accounting aspect (appearing at times and without consistency) was a step in the right direction, but he did not move the conversation forward enough. His Clarkian narration in which capital is productive and therefore interest is the price we pay for increasing our capacity may well be saved, provided we use the term "money capital" and extend monetary reasoning in the following way: Money capital is operationally productive because money is an economic instrument that opens the door for effective factor allocation. Without money countless production possibilities and production improvements simply could not take place. It should not be surprising then that present money has a certain price in the market for producer goods, a price we call "interest." Present money allows for bidding in factor markets, so entrepreneurs are ready to pay for this possibility of allocation (they pay the cost of money capital, which is interest). Knight was not eager to take that step, however, and instead argued about some productive forces hidden in his mythical concept of capital. Paradoxically then, while an eager critic of Böhm-Bawerk, he was too Böhm-Bawerkian in treating capital as something separate from money. Moreover, at one point he moved quite close to Böhm-Bawerk, when he stated that "time" should be considered a specific homogenous factor of production related to the payment of interest. Doubling the time involved in production (embodied in an increase quantity of capital goods) will significantly increase productivity (Knight 1931, p. 198). This argument sounds a lot like Böhm-Bawerk's third argument about the productivity of longer processes of production (which indicates that pushed to the wall Böhm-Bawerk believed in the productivity theory of interest).

On the negative side, Knight was too much focused on a stationary analysis. Under a condition of no change it is natural to treat production and consumption as if they were simultaneous. If preferences and needs stay constant and are constantly satisfied by progressively increasing output, then capital theory is almost useless, since there is no challenge of properly allocating factors (as they are already properly allocated). Capital restructuring is not a challenge. He overly neglected the real possibility of capital consumption—which is surprising when we realize that during his life (including when he wrote), he witnessed tremendous capital consumption: during World War I; in some of the Western European countries after World War I, in countries where various forms of socialism were introduced; and during the Great Depression in the United States. Even if he were right that the continuity model of production and consumption is useful, he still should not have neglected cases of societies where capital was consumed. Calling them "decadent" or "perverse" was a poor substitute for sensible economic analysis (Machlup 1935, p. 808).

During the whole capital debate in the 1930s, it is noticeable that both sides focused on the weakest points of the opposing case. Machlup pointed out to Knight the possibility of capital consumption (Machlup 1935, p. 808); and Knight emphasized that the interest rate cannot be related to the concept of length of production in any meaningful way (Knight 1935a, p. 808). As we will see, both arguments may well have been correct.

FISHER

Irving Fisher was the last important figure who significantly contributed to the neoclassical theory of interest. In fact, he may well seem the most important one, especially when we read modern microeconomic textbooks. If the chapter on the interest rate appears, it usually deals with the interest rate in relation to a consumer's decisions on spending their income today and tomorrow. Fisher moved away from the Clarkian-Knightian exclusive emphasis on the productivity side of capital by injecting "impatience" into his framework. In this case, the title says it all: Fisher's book is called *The Theory of Interest as Determined by Impatience to Spend Income and Opportunity to Invest It.*

We see the concept of time preference in the beginning of the book, where Fisher criticized the exploitation theory of interest. He accurately restated a Böhm-Bawerkian example of a group of laborers who are waiting for the final product. Socialists have stated two separate propositions. First, the costs of production are always lower than the value of the final product. Second, costs of production ought to be equal to the value of the final product for justice to prevail. Fisher gives a thought-provoking example of a colony of laborers who are sent to western and unpopulated lands. They could build roads there or irrigate land without the aid of borrowed capital. They would be doing it entirely on their own, without any capitalist "robbing them." Yet the truth is that they would become capitalists themselves since they would have to wait a long time for the completion of the final product. If they borrowed capital, they could use it to finance their current needs, and the financing would more or less reflect the discounted value of the product, which should be ready in a few years' time (Fisher 1930, pp. 49–52).

As a partial disciple of Böhm-Bawerk, Fisher was attentive to the problems of naïve productivity theories.[6] Their two biggest problems lay in confusing physical productivity with value productivity and neglecting heterogeneous quantities in real production (Fisher 1930, p. 54). Just because a machine is productive in the physical sense (it leads to a larger amount of wheat produced), it does not preclude the possibility that the value of the machine could be equal to its future contribution to production (in which case interest would be zero). Additionally, there is no way to create an objective index of physical usage of factors that could then be compared in real terms to quantity of produced goods. Only monetary value can serve such a function.

Well-grounded productivity theory can be reconciled with other theories of interest. Time-preference theory is one of them. Time preference is a synonym for impatience (Fisher 1930, p. 66). Impatience, or time preference, is a systematic undervaluation of future income; it is a preference for income in the nearer future rather than deferred income, or more remote income. Fisher openly and thoughtfully chose to focus on how income is valued, not on fuzzy concepts of "future" and "present" goods (Fisher 1930, pp. 63–65). Furthermore, he cleverly avoided discussing the existence of interest. Interest as a discount of future income always exists because even zero interest or negative interest is still interest (Fisher 1930, pp. 67–68).

The role of impatience in shaping interest depends on four factors: (1) amount of income, (2) expected distribution of income in time, (3) composition of the budget, and (4) probability (Fisher 1908, p. 71). Consider some examples: (1) If income is lower, then the preference for current rather than future income tends to be higher. (2) If income is increasing, then the preference tends to be high, since when the income comes in the future it will get relatively abundant. (3) A change in the composition of the budget may affect impatience. (4) Naturally risk and uncertainty also come into play (Fisher 1930, pp. 72–77). There are also other "personal" factors that contribute to time preference (Fisher 1930, p. 89).

Time preference is not the sole factor, however. The other factor represents productivity in some sense, but Fisher was mindful of problems with this term. He started off by clarifying the language. The word "productivity" is not proper because one needs to avoid concepts of physical productivity, the notion that capital produces income, or the idea that costs are causes of prices. Therefore the term "investment opportunity" seems to be much clearer and fits the purpose much better (Fisher 1930, pp. 150–151). It also departs from previous fallacious ideas. Investment opportunity is to be understood in relative terms. An individual may compare various production projects in terms of their possible returns (Fisher 1930, pp. 151–152). Israel Kirzner, for his part, calls Fisher's theory a "productivity of waiting theory" (Kirzner 1993, p. 169).

For example, let us assume that over many years we compare two types of investment projects. In the first one, we earn annually 450 units of money. The second one first gives us 300 units after three years, and from then on it gives 500 units of money. We can take these opportunities as given by current conditions, which affect our choices. Naturally the key factor is the interest rate. Depending on it, one or the other option becomes more attractive.

The following quote adequately summarizes Fisher's stance:

> We are constantly confronted with the opportunity to choose one income stream rather than another. We inquire *what difference it makes* whether one or the other alternative is chosen. We find often it makes two kinds of differences, advantages and disadvantages. If we start with the option which has the more immediate advantages and ask whether it is or is not worthwhile to give up this option and adopt the other instead, we may call the proposal so to do an *opportunity to invest*, i.e., to incur certain disadvantages or, as they will hereafter be called, costs, for the sake of certain advantages or, as they will hereafter be called, *returns*. (Fisher 1930, p. 154)

Impatience and opportunities seem to work for Fisher like Marshall's scissors. Both of them determine the level of interest rates. If we become more impatient with our spending, this will exert upward pressure on the interest rate. If we decide to invest more and exploit current investment opportunities, then the law of diminishing returns starts to apply and puts downward pressure on interest. Both forces work at the same time and influence the height of interest (Fisher 1930, pp. 176–177).

One possible criticism could be directed against Fisher. If assessing investment opportunities requires interest in the first place, aren't we taking it as given rather than explaining it? Don't productivity explanations have to be wrong, then? Fisher responded to this by stating that he is in "both camps." Investment opportunities produce a rate of return that has to equalize with subjective levels of impatience, just like supply equalizes with demand. It is a fact that objective technological factors do affect interest rates (Fisher 1930, p. 182).

Fisher strengthened his argument by giving unrealistic but thought-provoking examples of cases where rigid physical productivity has to set limits on interest rates, no matter what the level of patience is. Following Harry Brown he lets us imagine a Robinson Crusoe case where the rate of return on everything is set at 10 percent. Under that rigid and absurd condition, interest also has to be set at this level (Fisher 1930, p. 182). Fisher later on in the book gave his own cases, cases where the physical return is rigidly fixed at zero or even negative rates (e.g., the hardtrack example) (Fisher 1930, pp. 186–191).[7] Quite similar examples were given by Leland Yeager with his imaginary machine that could automatically produce 50 percent more of anything that was thrown into it (Yeager 1979, p. 208).

Knight believed the contrary—that this type of reasoning actually proves the correctness of productivity theory—since conditions of particular exchanges set the terms of trade. Therefore, if conditions outside of trade determine the terms of trade, production conditions determine interest (Knight 1931, p. 181).

Overall, Fisher treated interest as a practical subject that needs an empirical focus. He did not really see the difference that many other economists at his time highlighted, a difference between "determining" forces of interest and fundamental "causes" of interest (Fisher 1930, pp. 13–14; Kirzner 1993, pp. 183–184). Or perhaps it is better to say that he did not care about this difference for carefully articulated reasons. That was the essence of Böhm-Bawerk's criticism of the first edition of Fisher's book (Böhm-Bawerk 1959, vol. 3, p. 192). Böhm-Bawerk endorsed the book as compact and profound. Additionally, the theses presented in it were "properly understood," and were "indeed correct" (Böhm-Bawerk 1959, vol. 3, p. 192). Nevertheless, according to the Austrian, not all determining forces are to be seen as causes of interest.

NEOCLASSICAL FOUNDATIONS AND MODERN MICROECONOMICS

Clark, Knight, and Fisher were the most important figures in the history of neoclassical economics who dealt with problems of capital and interest. They mostly emphasized productivity factors in determining interest, but more importantly their approach to capital structure led them to illustrate how to homogenize heterogeneous capital resources. It may be debatable that there is one neoclassical presentation of theory of capital and interest, but the characteristic feature of modern microeconomics comes from the works of those thinkers and their neglect of capital restructuring as a building block for macroeconomic analysis. Despite an initial interest in debating those problems, the modern microeconomic consensus seems to have completely forgotten about its roots. What stayed are merely the Clarkian, Knightian, and Fisherian conclusions: that interest is a feature that has something to do with allocating income between now and the future, given technological constraints manifested in productive investment opportunities. Unfortunately, time as a potentially discoordinating factor in pricing and production plans has not received the special treatment that it deserves.

AUSTRIAN THEORIES OF INTEREST

Böhm-Bawerk

Eugen von Böhm-Bawerk's contributions to economic theory are numerous. Most of his scientific project was built on subjective fundamentals in the theory of pricing. His main enemy was centuries-old materialist and physical streams of thought. His opposition is well documented in the first volume of his treatise on capital and interest, where he systematically refutes existing theories of interest. At some points he overstates his case and neglects clear forerunners such as A. R. J. Turgot. The grand goal of Böhm-Bawerk cannot, however, be denigrated: to supplement the theory of pricing with the subjective theory of value.

Interest theory in *The Positive Theory of Capital* is just another manifestation of Böhm-Bawerk's pursuit of his grand goal. His interest theory aimed to base itself on the concept of subjective value, or the "value spread," to be precise. He starts off with a general statement: Present goods are worth more than future goods. Yet the future is always related to our actions, since economization is directed at the future. We are not indifferent about when to choose and when we will reach our goals (Böhm-Bawerk 1959, vol. 2, p. 259). With these opening words we are already assured that the whole theory will be built around the concepts of human action, valuation, and creative imagination: "Imagined future emotions are comparable" (ibid, p. 261). While focusing on possible scenarios he is also clear we should not include uncertainty in considering interest since uncertainty is present in all circumstances to varying degrees. Overall, present goods are expected to be more valuable than future goods, ceteris paribus—that is, under similar conditions and with goods of equal quantity and quality. Since subjective valuation of goods translates into exchange values, the case of interest—present goods versus future goods—will not be an exception: positive monetary interest directly results from undervaluing the goods we do not yet possess (ibid, p. 263).

To strengthen the main point, Böhm-Bawerk details three causes of undervaluation. The first cause stems from the difference in supply and demand between the markets for future and present goods. At first, it may be unclear what Böhm-Bawerk means, but after a long paragraph it becomes clearer:

employment opportunities for goods determine the value spread. Most goods are durable to some extent. Therefore, they can be consumed at different time periods. A future good can be consumed only after it is acquired in the future. A present good usually can also be consumed in a future day and on the days after that. Yet it has a certain advantage over the future good: it can be consumed before acquiring the future good. From this we clearly see a great feature of a present good: it can have all the advantages of a future good, plus the possibility of consuming in the present or not-so-remote future (Böhm-Bawerk 1959, vol. 2, pp. 266–267).

A book received today has all the features of a book received in a year. Plus it can be consumed within the less remote time of the upcoming twelve months. Such additional utility of the present good can hardly be underappreciated in seeking to understand the value spread. It becomes more obvious when we talk about a universally marketable good, money, a homogeneous commodity accepted by virtually all market participants. Money in 2016 has exactly the same features as money received in the future—say, 2017. Plus it can be used between 2016 and 2017. There is nothing surprising about the additional value of money in 2016 over money in 2017. Goods that can be depleted or that are short lived are of course a different case (Böhm-Bawerk 1959, vol. 2, p. 268).[8]

Second, future wants and the means used for satisfying them are permanently undervalued. Böhm-Bawerk starts off with the extreme examples of children and primitive tribes, only to then argue that such a phenomenon is present in all societies, though to a different extent. Böhm-Bawerk here ventures beyond typical economic thinking, since he mentions topics in physiology and cognitive theory. While imagining the future (to compare future goods to present goods) we are playing with abstractions and pictures, which we perceive inadequately. The limitation of a human mind seeking to properly grasp future reality is no surprise. Since the imagination is imperfect, we underestimate the future marginal value of goods (Böhm-Bawerk 1959, vol. 2, p. 269).

Besides this crucial imperfection of the human mind is an issue of sensations and temptations, a "lack of willpower": people are often tempted into seeking satisfaction from present consumption at the expense of the future. Beyond the drive to satisfy ourselves in the present, humans are generally uncertain of the future. We do not know if we will live to tomorrow or next year. The more sure we are of death, the less we value the future. Therefore, carpe diem, or gaining utility as soon as possible, may actually seem like a reasonable choice. Yet even healthy people, while more predictable in their choices, know that the future is remote, and remoteness means uncertainty in seeing the future. Hence, the second cause can actually be reduced to three subcauses: the limitation of the human mind in picturing the future; lack of willpower; and general uncertainty (although it was meant to abstract from it) permeating everyday choices (Böhm-Bawerk 1959, vol. 2, pp. 270–271).

The third cause is the most complex one and has led to many controversies. "In general," present goods are more suitable for satisfying wants because they are technologically viable. That is, it is a fact of "experience" that longer processes of production (which create future goods) are in general more productive.[9] With this notion Böhm-Bawerk (wholly aware of the fact) actually opens the back door for productivity theories, which he so vigorously criticized (Böhm-Bawerk 1959, vol. 2, p. 273). Present goods, when employed for more remote uses, result in more fruitful production. Such productive superiority manifests itself also in a surplus value.

The third cause appears to be in the spirit of older productivity theories because it is based on technical, not valuation, considerations.[10] Production takes time; labor and land inputs are transformed into capital goods, which then yield returns in future years. While criticizing productivity theories, Böhm-Bawerk argued that any productive power of capital goods can be imputed to its current price. Even if some tree is so productive that it will yield 1,000 times more in the future, its present price can simply be bid up to reflect such productivity. There is a difference between value productivity and technological productivity. Physical productivity is already included in the value of the machine. Naturally value productivity is in some indirect way derived from physical productivity. The question about interest is why the full value of the future product is not fully imputed to the means of production (Fetter 1914, p. 244). Such a fact appears to have nothing to do with productivity.

That is why Böhm-Bawerk, by presenting his third cause, may have countered his other contributions. What is worth mentioning is that he states that the third cause works independently of the other two causes. Does Böhm-Bawerk's third cause really represent typical productivity theory? At first this may seem so, but closer inspection reveals this may not be the case. Note the following:

> For if the value of a unit of product were the same in all periods of time including even the remotest, then obviously the most abundant product would also be the most valuable. But since the most abundant product is to be obtained by the lengthiest roundabout processes lasting many decades, then the economic center of gravity for all present means of production would fall in the extremely remote future. But we know that to be contrary to the realities of life. . . . For if every utilization for future periods were not only technically but also economically more remunerative than utilization for the present or for a near future, then people would naturally withdraw the bulk of theirs goods from the service of the present.
>
> This point furnished the most conclusive proof that this third cause of higher value of present goods is completely independent of the other two previously discussed. (Böhm-Bawerk 1959, vol. 2, p. 280)

The above quote makes a lot of economic sense, of course, but it is dubious that such an argument for a third cause is really based on higher productivity of roundabout processes of production. The truth is that the statement would be as sensible even if roundabout processes had the same productivity as shorter processes. Moreover, it would make even more sense if longer processes were less productive. What is hidden in the above quote is what Böhm-Bawerk was emphasizing from the very beginning: a value discount, a strong subjective force in people's minds that works on all levels of human activity. Aside from labor and land there is, therefore, some third factor of production that leads people to forgo various alternative employment options in favor of other ones. Dorfman with some regrets proposes to call this factor "waiting" (Dorfman 1959, p. 359).[11] Probably that was why Hayek was eager to agree about the role of productivity in explaining interest, but under a sort of stationary state: an "evenly progressing economy." Once we abolish such a limiting feature, "time preference takes charge" (Hayek 1945, p. 25).

Even if we put aside the two first causes—undervaluation of future wants and broader opportunities for present goods—there appears to be something fundamentally rooted in everyday choices, much more than with the other causes, leading to the discounting phenomenon. Perhaps, contrary to Böhm-Bawerk, it would make more sense to argue that there is just one cause of interest: a subjective value discount associated with the passage of time. As stated in the beginning of the chapter, in general, future goods are discounted by human beings, and it is true universally. Such an approach was later undertaken by Böhm-Bawerk's followers.[12]

Mises and Pure Time-Preference Advocates

Ludwig von Mises's approach to explaining interest is perfectly in line with his extension of Böhm-Bawerk's theory of pricing. Böhm-Bawerk understood well that the valuation process is subjective and a driving element in the pricing process. However, he sometimes relied too much on psychological explanations. This applies at times to his theory of interest also. Mises's contribution was to develop a pricing theory not based on states of mind, emotions, or psychological attitudes. The purpose was to base it on real choices. Hence, a natural result of his framework: the praxeological theory of economics based on real action and choices that materialize in people's surroundings. No different was the case of the theory of interest, which was to fully depend on subjective value—time preference, in particular. It is important to note that Mises's story of time preference is radically different from Fisherian and neoclassical stories of time preference. In the neoclassical case, it is a function of the distribution of consumption over time, which is uniform when the rate of time preference is zero (Garrison 1979, pp. 87–88). Such a function can be skewed more in the direction of the future (negative rate), or more toward the present (positive rate). In any case, time preference for the neoclassicals is not a feature of economizing in the praxeological framework as understood by Böhm-Bawerk's main follower.

What is the praxeological aspect of economizing? People always strive to satisfy their preferences as soon as possible, or out of necessity at later points in time, but no later than necessary. Time is a scarce factor, which like any other factor needs to be economized on.[13] People could always invest all their income to the remote future, bringing more production, but they decline to do so and prefer a smaller income compared to tomorrow. Impatience may have something to do with this, but praxeological explanations do not have to be based on it. The crucial element is *satisfaction* at closer or later dates (Mises 1966, p. 486). It is similar to physiological aspects, which are secondary and not essential. Naturally survival in the future requires survival today, but economics deals with actions as such, not with motives like that directing the course. In explaining market demand we do not reduce goods and services to proteins, fats, and carbohydrates to relate them on a purely physical level to satisfying demand (Mises 1966, p. 487).

Mises does not deny that the psychological factors mentioned by Böhm-Bawerk shape people's preferences. Nevertheless, they affect various people at various times differently. Moods and emotions are not fixed and eternal. Some people are more concerned about the future, others less. Despite the existence of such emotional influences, they are not universally true.[14] There are people who clearly undervalue future needs, but one can envision their opposites (Mises 1940, p. 440).

There are many examples of future-orientation and overvaluation of future goals. While criticizing Böhm-Bawerk's psychological approach, Mises discusses his version of consumption-based time-preference theory. Because they need to consume, people demonstrate positive time preference:

> In acting, one must always, without any exception, value a satisfaction at an earlier point in time more than the same kind and amount of satisfaction at a later time. If this were not so, then it would never be possible to decide in favor of a present satisfaction. Whoever uses or consumes anything, whoever seeks by acting to relieve to a greater or lesser extent a felt uneasiness is always expressing a preference for an earlier over a later satisfaction. Whoever eats and consumes anything is making a choice between a satisfaction in the immediate future and one in a more distant future. If he were to decide differently, if he were not to prefer the earlier to the later satisfaction, he would never be able to consume at all. He could not even eat and consume tomorrow, because when tomorrow became today, and the day after tomorrow became tomorrow, the decision to consume would still call for valuing an earlier satisfaction more than a later satisfaction. Otherwise, consumption would have to be delayed still further. (Mises 1940, p. 444)

There are a couple of problems with this explanation. The first one concerns the possible exceptions Mises himself mentions. Don't people exist who actually postpone consumption all the way until their death? Suicides, masochists, and so on are also acting individuals; they also take attempts to remove "felt uneasiness." So too is the case of any person deciding not to consume anything at all, by delaying consumption till the very end. Can we say those people have negative time preferences because they are not interested in consumption at all? Is any consumption needed in order for time preference to be positive? The above long quote would sound more plausible if it was more oriented toward action—rather than consumption. As Garrison notes, time preference is a feature of action (not consumption) (Garrison 1979, p. 89).

Additionally there is a side problem in Mises's statement that originary interest is a "ratio of value" and a "ratio of commodity prices" that under equilibrium is "equalized for all commodities" (Mises 1966, p. 526). Huerta de Soto in a similar spirit says the interest rate denotes the market price of present goods in relation to future goods (while in reality it is the market price of present money in relation to future money) (Huerta de Soto 2006, p. 285). What are the problems with such an approach? First, the term "ratios of value" is misleading since value is not measurable and it would be hard to arrive at ratios of something that cannot be expressed in numbers. Second of all, the same price discount for all goods would exist under a very specific equilibrium construct known as the evenly rotating economy. Yet, in that construct, interest on all commodities is equalized not by the mechanisms of the model but merely by the assumptions of the model: everything is the same because everything is the same. It is worth noting also that money does not exist in the ERE; hence, there is no monetary interest at all. There is also a third problem related to this: one could imagine stable equilibrium conditions in which the ratio of commodity prices is different than the interest rate in the market.[15]

Let us put aside those details and return to the fundamentals of action. By virtue of taking any action, people demonstrate their valuation of time, which needs to be economized on. Any choice made by an individual represents a will to act now rather than later. With this adjustment, all of Mises's points become more universal. After all, a choice is always a choice to act now—not later, not in the distant future. Hence, time is always valued as a scarce good that is in irreversible flux for humans. Yet, despite such adjustment, there is still a gap between making time preference an element in a pure theory of action and making it a prerequisite for physical monetary surplus. Actually praxeological time preference does not imply positive time preference (Gunning 2005, p. 106).

Consider a typical interest exchange where 100 units of money are given up in order to receive 105 units of money a year from now. The receiver of 105 units, by virtue of their choice of cashing out, demonstrates a preference for receiving the money in twelve months' time—not in thirteen months, fifteen months, or longer than that. Such a clear preference for accepting the good sooner rather than later comes from the praxeological nature of exchange as action occurrence. Nevertheless, there is no clear bridge between a preference for sooner rather than later and a physical surplus of money in interest payments. The transaction could well be 100 units of money today in exchange for 100 units tomorrow, such that monetary interest is zero. Or interest could even be negative: 100 units today for 95 units tomorrow. We do not argue that such an exchange is likely to happen or is normal: there are good reasons why a physical monetary surplus does occur in interest payments and good reasons why it leads to beneficial results in the market process. But there is no a priori, or praxeological, reason why zero or negative money interest should not happen because of some particular notion of time preference. There is obviously some missing link between the two (Hülsmann 2002, p. 81).[16]

Here we reach the fundamental problem of most interest theories developed in the nineteenth century—including the neoclassical theory: the gap between the pure, "originary" interest concept and the empirical reality of monetary interest. The whole reason why theorists invented the concept of originary interest was to direct our attention to some fundamental variables, which in turn were meant to explain a real-world, empirical fact: positive money interest, a physical monetary surplus, an actual difference between monetary inflows and outflows manifested universally in all sectors of the economy. Originary interest would explain why we have monetary surpluses and would also explain why such surpluses cannot be abolished. (There were also sociopolitical reasons for debating the issue.)

Unfortunately the gap between monetary reality and praxeological considerations was not filled. There are serious reasons to doubt it could be. Valuation is subjective, nonmeasurable by an outside observer (or even by decision makers themselves). It cannot be added, subtracted, objectively registered, interpersonally compared, and completely assessed (Cuhel 1907). There is no reason why a particular subjective valuation has to always result in physical surpluses of money. I am not arguing that such surpluses are not economically sensible. I am arguing that subjective value-theory considerations do not make positive monetary interest necessary.

In discussing originary interest, we can define original or pure time preference various ways and discuss its features. It may never perhaps be possible to describe pure time preference in such a way that it always has to be "positive." Nevertheless, even if we succeeded in such an attempt, there is no a priori reason why positive pure time preference would not result in zero or negative money interest rates in the market. Kirzner (1993, p. 118) appears to agree with this when he notes that the whole approach of originary interest was never meant to explain the (heights of) existing market interest rates but only the phenomenon of interest (Kirzner 1993, p. 118).[17] We can safely accept such equivocation, but we also should acknowledge, then, that any originary interest concept is compatible with any market rates (positive, negative, or zero). Henceforth, a full and sensible integration of originary interest and real money interest rates is possible, but originary interest appears to fail in the task for which it arose centuries ago: to economically "justify" the existence of positive money interest rates—or as antimarket critics called them "usurious" rates.

The above applies to both psychological, Böhm-Bawerkian theories and Misesian, praxeological theories. It is similar with Guido Hülsmann's approach, with interest as a value spread between means and ends. Originary interest is seen as a fundamental value spread present in every action between means and ends (Hülsmann 2002, pp. 86–87). By their very nature, means are always given up in order to arrive at certain valued ends (to slightly correct Hülsmann here, people are not really choosing between means and ends but between two conflicting ends). For example, constructing a vehicle requires assembling it from various parts. All parts in the technological process are together valued less than the final assembled product, the vehicle—not only in terms of monetary prices, but even in terms of fundamental value (again, actually it is not the means that are valued less, but alternative goals for the means are valued less than the goal, the vehicle's contribution[18]).

Hülsmann's means-ends framework with the above minor corrections appears to be a sensible and coherent set of statements about preference, action, and profit, or what he sees as interest. The primary goal set by acting individuals is always about the alternative goal that may be pursued with the available means. Despite the truth of that statement, such a value spread—just like psychological time preference, praxeological time preference, or productivity—cannot universally lead to monetary surplus in production processes. Hülsmann is quite aware of that fact (Hülsmann 2002, p. 93).

There is also another factor, one that suggests his theory is less superficial—because it does not rest on general equilibrium constructs taken to the extreme. With typical time-preference theory, one has to assume very sophisticated and quite unrealistic clauses about the other things being held equal: people compare two identical goods that are nonperishable and do not change while the circumstances surrounding them also stay the same, except for the passage of time, which happens under full certainty and predictability of future states of affairs (Lewin 1997, pp. 5–6). Such an imaginary construct may be a good thought experiment, but even in thoughts there are some inherent contradictions that are too problematic.

It is worthwhile to note Gunning's perspective on Mises's concept of time preference (Gunning 2005). He convincingly argues that many of Mises's followers (Roger Garrison, Murray Rothbard, Israel Kirzner, and Bettina Greaves) were constantly seeing more in Mises's case than what it actually says. Indeed, after clearing the writings of Mises's followers from one's mind, while reading passages from *Human Action* the reader may get the impression that Mises's statements are very broad, general, and at most times noncontroversial. There is, however, one deficiency of such a reading: those statements are, then, detached from the central controversies over interest income as a payment for capital.

Rothbard and Market Pricing of the Interest Rate

Murray Rothbard deserves special mention because of his presentation of how the interest rate is competitively shaped in the market process by suppliers of money capital and receivers of money capital. The presentation is not based on any loanable-funds theory. Rothbard actually argues that loanable funds are traded in a side market and are a manifestation of existing interest rates throughout the economy. Rothbard in his framework adhered to what he called pure time-preference theory. Despite this classification of his own, we may see some important differences between him and his Austrian forerunners. First, in his history-of-thought textbook, he does not agree with Böhm-Bawerk's arguments against all abstinence theories.[19] He actually says abstinence theories are quite close to pure time-preference theories since their main focus is the passage of time.[20] Time preference accounts for the disutility of waiting (Rothbard 2004, p. 49). One can therefore state that Rothbard saw himself as a presenter of the broader tradition of analyzing interest.[21]

Second, although Rothbard does go into details about the exact meaning of interest as originary, it is only part of his work on interest. While discussing the fundamentals of action he assumes future goods are discounted in value compared to present goods. The shorter the passage of time needed to satisfy preferences and achieve the goals, the better. Misesian traits are clearly visible in those passages (Rothbard 2004, pp. 15–16). From then on, Rothbard starts to develop his bargaining theory of interest formation in the market, and in this lies his great contribution to interest theory: treating interest like any other price formed purely by actors in the market.[22] Hence, third, the reason why Rothbard adheres to what he called the pure time-preference theory is that he believed the price spreads to be fully shaped by people's preferences and choices. The chapter "Time Preferences and Individual Value Scales" starts with particular preferences and possible supply and demand schedules, concepts to be developed later in the "time market" (Rothbard 2004, pp. 379–380). Time valuations become a universal feature of all production and consumption processes, which prepare the way for capitalization to appear everywhere.

Naturally the idea that time has a monetary value included in all pricing processes is nothing exceptional, since it appears in economics, the theory of finance, and so on. Rothbard, however, is actually the first to build the whole monetary-pricing theory of the productive capital structure. All this starts from subjective time preferences, or to be more precise, from individual preferences about monetary returns, preferences that stand above the financial market, the banking sector, and the loanable-funds market. None of those three markets produce interest-rate phenomena. Preferences do, and they find their way into those markets. Rothbard does not assume that monetary interest already exists and then describe how preferences respond. Rather than assuming the intertemporal price, he attempts to explain it fully in terms of people's choices, which are prior to any market exchanges, including exchanges in the time market (Lewin 1997, p. 2).

Paradoxically, by staying somewhat away from the nineteenth- and early twentieth-century approaches to interest as a nonmonetary fundamental, and by focusing on placing monetary interest in the pricing framework, Rothbard has made monetary interest more fundamental than ever—at the center of the whole market process. That is not, of course, to say that preferences are everything. Markets' functioning—along with the height of the interest rate—can be reshaped or disturbed by the working of various factors, including government intervention. Such forces and influences do not undermine the basic notion that monetary interest is produced by suppliers and demanders of present money and future money.

Extending Rothbard: Money is Productive

Another way of looking at the time market and strengthening Rothbard's vision would be to consider money as a productive good—not physically productive, but value productive. Many Austrian works emphasize that money is a good demanded in cash balances with its "yield" given by holding it (Hutt 1956). Money then offers present utility to its holder and possible utility to its potential purchaser. It is no surprise that giving up money is giving up a valuable good; hence, the reward is expected. Acquiring it means receiving a valuable good, so there is readiness to pay a price for it. Also, the concept of productivity in Austrian works is considered subjective, not objective. Any commodity or service traded in the market receives its deserved value par excellence. No direct physical productivity is required for market valuation.

By connecting those two issues, Robert Murphy appears to have found a sensible empirical notion of what interest is: a payment for a productive good (Murphy 2003, p. 171)—as simple as that. Owners of money are renting it out just as owners of machines are renting them out and owners of bodies are renting out their labor services. In such a way, Fetter's theory of rent—praised many times by Rothbard—could be extended and applied to the theory of all prices universally, including the price in the money market:

interest. Combining all factors of production results in higher economic value, since production is creation of economic value (Sanders 1896, p. 503). Each addition of value could be theoretically ascribed to specific factors, including ownership of money capital. The current usefulness of present money is unquestionable; hence, there is a market price for it. Present money allows current demanders to be financed in the time market to pay out necessary wages and rents for capital goods. Such a productive function of money cannot be doubted. Then there is no surprise that the current market price for such a function is neither zero nor negative—at least in the usual market circumstances. As the experience of negative rates after 2008 teaches us, the conditions for renting the money may be so influenced by various policies that such rent can become at times negative.

One of the early critics of Böhm-Bawerk attempted to reformulate his theory in terms of opportunity cost and possible alternate employments in a similar manner to the above:

> It is evident that capital is of great service in production, and that the benefit—other things being equal—is proportional to the duration of the service. A machine which will save $100 expense in one month will save another $100 the next mouth, and so on so long as its efficiency is unimpaired. Money capital may always be invested in forms of this kind, which, like the economy of machinery or the comfort of shelter, will bring a return proportional to the duration in time. Hence it is that the surety of $100 next year is not worth so much as $100 in hand; for the money in hand can be so invested as to administer somewhat to our comfort or profit, and still be worth $100 at the end of the year. It is the usefulness of capital, for the most part, which makes present goods worth more than future goods, and gives rise to interest. (Green 1891, p. 364)

Another author, Francis Walker, argued that Böhm-Bawerk's criticism of productivity theorists could be seen as a further development rather than a full rejection. After admitting that he is not very knowledgeable about interest (Walker 1892, p. 399), Walker tries to interpret the productivity argument as a very broad one: the use of capital in production contributes significantly because it allows for the creation of a larger amount of goods and services with higher aggregated value (ibid, p. 404). Hence, capital theorizing always bears some relation to the concept of productivity. Naturally, there is a missing element—for there is a difference between capital and capital goods. While discussing productivity, Böhm-Bawerk and others emphasized that physical productivity gains are to be associated with tools, machines, and other capital goods, which receive their marginal products. What remains to be explained is interest as a difference between future revenues and current prices. Here is where the difference between capital and capital goods enters. Nevertheless, the argument about increases in the value of production could be extended. Capital is also money productive and allows for creation of value that otherwise would not exist. To emphasize this we have to move back to the monetary side of production and pricing. Money is the necessary means to start production processes (sort of similar argument could be given for payments under barter).

Reformulating money as a productive good (perhaps even a fourth factor of production[23]) allows us to answer fully the initial Böhm-Bawerkian question about interest theory: Why is full value of a final product not imputed entirely to the factors of production? Why is the ability to produce not fully reflected in the price (Garrison 1988, p. 165)? Simply because by asking the question we committed a mistake and missed something when describing an imputation process. The value is fully imputed! Future rents of a productive machine are not fully reflected in its current price because there is an additional factor—money—that allows us to build the machine. Without this money the machine would not be built; hence, any potential future rent would not appear to the owner either. In other words, to gain utility from future services of a machine one cannot only build a present machine. Present money also is needed to finance other complementary factors of production to create it. And money in here is just as complementary as other necessary production goods, without which the process of production and value creation could not happen. Therefore, it "rightfully" receives its share in the imputation process, a specific type of rent called interest. I will inquire in the second chapter into how the height of this price depends on the productive structure.

Money plays a special role in determining the interest rate. In the typical equilibrium, Böhm-Bawerkian and Misesian framework, one discusses the relationship between "future" and "present" goods without going into the details about what exact types of goods are being discussed. Yet it would be interesting to learn whether there is a higher systematic discount between future and present nonmoney goods than between future and present money. The very special nature of money is that it is a highly marketable good universally accepted and desired at all times. Within money lies a productive potential to start any production process now or in the future, and the potential to bid away the factors of production into desired processes. Such a feature of money can well explain its additional productive function, one manifested in the interest-rate market. Money has the biggest reallocation power of all. No surprise then, that there is a premium of present goods over present money (Watkins 1928, p. 378).[24] Hence, the marketability and universality of money as compared to nonmoney goods expands in time, which leads to growth in its value, manifesting itself in the interest rate. Money is simply productive in every economic sense of the word.

In this way, we also reach a full circle with the Knightian-Clarkian notion of capital as something productive—but only if we treat money capital as productive and hence leading to positive money interest.

Neoclassical and Austrian Exercise in Pure Theorizing of Interest: A Summary

What was the characteristic feature of the early marginalist discussions of interest? A focus on finding a fundamental phenomenon outside of monetary and market transactions, a phenomenon deeply rooted in something inherent in the nature of man or reality, a phenomenon that would not be immanently linked to existing institutions such as money or private property. Neoclassical attempts were more focused on productive powers. Austrian contributions were more centered on people's subjective preferences. All those considerations led to the acceptance of the notion that there are some underlying crucial factors for setting the interest rates in some "accordance." Such a state of affairs has not been shaken by obscure debates between Knight, Machlup, and Hayek. The general notion was set, which can be well summarized by words from the most famous textbook of the twentieth century by Samuelson and Nordhaus:

> Investment in capital goods involves forgoing present consumption to increase future consumption. Consuming less today frees labor for making nets to catch many more fish tomorrow. In the most general sense, capital is productive because by forgoing consumption today we get more consumption in the future.
>
> Fisher described the interplay between the interest rate and innumerable other elements of the economy. Yet the basic determinants of the interest rate, Fisher showed, were two fundamental pillars: impatience as reflected in "time discounting" and investment opportunity as reflected in the "marginal rate of return over cost."
>
> We can use the classical theory of capital to understand the determination of the rate of interest. Households supply funds for investment by abstaining from consumption and accumulating savings over time. At the same time, businesses demand capital goods to combine with labor, land, and other inputs. In the end, a firm's demand for capital is driven by its desire to make profits by producing goods. Or, as Irving Fisher put the matter a century ago: *The quantity of capital and the rate of return on capital are determined by the interaction between (1) people's impatience to consume now rather than accumulate more capital goods for future consumption (perhaps for old-age retirement or for that proverbial rainy day); and (2) investment opportunities that yield higher or lower returns to such accumulated capital.* (Samuelson and Nordhaus 2010, pp. 291–293)

The solution was there: interest is tied to capital's function of representing either time preferences or the productive powers of capital (or both to different extents). Despite such a consensus, the debates about interest were far from over. The next serious attack came in the famous reswitching debate, which will be the subject of the second chapter, and which will allow us to see how interest rate is formed in the production structure.

NOTES

1. Compare this to Roger Garrison's statement on the capital structure, which may sound similar in some respect: "The time dimension . . . has a double interpretation. First, it can depict goods in process moving through time from the inception to the completion of the production process. Second, it can represent the separate stages of production, all of which exist in the present, each of which aims at consumption at different point in the future. This second interpretation allows for the most straight forward representation of the relationships of capital-based macroeconomics" (Garrison 2001, p. 47).

2. In fact, a lot of the quarrel between Clark and Böhm-Bawerk can be seen as a quarrel about different definitions of capital. Compare Skousen 1990, pp. 28–35. The confusion about terms surrounding the concept of "capital" is also well documented in Fetter 1900, pp. 8–12, passim.

3. Knight sounds here almost like Murray Rothbard. Compare: "We must keep in mind the vital fact that the concept of a 'good' refers to a thing the units of which the actor believes afford equal serviceability. It does not refer to the physical or chemical characteristics of the good" (Rothbard 2004, p. 69). See also Rothbard's discussion of Frank Fetter's theory of rent (2004, pp. 488–495).

4. Yet, as one of the critics stated, the whole concept of interest as a result of "productivity of capital" rests on some notion of equilibrium (Somers 1941, p. 501).

5. Knight argues that Böhm-Bawerk's third reason for interest (greater productivity of longer processes of production) is productivity theory in disguise (Knight 1916, p. 294).

6. As Herbener argues (2011, pp. 37–38) Fisher can rightly be seen as a follower of John Rae and Böhm-Bawerk (see also Dimand and Geanakoplos 2005, pp. 4–5).

7. Kirzner (1993, p. 184) argued that pure time-preference theory actually does not have to disregard the role of productivity in subjective considerations on interest (in the intertemporal pricing process). Garrison, on the other hand, argues that under the conditions in those examples no exchanges and transactions exist; therefore, the questions about interest become irrelevant (Garrison 1979, p. 92).

8. This is not the case, for example, when we have current money (say, in 2016), which can be stolen by someone. We could accept negative interest (which actually means: pay for the service) in order to secure the money to safely use it later (for example, in 2017).

9. Böhm-Bawerk treats his statements of roundabout productivity as just depictions of a fact of life, a very general rule, and offers real-world examples of it. Therefore, unfortunately, the status of the roundaboutness proposition remains unclear and cannot be fully settled (see Buechner 1989, pp. 503–504).

10. Also, Böhm-Bawerk probably without noticing is leaving the realm of the stationary model. When we consider future increases in the amount of produced goods and services, we cannot argue that the ceteris paribus notion is in place, since conditions are systematically shifting (Bernholtz 1993, p. 26).

11. Clark of course, called this "abstinence" theory, which intensified the previously mentioned heated capital debates in the nineteenth century (Clark 1895, pp. 98–99). The uncertain meaning of "waiting" and "abstaining" created a lot of confusion about the nature of the capitalist process. In a developed capitalist economy, do we actually have to wait through the whole process of product creation, from the very beginning till final consumption? Well, yes and no (see Taussig 1908, pp. 339–240). See also the previous chapter on the neoclassicals.

12. It is also worth noting that some of the criticisms of Böhm-Bawerk are directed against expositions by others, and not by Böhm-Bawerk himself. Such is the case for example with Hirshleifer (1967), which is based on simultaneous equations among wage rates, the value of the capital stock, the period of production, and a particular rate of interest (Hirshleier 1967, p. 191). Böhm-Bawerk neither built such a framework nor based his model entirely on the concept of one good. Possible confusion may come from Dorfman, who named his contribution "Böhm-Bawerk's exposition," whereas it was more of a further development (in the neoclassical framework) than just a graphical presentation (Dorfman 1959, p. 154). For a more modern example of the neoclassical approach to time preference as utility functions, see Becker and Mulligan (1997, p. 734). Another such example is the work of Koopmans aiming "to define preference for advanced timing entirely in terms of a utility function," or to simply make an attempt to translate Böhm-Bawerk's discussions into mathematical functions (Koopmans 1960, p. 287). Unfortunately, during the process a lot is lost in translation, especially in light of the fact that Dorfman seems to downplay the crucial element of Böhm-Bawerk's insights about the interest rate: time preference! (See Neuberger 1960, p. 150.)

13. Moreover, time in a praxeological manner is being treated differently than in the neoclassical framework (or physical). It has sometimes been said with exaggeration that in neoclassical economics there is "no time." While an overstatement, it contains a kernel of truth. The neoclassical framework is not timeless, but it is impotent in capturing dynamic change (Boland 1978, p. 242).

14. Actually Böhm-Bawerk's reasons at times sound less psychological, more cognitive. His discussion on how people think about the future and create abstractions in their minds sounds less psychological and more like inquiries about the thinking process.

15. For example, assume that one present apple trades for one present orange and for two claims to future apples and half a claim to a future orange (Murphy 2011, pp. 4–5). At the same time, a present orange naturally trades for half a claim to a future orange, two claims to future apples (therefore, one claim to a future apple

trades for one-fourth of a future claim to an orange). We are assuming equilibrium conditions—everything is foreseen and balanced and there is no place for arbitrage. Why is that example puzzling? Because here we have multiple natural real interest rates that are not uniform. Therefore, it would be safe to simply drop the notion of originary interest as equalized in all ratios of commodities, for it need not be so.

16. As Robinson comments on a hypothetical primitive economy: "Suppose that some hunters wish to consume more than their kill, and others wish to carry consuming power into the future. Then the latter could lend to the former to-day, out of to-day's catch, against a promise of repayment in the future. The rate of interest (excess of repayment over original loan) would settle at the level which equated supply and demand for loans. Whether it was positive or negative would depend upon whether spendthrifts or prudent family men happened to predominate in the community. There is no a priori presumption in favour of a positive rate. Thus the rate of interest cannot be accounted for as the 'cost of waiting.'" (Robinson 1953, p. 87)

17. Kirzner also notes that productivity aspects can influence rates of interest, even though the main cause for interest is time preference. In a similar manner, Fetter states that time preference dominates the alternatives and decides about choosing most productive technologies (Fetter 1914, p. 259). For the same reason, he remained skeptical about Böhm-Bawerk's third cause and pointed to various non sequiturs in Böhm-Bawerk's lines of reasoning (see Fetter 1902, pp. 165–172).

18. Hülsmann attempts to differentiate between the concepts of "gain" and "interest" (Hülsmann 2002, p. 90). To do this he uses an example in which there are intermediate goals and goods: Brown sells the garden full of flowers to gain a kitchen, allowing him to produce meals. A kitchen is apparently the means, the meals the goal. The exchange of garden for kitchen is gain. Yet this is a definitional quarrel. Why not just say that the garden becomes the means for having the meals? It is just like how the wheels of a car are the means to move around the city. Certainly they are an indirect, intermediate means, but in the end they receive their value as intermediates. Similarly, in the garden example, the possibility of exchanges opens the possibility for a higher end to be satisfied. Hülsmann confirms this later on in his paper in the section "Manifestations of Means and Ends in Consecutive Actions": "All intermediate evaluations are made in light of the overarching evaluation of the final good, and all exchange ratios (prices) are formed in light of the exchange ratio (price) in the final transaction. In other words, there is a hierarchical value-relationship between the ultimate goals and the means to attain them" (Hülsmann 2002, pp. 95–96).

19. "Despite Böhm-Bawerk's uncharitable strictures on the more highly developed abstinence theory of Nassau Senior, there is not a great deal of difference between the abstinence view and the later, and more sophisticated, Austrian theory of time-preference" (Rothbard 1995, p. 138). Also very strongly commenting on Turgot: "One of the striking examples of injustice in the historiography of economic thought is the treatment accorded to Turgot's brilliant analysis of capital and interest by the great founder of Austrian capital and interest theory, Eugen von Böhm-Bawerk. In the 1880s, Böhm-Bawerk set out, in the first volume of his *Capital and Interest*, to clear the path for his own theory of interest by studying and demolishing previous, competing theories. Unfortunately, instead of acknowledging Turgot as his forerunner

in pioneering Austrian theory, Böhm-Bawerk brusquely dismissed the Frenchman as a mere Physiocratic naive land-productivity (or 'fructification') theorist. This unfairness to Turgot is all the more heightened by recent information that Böhm-Bawerk, in his first evaluation of Turgot's theory of interest in a still unpublished seminar paper in 1876, reveals the enormous influence of Turgot's views on his later developed thought. Perhaps we must conclude that, in this case, as in other cases, Böhm-Bawerk's need to claim originality and to demolish all his predecessors took precedence over the requirements of truth and justice" (Rothbard 1995a, p. 402).

20. On the other hand, Böhm-Bawerk's perspective can be justified by the fact that all those predecessors did not have a proper utility theory, but instead relied on the older, cost-of-production theory, mostly irrelevant in the ending years of the nineteenth century (Bernholtz 1993, p. 49).

21. One of the early critics of Böhm-Bawerk argued that the Austrian overstated his case in the first volume of the treatise and created great expectations about what he might explain in the second volume. In reality it turned out that the proposed explanations may actually appear as a combination of both productivity and abstinence arguments about interest known from previous writers but in much different and primitive forms (see Hawley 1892, p. 306).

22. Before that, he actually uses a slightly problematic concept of "rate of time preference" detached from monetary prices and rooted in the valuation process (Rothbard 2004, p. 62). "Rate" could assume something measurable to discount, which in the case of subjective valuation could not be the case, which Rothbard was perfectly aware of.

23. One could counterargue that money just facilitates the true factors of production. Yet such a response would be very materialistic and eventually self-refuting. For example, we treat logistics and transportation services as factors of production. The same is true with managing and directing the processes of production. Why then not treat an even-more-essential element—money—as also a factor of production (receiving its rent)?

24. The phenomenon of undervaluation of future commodities because of inventory deliveries (compared to more liquid instruments) is known as convenience yield. Under regular circumstances it results in normal backwardation—where the price of a future contract sells below the future spot price.

Chapter 2

Challenges Concerning the Structure of Production

Capital-Reswitching Puzzles: What in Production Can Be Measured?

Analyzing interest within the capital structure leads to questions about the amount of capital, accumulation of capital, and "length of production," the last of which will be a subject of the later parts of the chapter. How does the interest rate relate to the number of production stages and the overall length of production? Before we proceed with that question, I will start with the famous reswitching debate. The reasons for considering this slightly archaic discussion are simple: The reswitching critique was perhaps the main challenge for capital theory in the twentieth century, and it has not been successfully resolved (though some may certainly dispute this). Additionally, starting with the critique will be convenient for us to see where thinkers neglected critical problems when I offer the example of a negative relationship between the height of the interest rate and the length of production. By seeing their errors it becomes possible to correct them while presenting the concept of capital structure and to include in capital theory insights from the reswitching debate. At the same time, I plan to adapt the concept of reswitching to the monetary framework. In other words, rather than start with existing ideas only to demonstrate their incompleteness by keeping in mind the challenge and the mistakes of the reswitching debate, it will be easier to develop a proper capital theory from scratch.

The capital debates dwelt mainly on the neoclassical production function. Apparently well-established conclusions in the profession coming from the Hicksian view of the pricing process were the following: (1) Cobb-Douglas functions, where output is determined by two distinct aggregate variables, labor and capital (in addition to rest, which remained unexplained), exist; (2) both of those factors earn their marginal returns, such that the wage rate depends on the marginal productivity of labor, while the return on capital depends on the marginal productivity of capital;[1] (3) the rate of interest (i.e., profit on capital) is related to the relative scarcity of capital, meaning that its abundance should lead to lower returns, its relative scarcity to higher returns (Pressman 2005, p. 422). From these basic, though at-times-questioned, lines of neoclassical reasoning, many flowers blossomed. If the production-function approach has withstood criticism, the Clarkian task of unifying the theories of capital and capital goods (production on the one hand, and distribution on the other) has been successfully completed (Laibman and Nell 1977, pp. 878–879).

The reswitching debates started off with Joan Robinson's (1953) famous publication on the production function. Yet perhaps the clearest exposition of the reswitching challenge can be found in the summary by Paul Samuelson, who suggested that the capital structure is an example that validates the "simple story" of William Stanley Jevons, Böhm-Bawerk, and Knut Wicksell—a story of how lower time preference (i.e., greater abstention from consumption) favors more productive and longer processes of production (Samuelson 1966, p. 568).

The debate's initial presentation of reswitching came in Pierro Sraffa's treatise (1960, ch. 12). It began with the ordering of various techniques in the production process. It is not possible to order all of them according to some monotonic transformation in relation to the rate of profit. The implication is that a fall in the rate of interest may initially lead producers to drop one technique, A, in favor of another technique, B, but further reductions in interest can lead to the reverse change: a move from technique B to technique A (Pasinetti 1966, p. 503). This means it is hard to capture the one-way dependence of the rate of profit with such concepts as, for example, length of production, amount of waiting, or amount of accumulated capital. Levhari (1965) attempted to rebut Sraffa's argument by claiming that Sraffa's claim does not hold for the whole economy. Yet, as it turned out after the debate's series of publications, Sraffa's example is fine, as proven by Samuelson's concession in what is probably the best exposition of the reswitching challenge.[2]

Let us proceed with Samuelson's example. Imagine a simple choice between two production techniques (Samuelson 1966, p. 569; compare also with Wright 1975, p. 21). Technique A requires the producer to invest two labor units in the first period, zero units in the second, and six units in the final stage (a good can mature without any labor needed). The final value, with the interest rate symbolized by r, is as follows:

$$2\,(1 + r)^2 + 0\,(1 + r) + 6$$

In technique B, seven units of labor are applied in the second period and no units in the third and first periods (therefore, the process is shorter). The final value is the following:

$$7\,(1 + r)$$

How does the height of the interest rate affect the choice of alternatives? As the example proves, there is no uniform relationship between interest and the length of production. When the interest rate is higher than 100 percent—for example, 200 percent—technique B will be chosen (with twenty-one units of labor instead of the twenty-four units in A^3). When the interest rate falls below 100 percent, the case changes. New levels of time preference (or whatever determines interest) now favor technique A over technique B, which could mean the production structure is changing toward more "roundabout" processes of production. Yet, there is a boundary. When the interest rate falls below 50 percent, technique B becomes profitable again—hence the "reswitching" in the capital structure.

This consideration apparently leads to a staggering result: the interest rate is not systematically related to the length of production or the amount of capital. The production function does not behave like a typical set of demand and supply curves for capital—at least not in the way the "simple story" was told for decades. Naturally, reswitching had been admitted as a possibility, since it was obviously drawn from theory. Another issue would be finding reswitching in reality—a task that was not successful. Hence, reswitching appeared to be similar to a positively sloped demand curve: possible in theory, difficult to find in practice (Han and Schefold 2006, p. 745).

It comes as no surprise that Samuelson, with his pedagogical gift, offered the clearest exposition of reswitching. We should, however, keep in mind that reswitching in itself was never considered a very big issue, but only a symptom of some tension in then-prevailing currents of thought. Why? Because it is a highly technical problem about how various modeling techniques work. As Robinson noted after some time (in an article with the telling title "The Unimportance of Reswitching"), the whole debate, like many others in economics, was about confronting conclusions and arguments without going back to the basics: the assumptions of models (Robinson 1975, p. 32). A large literature is full of almost purely mathematical a priori exercises, with only occasional, weak attempts to actually make them empirically workable. Consisting of purely logical inquiries, the capital debate was a little overblown. All the heat it generated came because of the problematic assumptions in theorizing about monotonic transformations.

Going back to fundamentals, Robinson, in an early publication on the topic, was not really focused on the issue of switching techniques but on problems related to measuring capital and the neoclassical approach to economic theorizing. These were the times when the Solow model was on the rise and Cobb-Douglass functions appeared in most places with parallel microeconomic distribution theories.[4] A typical presentation of neoclassical thinking may be found in Swann's model: labor is homogeneous and expressed in labor hours, undifferentiated land expressed in acres. Capital similarly is made of "meccano sets," which do not wear out and can be easily assembled in various combinations without incurring huge costs. Various products could be created with many possible combinations of all three factors (Swann 1956, pp. 343–344). Robinson was commenting on precisely these types of assumptions. While addressing the features of production functions, the literature somehow omitted the question of how capital is measured. The result was that sloppy thinking was passed on to the next generation, as students became professors (Robinson 1953, p. 81).[5]

Why is measuring capital so important? Measurement is needed because in neoclassical economics, capital needs to be defined in nonmonetary terms. The only way to measure capital in practice is to assess its monetary value. Yet, the monetary value depends on the interest rate and discounting of future revenues (thus assuming away the problem of the disequilibrated nature of capital in the real world, where many investment plans are in conflict). Therefore, in order to assess monetary value, the interest rate is needed. But if interest is needed, then capital measured in money terms cannot explain interest. Interest has to be assumed and known before doing the measuring. If that is the case, then the whole idea of describing a production function and explaining the interest rate in the neoclassical framework is completely circular. The interest rate cannot be explained in relation to existing capital because the concept of existing capital relies on knowing the interest rate in advance.

In a sensible response, Solow argued that measuring capital is not a true problem. Not the diversity of capital, but putting together the past, present, and future is what challenges capital theorists. With capital—equilibrated—theorizing there is always something "foolish" in assuming perfect foresight (Solow 1955, p. 102). Indexing the quantity of capital is one such foolish assumption because it could allow for intracapital substitutions against changes in the labor input (ibid., p. 103). Solow here is (probably unintentionally) echoing Hayek's comment on marginal rates of substitution under socialism: if we knew all possible combinations of production and also the relative influences of all factors on output (i.e., how much of factor A can be substituted with certainty for some amount of factor B), then the problem becomes technical. Similarly, the question of the quantity of capital would not even arise, since capital would be perfectly allocated without additional interference.

Sen also opines that measurement is not the main issue (Sen 1974, pp. 329–330). He points out that even with a measurable unit of capital, a problem of comparing utilities and prices remains.[6] Hence, the model has to be even more unrealistic than just assuming measurable capital: For example, it must assume also one homogenous good, or it must assume surrogate production functions with equal factor intensity.[7] There are other ways, such as assuming the rate of profits is equal to the rate of growth (as in Solow's model). In any case, the assumption of measurable capital is just the beginning of the unrealism in neoclassical modeling, not the end of it.

One of the important conclusions from studying capital is that there is no fixed relationship between the "amount of capital" and interest rate levels. There are also no fixed relations between labor and capital that derive directly from some production function. When we assume given technological conditions and a given length of production, the same techniques can be used at the same interest rates. Valuations of capital and capital per employed unit may not behave as neoclassical functions as they should. Even without reswitching between the techniques, there may not be an inverse relationship between the rate of interest and capital abundance (Harris 1973, p. 104).

If the relationship between the quantity of capital and the interest rate could not be settled on, why then there is the continued success of Cobb-Douglas and the constant use (up to this day) of the neoclassical approach? As usual, instrumentalism prevails. The framework is used because it is useful for empirical work and policy considerations, despite its obvious—and well described—theoretical flaws (Filipe and Adams 2005, pp. 429–430). Samuelson lamented that Cobb-Douglas should be critically and empirically examined in light of accounting identities (Samuelson 1979, pp. 923–924). Filipe and Adams do precisely this and conclude that Cobb-Douglas functions are like exercises in accounting (Filipe and Adams 2005, pp. 441–442). Their existence cannot be confirmed in reality, as with "perfect" neoclassical markets or returns to scale, because they cannot be "tested" and hence refuted (or corroborated). They are ways of thinking and picturing. In fact, the neoclassical argument cannot be differentiated from a mere tautology (Shaikh 2005, p. 449). Statistical data on wages and industries can always be fit into those functions—quite elastically, I may add.[8]

Fisher's conclusion appears to make a lot of sense: aggregate production functions are just as imaginary as imaginary numbers (Fisher 2005, p. 489). How then are we to assess the actual correspondence between the statistical data of income shares and the aggregated production functions? The same year that Solow published his Nobel Prize–winning article, Phelps Brown published his critical evaluation of the Cobb-Douglas function, where he observed, by analyzing equations, that shares of earnings and elasticity are two sides of the same coin (Phelps Brown 1957, p. 557). They are derived from an identity, and hence the equations cannot really be tested against the data (Filipe and McCombie 2005, p. 470).

The study with its far-reaching conclusion of the reswitching debates therefore has very strong implications for modeling: there are no fundamental, underlying "real data" that could successfully determine the nature of capital, the structure of production, and the rate of profit. Capital and interest are necessarily linked to social institutions and to the monetary economy, not external, material, or physically measurable. Institutions and capital cannot be separated. Overall, this leaves us at the next step in capital theorizing: the monetary approach. As Robinson commented:

> This leaves the question where it began. "Capital" in the statistics is a sum of money. Estimates of the dollar value of capital represent equipment, stocks and work in progress committed to industrial production, reckoned at dollar prices. A piece of equipment or a stock of raw materials, regarded as a product, has a price, like any other product, made up of prime cost plus a gross margin. These costs (direct and indirect) are composed of wages, rents, depreciation and net profit. The amount of net profit entering into the price of the product is, obviously, influenced by the general rate of profit prevailing in the industries concerned. Thus the value of capital depends upon the rate of profit. (Robinson 1971, p. 601)

What is the institutional aspect implicitly or explicitly present in discussing the pricing of capital? Profits and interest exist in the current form because there is private ownership of the means of production and monetary calculation based on it (Robinson 1953, p. 87). Such an observation may have something to do with ideology, since property is not only an economic concept but a normative and political concept. Although the economic consequences of differing political orders may be discussed, it may be difficult to completely put aside normative values while discussing them. That at least was Harcourt's position, though he went a bit too far in suggesting that one's views about the pricing process probably reveal one's ideology of markets and private property (Harcourt and Cohen 2003, p. 210). If you believe in the neoclassical marginal theory of pricing, then very probably you are more or less a supporter of the market system. Most of the representatives of the debate, however, would not share Harcourt's view and should not be seen as ideologically biased (Stiglitz 1974, p. 901).

Why was it such a big deal to create production functions, functions that could well describe production and distribution? Because "capital" could now be recognized as a separate factor of production, independent of distribution, and then production could justify distribution in some fundamental sense. For some of the Marxists, the neoclassical failure to justify distribution in this way was seen as a sort of victory, since talking about capital was not about some objective underlying variables detached from society. It was about the rules of the game, about institutions, about the way society is organized, and not about mythical concepts of objective scarcity translated into equations and then prices (Bhaduri 1969, pp. 532–533). In other words, the neoclassicals failed to continue with the undertakings of Böhm-Bawerk, Clark, Fisher, and others: searching for the fundamental causes of interest. Similar is the case of the whole pricing process, where prices were understood to only reflect inherent technical conditions and the exchange mechanism understood to allow for perfect allocations (Robinson 1967, p. 77). Yet it turns out that Kirzner appears to have been right all along: theorizing about interest is not about finding something causing it to exist at certain quantitative levels. Theorizing could perhaps only be qualitative in this aspect—about finding general variables that cause interest to simply exist, not exist at mathematically definite levels.

While it is certainly true that there is an ideological aspect, it is not necessarily true that admitting the connection between ownership of capital and capital owners' income must in some way signify a slightly negative attitude toward private property. One should not forget about the representatives of the Austrian school, who would share most of Robinson's reservations about the neoclassical functions (or even exceed them). One can study the works of Hayek and Ludwig Lachmann to see that their approach to aggregated neoclassical functions was much more critical than the Sraffians later on. They came before the whole debate started and offered deep insights into the problem with neoclassical views on capital. Moreover, one can refer to their teacher, Ludwig von Mises, who in the 1920s and 1930s, in fact, built the whole argument about the innate and inseparable relationship between prices and property: the famous calculation argument against the possibility of an effective socialist system. He certainly would have wholeheartedly signed on to the statement by Robinson about the fallacy of the production function, which holds that it is "possible to specify purely technical relations, not involving prices, in a human economy" (Robinson 1955, p. 71).[9]

Initially the challengers in the reswitching debate concluded that in general, with given technological knowledge, changes of technique that are caused by interest rate shifts cannot lead to any general statements about the amount of capital per unit of labor. No matter how capital is measured (or mismeasured) in modeling, various new ways of producing may require less or more capital per unit of labor (Pasinetti 1966, p. 514). Naturally this point addresses the Solow model and the neoclassical functions more than Böhm-Bawerk's arguments about the length of the production process. Moreover, Böhm-Bawerk's and Wicksell's failed attempts to specify an "average period of production" were similar to attempts to separate a fundamental capital variable from capital distribution (Garegnani 1966, p. 563).[10] In fact, the general reswitching critique also applies to Böhm-Bawerk: lower or higher interest rates are compatible with either longer or shorter production processes—as, in the third part of the chapter, I will attempt to show and therefore to slightly extend the reswitching challenge.

Samuelson's example of reswitching suffers from a fundamental flaw: one homogeneous unit of labor is being allocated between various ways of producing goods. Additionally, this unit is considered a measure of the amount of invested capital (as corrected via a particular interest rate). Yet one of the conclusions of the reswitching debate was to suggest that we should abandon such an approach, at least if we are to take seriously its broad implications. There are no objective factors to which capital could be successfully and deterministically reduced. How are we to make sense of the example? We can simply switch units of money for the labor units.

Let us again compare two different ways of producing a particular good. Recall that technique A requires two units of money in the first stage of production, zero units in the second stage, and six units in the third stage. Technique B requires zero units in the first stage, seven units in the second stage, and zero units in the third stage (notice that production itself only takes two stages because it is a shorter production process, where the good is maturing in the second of these stages). A purely monetary approach to the problem of reswitching can help us capture the essence of the problem from the perspective of the investment process and overall length of production from monetary perspective. Technique A requires a budget (including the value of money over time):

$$2\,(1 + r)^2 + 0\,(1 + r) + 6$$

Technique B also requires a budget:

$$7\,(1 + r)$$

How does reswitching happen in the monetary framework? Exactly the same way. At a 200 percent rate of interest, technique A requires twenty-four units of money:

$$2\,(1 + 2)^2 + 6 = 24$$

Technique B requires twenty-one units of money. A, the longer production process, consisting of three stages, is more costly. Therefore, it is better to select the shorter process. Now assume the interest rate falls to 100 percent. The budgets are equalized: they both are at fourteen units of money. As the interest rate falls below 100 percent, it becomes less costly to switch to technique A, the longer one. It could appear, then, that the interest rate is negatively related with the length of production. A lower interest rate leads to a longer process. Yet, in this example, the relationship starts to break down once we move closer to a 50 percent interest rate. At this rate, the budget for technique A is 10.5 units of money, exactly the same as the budget for technique B. As the interest rate falls below 50 percent, technique B becomes cheaper again—hence, the label "reswitching." Surprisingly, a lower interest rate favors a shorter production process at some point; hence, we cannot find a satisfactory unidirectional function relating the interest rate to the length of production. It is because the solution depends on an additional variable: the capital-to-labor ratio at various scattered stages—a subject of our next subchapter, which offers a monetary solution to the reswitching issue.

FACTORS OF PRODUCTION AND ORDERS OF GOODS

Traditionally, capital goods used for production were divided into two general categories: goods of "higher order" and "lower order." The categories could be subdivided further (i.e., first order, second order, third order, etc.) because the difference between categories is a matter of degree. Put differently there are "final" goods (also known as consumption goods)—goods of the "lowest" possible order—and goods less or more remote from that final stage. The essence of capital theory lies in explaining how goods of higher order are transformed by social and economic institutions into goods of lower order. The process ends with final consumption. Despite all the various subdisciplines in modern economics, economic theory in general is centered around this process. So-called imputation theory is illustrative at explaining how prices of goods of different orders are formed in the market economy (Menger 1976, p. 63).

The production structure can be divided into consecutive stages. Commodities and other goods that are closer to the consumer are examples of more-processed capital goods. With every stage of production, capital goods become goods of lower order. Less labor and less machinery are used for creating higher-order goods (as processing can be seen as cumulative). Every capital good—every good of higher order—can be reduced to other capital goods, labor, and natural resources. The reasoning cannot continue indefinitely. Working backward in time, the logical ending point is when there are no capital goods and only purely "primary" factors remain. At some point, basic capital goods had to be produced with only labor and natural resources. That was the hypothetical beginning of the capital formation. From that point on, capital goods comfortably found their place in the production process and started being used in all stages of production. Of course, as Knight would comment, this is a hypothetical exercise and a thought experiment. The characteristic feature of the market economy is that capital goods are constantly being produced with capital goods. There are virtually no processes performed by bare hands. Additionally, an older epoch of economic thinking overemphasized this idealized picture of "primary" factors of production at the expense of the most important factor, vindicated in the twentieth century: entrepreneurship (Klein 1988, p. 504).

Even though in theory the concepts of higher- and lower-order goods are logical and precise, applying the concept can lead to some empirical puzzles. An easy example concerning coffee seems a little too simple but remains illustrative (Mises 1966, p. 94). Let us say that a cup of coffee with milk and sugar is the final good consumed. By taking an individual's perspective, coffee without sugar and milk would be a sort of capital good, a good of higher order, at least relative to coffee with the additional ingredients. The perspective makes sense, but it is not relevant for empirical economic analysis. How are we then to decide which orders are of interest? In responding to real-world challenges, much more relevant is the division of labor among specialized industries. That is why the approach of higher- and lower-order goods must be applied to cases where different firms are engaged in various stages of production. Nobody is interested in the production of coffee with sugar at home. The perspective can be taken even with consumer goods that are consumed over a very long time span, which could make them almost like capital goods. As Boulding noted, cathedrals can be consumed for centuries and furniture for decades—much longer than their production process (Boulding 1977, p. 1).

The concepts of orders of goods are used just as the ideal types of "capitalist," "laborer," "landowner," and "entrepreneur" are used in pure theorizing. Even though in reality there is no man who is exclusively a capitalist, or laborer, or entrepreneur, we still derive those roles from real activities in order to present their function. In theorizing, we often treat them as separate functions. Similarly, we can treat coffee without sugar and milk as a final consumption good by putting aside the (perhaps a bit silly) question of whether it should be treated as a final good even though its owner plans to mix it with additional "factors of production." However we deal with that example, much more thought provoking are inquiries about the stages of production in the monetary economy involved in growing coffee plants and selling processed coffee beans at the grocery store.

Economics does not differ from other empirical sciences in the absolute basics. Although it uses radically different methods and models, one thing is the same: it conceptualizes the universe (Hamilton 1955, p. 97). Such a conceptualization was context dependent for a long time in economic thought. The burden of very old classifications is felt even today when we try to construct neoclassical models of growth, where one particular group of factors of production is put into one basket ("capital," "labor," etc.). The reality, however, is that such classifications are to a large degree artificial. They can also be very misleading, since they approach the problem almost from a physical perspective, neglecting institutional and social factors, which often can be decisive for economic development and decline (Belotti 1960, p. 74).

The above coffee example can be set aside. Nevertheless, an additional, somewhat Knightian objection to classifying orders can be raised. Knight argued that all three classical factors can be put under the heading of capital (Buechner 1976, p. 599). The problem is that capital goods are used constantly to produce other capital goods. It may not make sense to order them in a simple manner. Actually, this Knightian criticism cuts a bit deeper because it touches on a more fundamental fact: it is not possible to make a clear-cut distinction between land (natural resources) and capital goods. One possible historical way of making the distinction is to treat land and natural resources as permanent and ultimately given without the need to sustain them. Capital goods, on the other hand, needed some form of savings in order to be produced, and apparently no pure rent can be derived from using them[11]—only a basic return on capital resulting from the difference between current prices and future prices.

This approach works as long as we can safely assume that natural resources are permanent and renewable. The unfortunate truth is that they are not. Natural resources are being used up, as the basic laws of thermodynamics tell us (Georgescu-Roegen 1975, p. 368), even the so-called renewable resources (there is no such thing, actually). Goods once used up will never return. There is more to this story, as Frédéric Bastiat explained. Many thinkers in the nineteenth century argued that land and natural resources are natural gifts from God and therefore it is unjust for some people to take advantage of them by using (renting) them for their own benefit. Bastiat's answer in a nutshell was that the owner of the land always has to invest in owning and keeping his land (or at least had to invest in it in the past—assuming away the problem of theft and feudalism, of course). In fact, "nature" in itself has no value, but it becomes valuable once man starts to economize on it. The price of land, or "rent," represents the services rendered by the person owning land (Bastiat 2007, pp. 136–137). Therefore, with ownership of even the wildest possible land there is some associated capital formation. Some amount of time, energy, and resources had to be invested in the past in order to develop the land. What Bastiat was not aware of was that by responding in such a way he actually negated the existence of the factor of production that we call land. Rather we should treat it as a capital good. Let us also note here that Bastiat's insights were way ahead of the twentieth century, when neoclassicism finally triumphed and dropped land as a very special factor of production. The revolutionary nature of the Frenchman's vision can be fully grasped once we understand that even marginalists from Carl Menger to Alfred Marshall and Vilfredo Pareto were still faithful to the classical approach corresponding with an almost-Georgian vision where land deserves very special attention (see on this Foldvary 2008).

Bastiat's incompletely accepted revolutionary idea was a Knightian solution to the capital-vs.-land puzzle: there is no such thing as pure land. Yet we need not worry because even assuming there is no such thing as land as a primary factor, we can still create a separate concept of land (although we do not have to). Surely, we can argue in the spirit of Bastiat and Knight that only capital goods are used in production. Despite this, there is no universal capital good symbolizing them all. Capital goods differ, and varying capital goods are allocated and employed. We could name them capital good A, capital good B, and so forth. One of the capital-goods categories could be named “land.” This name could be assigned by us in the empirical analysis to give it a special place in our explanation. It is of course up to debate how we proceed at that point.

Bastiat’s step could mean attempting to have our cake and eat it too, just as in the case of higher-order and lower-order goods. We cannot objectively, once and for all, strictly classify goods into the latter two categories. How we classify them depends on what we want to describe. If we take the perspective of a consumer who wants to add sugar and milk, a cup of coffee can be seen as a good of higher order, and from the perspective of a theorist explaining the relationship between prices of coffee plants and cups of coffee, it is a good of lower order. In a similar manner, in the nineteenth and eighteenth centuries, it was useful to separate land from capital, or actually, landowners from capitalists. For some time those two social groups competed for the workers migrating to cities. As Clark Warburton noted, the categories in the nineteenth century seemed to fit perfectly the social aspects of life (Clark Warburton 1928, p. 65). Despite the fact that pure land did not exist at that time (and still does not), the idea was certainly beneficial. Therefore, although Knight was right about capital being a central figure that cannot be separated from the so-called primary factors, we do not have to fully reject those categories.

In fact, Schumpeter may have been quite right in observing that how we classify factors of production in reality is related to economic and social power. Therefore, the concepts are crucially embedded in political economy (see his brilliant analysis in Schumpeter 1954, pp. 544–570). As Dean and Kretschmer comment, the historical circumstances shifted and the classical approach faded away once land lost its relative share of the product and once “intellectual capital,” or various intellectual skills, started to play a more important role in production (Dean and Kretschmer 2007, p. 587). Naturally, there are serious differences between capital goods as the classical economists understood them and other forms of capital—intangible forms—as we understand them nowadays. One important difference is the more universal aspect of intangible capital and how it adapts to changing conditions, while classical capital goods are much more specific and related to concrete ways of producing things. Yet despite this difference, it seems understandable why the world “capital” has many more meanings and is attached to so many more economic activities (even with labor: we use the term "human capital"). It is for the simple reason that ways of increasing economic value and producing economic profits are more diverse than ever before.

It is not only difficult to find "pure" factors but also to put them into strict categories. As twentieth-century modeling developed, more labels were used. For example, apart from land, labor, and capital, we could have technology and "human capital" (Hippe 2013, p. 325).[12] Again, such is a matter of one's perspective and research focus. The above issues cannot be fully resolved with an a priori universal decision, since we are talking about teleological categories, which depend on particular circumstances.[13]

One possible problem with classifying goods into orders is that the unchanging production structure cannot represent the real world because in the economy things are constantly changing. Even with stable preferences, stable technology, and a fixed savings rate, natural resources (a special type of capital good) are being used up. That is why we cannot meaningfully picture an integrated, self-sustaining production structure in equilibrium (with no net savings involved, of course). This actually argues against any equilibrium construct, and it does not threaten what I have said about imputation theory in this subchapter.

One particularly attention-grabbing feature of the capital structure (one shown in the reswitching debate) is its heterogeneity. Factors of production are traditionally grouped into aggregates. Each of the aggregates can be seen as having a common unit. With labor, the case seems quite simple: labor hours express how much of that input is used in production. Naturally, though, there is a big puzzle about the variety of types of labor. After all, not every type of labor is the same. But setting this issue aside, the case of capital goods is even more hopeless, since there is not even a theoretical unit that one could use.

JEVONSIAN TRAPEZOIDS OF THE STRUCTURE OF PRODUCTION

Perhaps the first trapezoidal presentation of orders of goods placed within the production structure can be found in Jevons's *The Theory of Political Economy*. Jevons was focused on the interval between when labor is exerted and raw materials are applied and when the final consumer good reaches the buyer. In light of the concept of orders of goods, he associated any advances in production with new uses of capital: improvements increasing the interval are always associated with capital extensions (Jevons 1957, p. 228). Capital investments are consecutively dependent on the time horizon. Here Jevons distinguished between "amount of capital invested" and "amount of investment of capital," where the former is only about the pool of capital and the latter is the pool of capital placed in time: the quantity of capital and the length of investment (ibid., pp. 229–230). The structure itself can be presented as a trapezoid, as in figure 2.1.

Each consecutive stage adds to the existing capital structure; hence, capital value increases until the good reaches the final consumer. The value is imputed backward in the trapezoid, so that each stage is less valuable than the next one due to the contribution to economic value by adding capital. The total amount of productive expenditures is higher than consumer spending, even though each stage on its own is less valuable than the consumption stage. A quest for monetary surplus in the form of interest payments transforms capitalist spending into profits and revenues (Foster 1987, p. 105).

Jevons was focused on the capital aspect and monetary side of the orders of goods. Hayek, on the other hand, went into further detail and decomposed the trapezoid even further by separating original and produced factors of production (Hayek 1933, p. 233), as we can see in figure 2.2.

Each of the successive stages is supplemented with original means of production, labor, and land, which are apparently irreducible to other factors and treated as permanent in the process. The first stage of production uses original means and creates a product valued at eight units and bought at the second stage. We can treat the product as a capital good (or intermediate good—a term synonymous for the purposes of the chapter), later supplemented by additional original factors to create an intermediate good (capital good) with a value of sixteen. And so the process goes until the product of final value of forty units is created and sold to the consumer. The confusing element of a Hayekian approach to Jevons's scheme is that Hayek neglected interest payments. He presented only factor payments. Why? The explanation given is that it kept thing simple. It is disturbing, however, since adding interest payments would not complicate things much (as proven, for example, by Rothbard's path-breaking analysis discussed below). Nevertheless, Hayek decided

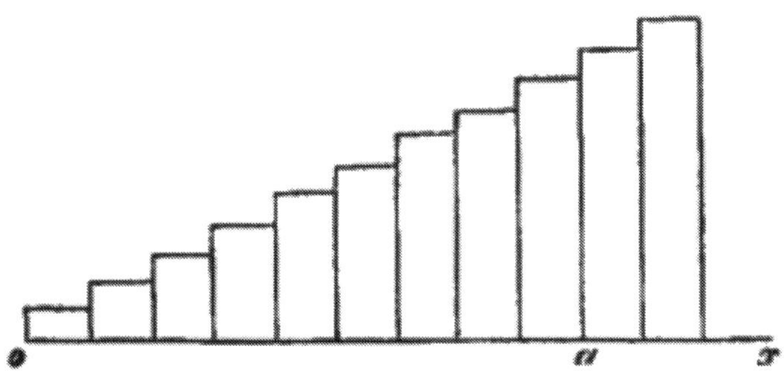

Figure 2.1 Jevons's Trapezoid

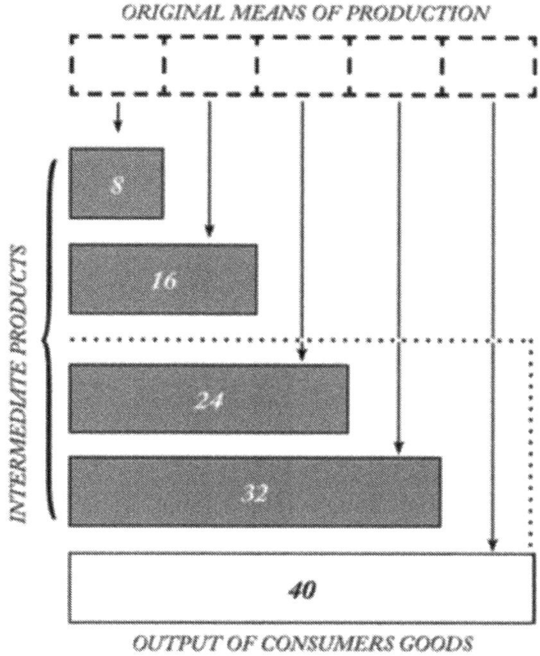

Figure 2.2 Hayek's Trapezoid without Interest Payments

not to include them when describing his theory of fluctuations. Apparently the distinction between fixed and circulating capital was the main issue.

What then was the objective? It was to demonstrate the extent and importance of the productive sector sustained by spending on intermediate goods. The typical national-income accounting approach, following Kuznets's contribution, includes consumer spending and a small part of investment spending. It does not include gross productive spending and most of the money supply circulating to maintain the capital structure. Here also lies the spirit of the capital debates between Knight and Hayek. If capital is permanent and renews itself without a problem from current flows, it need not concern us what can destroy it (except wars, perhaps). On the other hand, if Hayek is right and capital can be consumed with the capital structure destroyed, then such a presentation is crucial to notice, since it emphasizes the role of productive spending in the system. Most of the aggregate demand comes from such productive spending by capitalist and entrepreneurs. Naturally when I use the term "aggregate demand" here I mean the total volume of spending in the economy. This definition differs from aggregate demand as found in Keynesian models (Hansen et al. 1985, p. 288).

It is highly probable that the whole purpose of Hayek's *Prices and Production* was not really to present lectures focused only on business cycles, but lectures focused on movements within the production structure, movements that can be caused by different shifts, although mostly by credit expansion in the earlier production stages. Yet, various changes in the spending patterns in the trapezoid may cause it to shrink or expand.

The shortcoming of Jevons's presentation is that he did not include in his trapezoids detailed factor payments. He only analyzed interest payments in the investment process. The shortcoming of Hayek's presentation is that his trapezoids are focused on the distinction between capital goods and original means of production, while interest payments are omitted. Rothbard's greatest contribution to capital theory was to unify both approaches and place them in the context of the marginal-pricing process. A table developed by him decomposes all spending into the earnings of all the factors of production, intermediate and original ones, by including interest alongside labor and land (Rothbard 2004, p. 369). We have no reason to exclude any of them, especially if we want to construct a complete micro- and macroeconomic framework of the economy. Consider figure 2.3.

Final consumer spending of 100 units is divided in grey into, first, intermediate goods of 80 units of value bought from previous producers and, second, original-factor payments of 20 units, which include interest. The 80 units of intermediate goods are further divided into, first, 60 units of value of capital goods bought from the preceding capitalist, and, second, 20

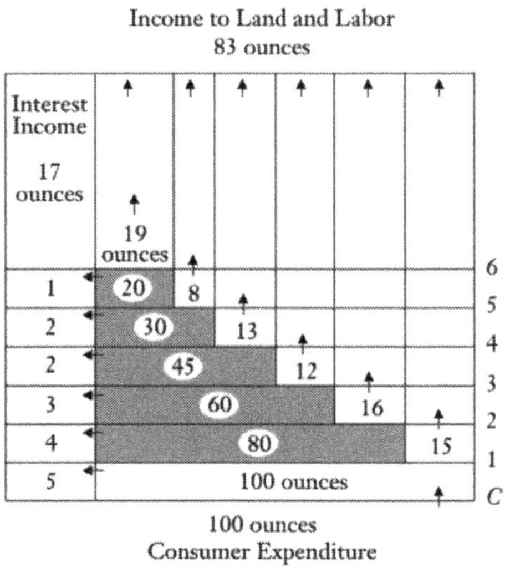

Figure 2.3 Rothbard's Trapezoid

units again of original factors, including interest. We will come back to this scheme in one of the next sections, where I analyze in detail the connection between interest and productive spending at each stage. For now it is sufficient to say that the whole concept of the productive structure developed in the following paragraphs was shaped by Rothbard's original contribution, which can hardly be overstated. It was the most comprehensive intertemporal circular flow at the time. Since the times of Quesnay, there were various approaches to describing "economic tables" of closed spending in the system. The economic tables sat alongside equilibrium analysis, where money changes hands with each of the rounds until we are back where we started (Johnson 1966, pp. 617–618). I do not mean to say the physiocrats' analysis is correct—to the contrary. We should not deny, however, their importance for the development of the economic theory of equilibrated monetary flows.[14] For many decades—even in the second part of the twentieth century—Quesnay received praise from different authors for his pioneering of the equilibrium model of flows as a forerunner of any attempt to conceptualize general equilibrium (Schachter 1991, p. 317), despite his analysis's many undeniable shortcomings.

The circular-flow diagram is usually ascribed in its present form to Frank Knight, although Knight himself did not state it was his own invention but referred to it as a familiar figure of "wheel of wealth." Don Patinkin studied the history of the graph and found its preliminary appearance in a couple of publications preceding Knight's treatment from the 1920s (Patinkin 1973, pp. 1041–1043). Rothbard's presentation is also a circular flow, but with an intertemporal twist, with the capital structure existing due to productive capital spending, something not seen in the traditional Knightian approach. Rothbard, therefore, turned the "wheel of wealth" and placed it in the framework of capitalist aggregate demand (see also a somewhat-Marxist treatment similar to this: Sekine 1981, pp. 301–303).

Such presentations are in accordance of Mill's famous fourth statement on the nature of capital: demand for commodities is not demand for labor. Various controversies arose about the meaning of this thesis, especially because of the development of the Keynesian model, where those two demands are quite interrelated. Nonetheless, the fundamental notion retains its place. Money spent in the system can either be directed toward consumer spending or productive spending (non-spending the money is a separate issue, discussed in chapter 3). Mill's statement does not invalidate the concept of derived demand and backward imputation theory—production goods still gain their value due to the creation of consumer value in the end (in terms of expectations, naturally). At the same time, larger amounts are expended on labor and capital goods because owners of money capital decide not to consume it for themselves (Johnson 1949, p. 533).

I also should describe the very important and impressive work done by Professor Roger Garrison, who has taken a much different route while discussing Jevonsian stages. Roger Garrison presented his approach less in monetary terms, which makes his take on Jevons much different. And he attempted to answer the reswitching problem from a much different perspective, one that deserves attention and that I leave for the next section (Garrison 2004, p. 28).

Garrison's framework consists of three interconnected elements creating a complete macroeconomic picture: the loanable-funds market, the production-possibilities frontier, and the *maybe real* structure of production. I emphasize the word "maybe real," because it is a clear break from Jevonsian tradition (from Jevons through Hayek to Rothbard) of presenting the stages as decomposed monetary flows. It is probably real because we cannot be sure what Garrison meant in his presentation: real or monetary structure? Importantly, Garrison himself may not have been fully aware of this problem, but as we will see below it is a quite plausible conclusion drawn from his presentations, though the presentations were not without paradoxes. Let us bring in the three building blocks of his capital-based macroeconomics (figure 2.4).

The lower graph depicts the well-known loanable-funds market, where the demand curve represents investment demand for credit and the supply curve represents savings preferences of money-capital owners. Above it is the production-possibilities frontier, which presents a tradeoff between consuming the available income and investing it. The index number for investments on the x axis corresponds with the index number for the investments in the

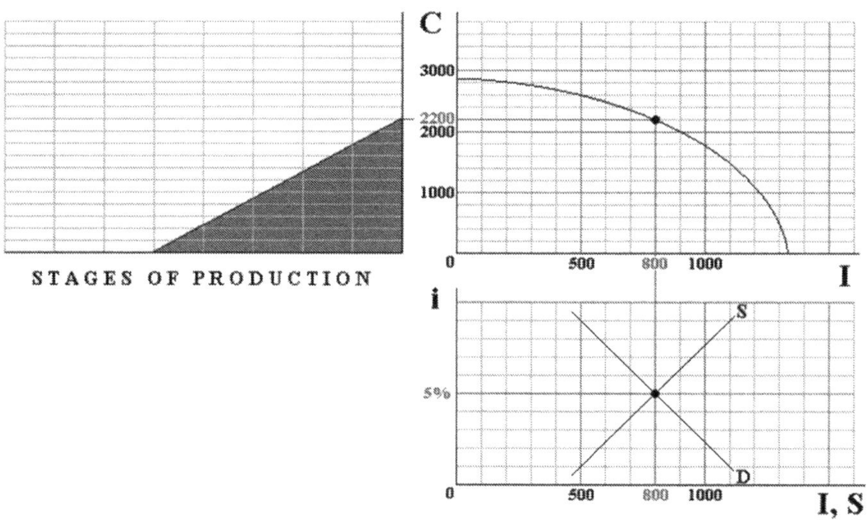

Figure 2.4 Garrison's Contribution

loanable-funds market on the x axis. The third graph presents a modified Jevonsian trapezoid, which Garrison calls the "Hayek's triangle." One immediately noticeable difference from Jevons's geometric figure is that it starts at the beginning of the x axis, so that it is truly a triangle, not a trapezoid. The vertical side of a triangle, on the right side of the third frame, corresponds with the amount of consumption on the production-possibilities frontier.

There are a couple of problems with this illustration. First, the dimensions are not consistent (Hülsmann 2001, p. 40). Loanable funds are depicted in monetary terms and then transformed into real terms on the production-possibilities frontier. Eventually we do not really know what the dimension for consumption in the structure of production is. Perhaps it was meant to be monetary, but as figure 2.5 proves, it simply cannot be monetary. Despite some dimensional problems, the issue could be resolved, but we need to supplement the graph with explanations of how the transformation happens. Perhaps the monetary pool of investments can be tied to specific production limitations present in the production-possibilities frontier, but we need to inquire further. Transforming the real into the monetary and the other way around is key. Without it no theory of business cycles is possible.

Second, there is no explanation of how a specific amount of consumption and investments given on the production-possibilities frontier can be transformed into a specific structure of production. For a detailed explanation of this problem, we have to wait for the last section in this chapter, where I demonstrate that a certain amount of savings-investment and certain levels

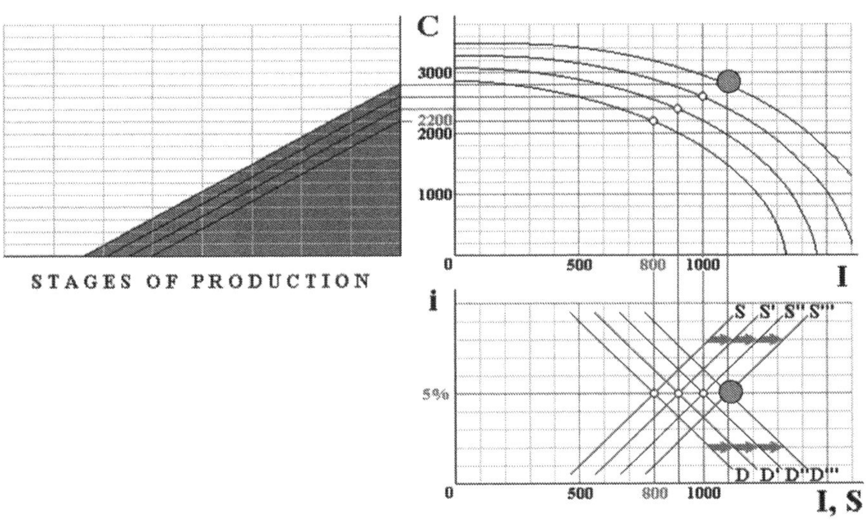

Figure 2.5 Garrison's Secular Growth

of consumption are compatible with various possible production structures (longer and shorter). The end result depends on additional factors that I plan to explain. Additionally, the "investments" on the production-possibilities frontier are one index number, which strongly aggregates them. At the same time, it is unclear how this one aggregate is decomposed into the harmonica-like structure on the third graph.

The third point, a detailed extension of the first one, is the strongest one. It is about the triangle being at some points in real terms, not monetary. With that we have to refer to the concept of secular growth (on some problems surrounding this concept see Salerno 2001, pp. 46–49). Figure 2.5 is a sample picture of sustainable secular growth in Garrison's framework.

Leaving aside the mechanics of growth and its illustration, one thing becomes clear: the triangle is getting bigger, the overall volume of spending increasing. If the triangle is meant to be monetary (as Garrison apparently wants it to be), then all monetary flows have to increase in total. They cannot stay the same. Therefore, additional money has to be spent. Where does the money come from? Either from monetary expansion and credit creation or from decreases in the demand for cash. To put it in monetarist language, either money supply (M) or velocity of money (V) has to change. Yet Garrison himself emphasizes that he assumes MV under such conditions to be constant: "The macroeconomics of secular growth . . . does not keep track of the relationship between the money supply and the general level of prices. Money and prices can be kept in perspective, however, with the aid of the familiar equation of exchange, MV=PQ. *For a given money supply (M) and a given velocity of money (V) . . .*" (emphasis added; Garrison 2001, p. 55).

For a given money supply and velocity of money, the triangle cannot increase its overall size. Therefore, Garrison's whole approach suffers from shortcomings—unless we are to conclude that the triangle is actually presented in real terms, which would require more in-depth analysis. If it is in real terms, then the framework breaks one of the fundamental rules of capital to which Garrison adheres and ingeniously presented at many times: lack of unit of capital. If the triangle is in real units, what are those units? Can we discount "real consumption" (on the *y* axis in the triangle graph) into the values of intermediate goods? If so, then the unit for capital is discounted real product. Naturally we need not go further into this, since the idea of measuring capital in such a way has to be abandoned. One reason for this is Garrison's own criticism. He calls measuring capital in real terms a "red flag":

> Capital is by its nature heterogeneous–and more radically so than other inputs. The heterogeneity is reflected in the various physical measures: lumber is measured in board feet, concrete in cubic yards, steel in metric tons, gasoline in

> gallons, and electricity in kilowatt-hours. "Machine-hours" are units that evoke some imagery of stereotypical capital equipment but hardly serve as a comprehensive unit. And capital in the sense of goods in process renders the issue of units hopelessly open-ended. (Garrison 2006, p. 12)

If the triangle cannot be in monetary or in real terms, what is left? The solution is to go back to Rothbard—to his fundamental integration of Hayek's intermediate-goods trapezoid and Jevons's capital-values trapezoid, not only because it integrates the previous contributions but because it adds another important one: monetary considerations. Keeping money and its velocity constant in Rothbard's trapezoid is consistent with the numbers and the shape of the graph, a feature we cannot find in Garrison, where some of the conflicts pile up.

Another two very important presentations of Jevons's trapezoid in the literature are Mark Skousen's book and Huerta de Soto's treatise (2006, p. 293). In both of those cases, we can actually say they are successfully restating Rothbard's contribution (which by no means is a defect—quite the contrary). In Skousen's case, the trapezoid is borrowed from *Man, Economy, and State* and in some places given a new presentation (Skousen 1990, pp. 187, 198). Quite relevant is Skousen's concept of "gross national output," which unlike gross domestic product measures total investment spending in the productive capital structure (p. 191).

These are all just Jevonsian starting points on how the production structure is to be pictured and how value is imputed through all the stages from future consumer goods to productive intermediate goods. There is a lot more to this, however, since one of the crucial prices in Jevons's trapezoid is of course the price of money capital: the interest rate, which directs resources into selected stages. Additionally, it certainly influences the way the production structure lengthens and shrinks. The subject of the next section is to present some unresolved puzzles in such an approach. And we will see how history completed the circle, or how developments based on the Jevonsian scheme have led the reswitching issue to reappear, but in a much more indirect manner.

The trapezoid route means production is not being treated as automatically fulfilling itself, since in reality investments are extended in time. As Kydland and Prescott emphasize, "Multiple periods are required to build new capital goods and only finished capital goods are part of the productive capital stock. Each stage of production requires a period and utilizes resources. Half-finished ships and factories are not part of the productive capital stock" (Kydland and Prescott 1982, p. 1045). Furthermore the notion of "time to build" in models helps to explain the serial correlations among and interdependence of various investment plans (Zhou 2000, p. 273).

SHIFTS IN JEVONSIAN TRAPEZOIDS AND THE RESWITCHING ISSUE

The development of the trapezoid demonstrated the importance of capital structure and presented the relationships within productive spending that could not be captured by a typical circular-flow diagram. To be precise: production structure is something like an intertemporal circular flow, an intertemporal *Tableau économique*, where flows take place in time and repeat themselves in an ordered sequence. It is a sort of Hicksian view of "complementarities over time" with integrated input-output flows, supported by the division of labor and perfect time coordination, connecting all the factors to one another (Scazzieri 1990, p. 24). Yet as with any other equilibrium model, this one is constructed to depict a specific change—in this case, changes in length due to interest rate adjustments.

Most of Jevons's followers attempted to show how a higher amount of savings—capital accumulated, broadly understood—causes the production structure to reorient itself toward more productive and more time-consuming processes (so roundaboutness becomes a key concept). The causal relationship was meant to be the following: a change toward more future-oriented preferences leads to a higher amount of savings, which in turn lower the interest rate and create a bigger pool of funding. The end result is more stages of production and overall a longer time to produce output. I now present sample graphics from the authors mentioned in the previous sections. In figure 2.6, let us start with Hayek (1933, p. 239).

Compare figure 2.6 with figure 2.2. In the latter, we only had four stages before the final consumption. In the former, we expand the structure like a harmonica: now six stages precede final consumption. At the same time, profit and interest margins are squeezed, although, again, Hayek does not consider the effect directly. At the previous moment, complementary factors of production supplement intermediate (capital) goods, contributing directly to the creation of economic value. One major aspect of the change is a shift in the production structure because consumer demand falls. This is something not envisioned by Jevons. I need to add here that notion on consumption decrease set the standard for decades and future followers, who were always focused on presenting all things happening at the same time: lower consumption, lower interest rate, higher savings, longer processes of production (i.e., processes with more stages). As we will see in the next section, all those changes need not happen in the same direction. My purpose is to alter the tradition and to break from a fixed approach, partially because of the neglected reswitching issue.

In Rothbard's case (figure 2.7), the trapezoid is extended because net savings boosts spending in the production structure, and at the same time interest margins are also narrowed (Rothbard 2004, p. 519).

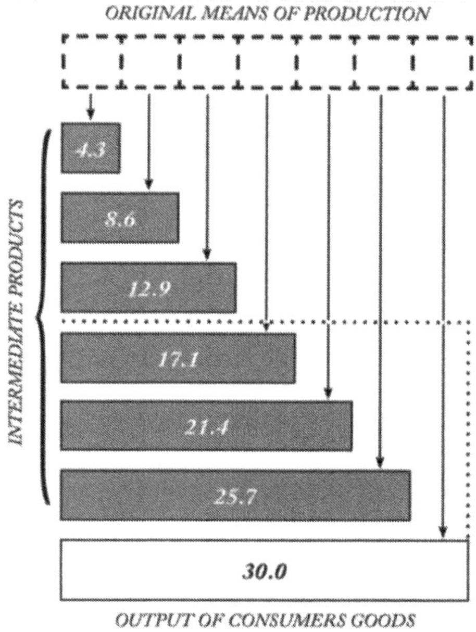

Figure 2.6 Hayek's Extended Trapezoid

The line AA (figure 2.7) represents the older structure of production, which is shorter overall (four stages of production before the final stage), has higher nominal consumption, and has a higher interest rate. The grey fields and the line BB represent the change triggered by lower time preferences: we have more stages of production (six before consumption), lower nominal consumption, higher productive spending in the structure, and lower profit and interest rates. Skousen reproduces the same graph (Skousen 1990, p. 254).

It is worth noting that Rothbard's approach here is not as rigorous as it could be, at least when compared to other chapters of his book. The graph is just illustrative. What we lack here is the same type of analysis as the analysis of equilibrium conditions (figure 2.3) with all factors of production spending corresponding to their net incomes so that we could see the full picture of the intertemporal circular flow. Using two distinct equilibriums with different interest and saving rates, we could see how a change plays out. Naturally we would not explain the changes with such comparative analysis. Yet we could compare final states of affairs just like we do with demand and supply curves.

Roger Garrison (2001, p. 62), in his original framework, also presented an extended production structure with lowered interest rates, but with even fewer concrete examples.

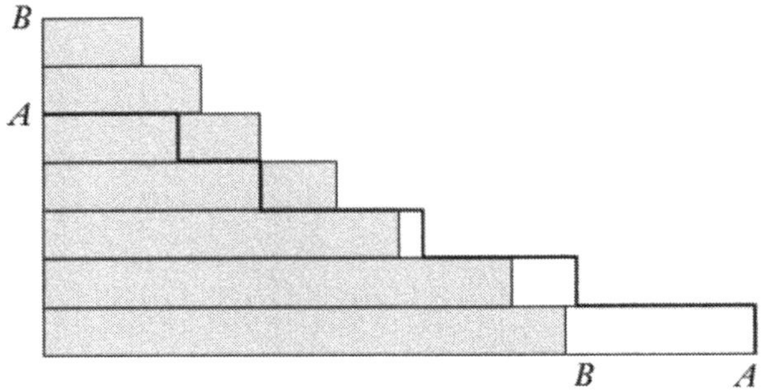

Figure 2.7 Rothbard's Net-Savings Effect

The bottom graph in figure 2.8 presents an increased willingness to save, which results in lower interest rates and lower consumption levels. The transformation along the production-possibilities frontier follows, and the production structure adapts to become longer. The characteristic feature here is again a triangular, not trapezoidal, structure. This assumes that the processes always start with zero expenditures (a break from Jevonsian tradition), which in reality is hardly the case. It additionally allows the structure to be extended. As we will see below, abandoning this assumption will lead to different results. But first, I present Huerta de Soto's last depiction on the matter (figure 2.9) (Huerta de Soto 2006, p. 340).

Huerta de Soto extended Rothbard's model in that he gave some example numbers to demonstrate two distinct equilibria and thanks to this, he was able to perform a comparative analysis (Huerta de Soto 2006, p. 334). The above graph is his theoretical summary of how the structure widens as more intermediate goods are used in the relatively earlier stages and also how the structure deepens because it adds stages that were not previously planned.

As we see, then, the Jevonsian tradition, which flourished in the twentieth century, presented the extension of the production structure in a largely unified manner. Unfortunately, it did not do so in a very rigorous way but had corresponding changes happening at the same time: lower nominal consumption, higher savings, lower interest rates, and more stages of production. It well described developing market economies with more and more stages, an increasing amount of available capital, and generally relatively stable decreasing interest rates associated with growth. Nevertheless, overall empirical correspondence with some general facts is not enough—especially once we consider the reswitching issue, which the tradition ignored for most of the twentieth century with few exceptions.

Samuelson lamented we cannot formalize a model in which there is a monotonic relationship between the length of production and the interest rate.

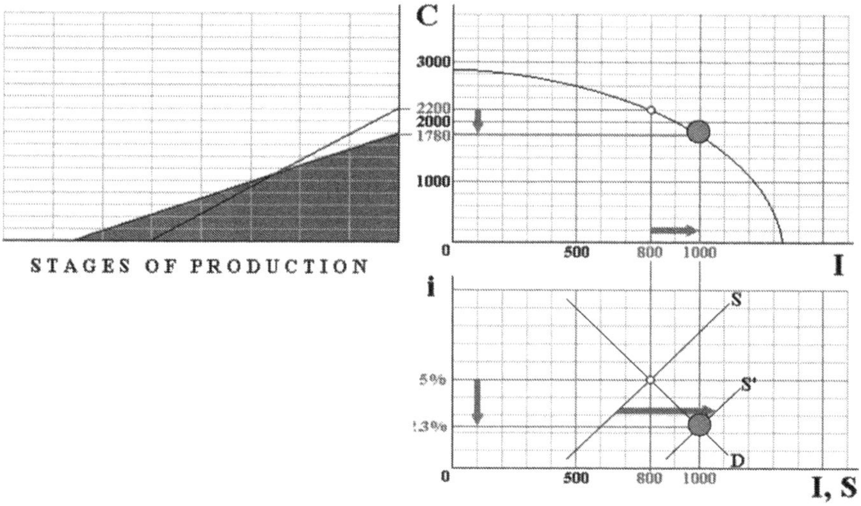

Figure 2.8 Garrison's Extended Triangle

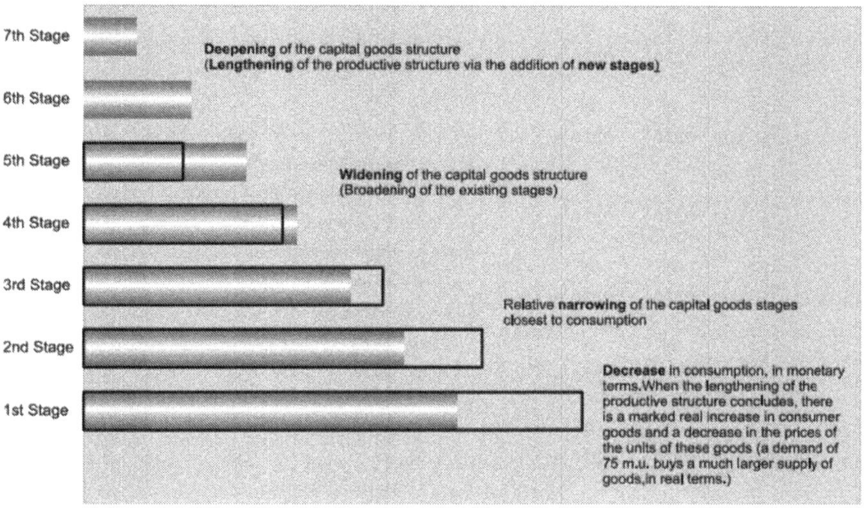

Figure 2.9 Huerta de Soto's Depiction of the Lengthened Structure

Multiple equilibriums are possible. What was the answer from the third side in the reswitching debate, the Austrian perspective working with Jevonsian trapezoids?

One possible argument from the Austrian tradition was about a variety of subjectivism. Reswitching works mathematically and numerically, but two different processes of production cannot be straightforwardly compared and objectively measured. Such was the argument made by Kirzner, who spotted the problem and tried to avoid it by referring to subjectivism:

> The cases that yield the capital-reversing paradoxes all arise from production processes involving more or less complex dating patterns for inputs and outputs. (In a stylized example made famous by Samuelson (1966), a given quantity of output can be obtained in year 4 from one technique that calls for the input of two units of labour in year 1, and six units of labour in year 3; or alternatively by a second technique of production calling only for the input of seven units of labour in year 2.) It appears obviously mistaken (or at least to involve an arbitrary and possibly misleading oversimplification) to wish to collapse the possibly incommensurable quantities of time associated with individually dated input components of a given complex production technique into a single simple unidimensional quantity of time. . . . Rather, we should understand that comparing the complex, multidimensional waiting requirements for different techniques simply does not permit us to pronounce that one technique involves unambiguously less waiting than a second technique. . . . What should be emphasized is that, from the subjectivist Misesian pure time-preference perspective, there is absolutely no need to assume any possibility for such unambiguous ranking. In this perspective, time is simply not viewed as an "objective" (or any other kind of) input. (Kirzner 1996, pp. 9–10)

The statement is fine on its own terms, but it looks more like a white flag rather than an answer. Kirzner clearly argued here that we cannot relate interest rates to the passage of production time. Therefore, the whole concept of a "more or less remote" future is entirely specific to the cognitive perspective of an actor. However strong the statement is, it suffers from a fundamental flaw: if we cannot objectively determine the length of production, then we cannot really argue that a lower interest leads to longer processes. It could well be the other way around. Such is the pitfall of ultrasubjectivism: none of it can really be known. If so, then it also cannot be known that a lowered interest rate leads to longer processes. It can go either way, and it all depends on a subjective perspective. Kirzner's point is an argument against all sides in the reswitching debate, not just one (Gordon 1997).

A related criticism from Roger Garrison was that the comparison presented in the reswitching debates is static in nature, whereas real-world market dynamics are more like processes not depicted in comparative discussions of reswitching. Garrison calls this "illegitimate use of comparative statics." (Garrison 1979a, p. 222)[15] He does not, however, explain why it is "illegitimate." While the exercise undoubtedly uses comparative statics, it is not really a big problem, no matter which perspective we take. After all, such comparative statics are no different from Garrison's own approach, where he used very static notions of loanable funds, the production-possibilities frontier, and equilibrated stages of production. Nonetheless, such statics do not necessarily make the procedure illegitimate. It depends on the purpose. Garrison's purpose was to show a negative relationship between the interest rate and the length of production. The purpose of the reswitching argument was to show that no such one-direction correlation can exist, at least in terms of two variables carefully selected in equilibrium reasoning: interest and length. Same tools, same method, same approach—just different results. How come in one case the method is illegitimate, while in the other it poses no problem?

Another point, made by Leland Yeager in a spirit somewhat similar to Kirzner's, was that in the various reswitching examples it is not clear what the amount of capital is, and therefore it is unclear how interest is related to it. So the controversy surrounding the competing presentations cannot be settled completely, since capital is related to interest and interest is related to capital. Yet, this is one of the points of the reswitching argument. Therefore, it does not really answer it but rather clearly reformulates it: capital and interest are tied together and cannot be separated. In Yeager's (1976, p. 345) own words, "Admittedly, waiting cannot be measured in purely physical terms, and the amount of it required in a physically specified production process does depend partly on its own price." Yeager also pointed out we do not have an answer about what in the model causes the interest rate to change in the first place (Yeager 1979, p. 193). That is correct, but no matter the answer, one lesson from the reswitching challenge remains relevant: multiple equilibriums are possible.

Yeager also makes the point that the reswitching challenge offered in Samuelson's example works as long as we use the notion of physical capital (Yeager 1979, p. 188; Yeager 1976, p. 323). Perhaps a clearer statement would speak of using measurable capital. Surely there are problems with reducing everything to either labor hours or some type of index (e.g., one related to consumption), since that is not how the capital structure is organized. Nevertheless, as we have seen, Samuelson's example can be easily "monetized" and turned into a pricing example (as Garrison did). Later on, Yeager again emphasized the need for "purely physical terms" in theorizing about capital and explained how waiting (as a factor) has to include not only the amount of time but the value and price of this time (Yeager 1979, p. 191). He uses the concept of "waiting intensity," which incorporates both the time element and the valuation element. Once again, it is not a very satisfying answer to the reswitching challenge, but more like a way of incorporating its arguments: the interest rate cannot be separated from capital. The "price of waiting" cannot be related to "waiting" because they are not separate but combine into "waiting intensity."

It is fine to construct such tautological statements. Nevertheless, Yeager cannot really have it both ways, since if we accept his premise, then we cannot say that interest is the price of waiting because then we would have circular reasoning. Interest depends not on actual waiting but rather on "waiting intensity," which is measured by interest itself. Here we have a full concession of Robinson's point. In exactly the same manner, Karl Marx tried to defend the labor theory of value: by making additional assumptions about how labor time is not really labor time but something like labor-time intensity, which is related to existing market prices. Similarly, "waiting" is not an independent time factor, but a theoretical concept that already includes time discounting (interest) in it.

Among other commentators, Skousen repeated the main arguments of Garrison and Yeager (Skousen 1990, pp. 118–120). Additionally, he commented that the whole reswitching debate was "wrongheaded" because Böhm-Bawerk's main point was that if a company engages in a longer process, then the process must be seen as ex ante more profitable. But that is a trivial statement that can easily be reversed: if the company engages in a shorter process, then it must be seen as ex ante more profitable. The statement is true but solves none of the problems raised in the capital debates. Further, Jevons's followers were attempting to draw a distinct and one-directional relationship between interest and the length of production: a negative relationship between interest and roundaboutness. The debate was definitely more than what Skousen suggests. Moreover, his own work is built around the idea that lowered interest implies longer processes of production. Such an idea is scattered throughout his book. Last but not least, Jesús Huerta de Soto also tried to answer the reswitching challenge by attempting to distinguish between "technique" and "length of production." Unfortunately, he did not advance his argument but merely stated it three times:

> Productive structure is lengthened *regardless* of whether changes or even reswitching occur with respect to the different specific production techniques. . . .
>
> [S]avings always causes, in prospective terms, a "lengthening" of the productive structure, irrespective of whether techniques which were only profitable at higher interest rates are readopted in a certain new investment process. . . .
>
> *It is therefore irrelevant whether or not to the new investment process incorporates techniques which, considered individually, may have been profitable at higher rates of interest.* (Huerta de Soto, pp. 573–575)

The one argument that supports those conclusions is that with every shift and change of circumstances, the system resets. All factors have a new life with every switch, so Huerta de Soto would not allow us to compare various ways of producing goods. Such a statement may be doubtful, but let us assume it is true. Taking a future-oriented perspective, we can still show a potential reswitching between two ways of producing a particular good, depending on the interest rate. We do not have to rely on bygones and include past costs in any way. The reswitching challenge can be presented in a forward-looking manner.

Moreover, the more we look into Huerta de Soto's statements, the more questionable they become. In a sense, he tries to completely separate the notions of "technique" and "length of production." But why? What if by "technique" we also mean length of production, as in the reswitching debate? A contradiction appears since, in Huerta de Soto's terms, we would have to state that the productive structure lengthens regardless of whether we choose a shorter production technique—even if all sequences of techniques are in sum taking shorter time! Put differently, we would have to state "savings always causes, in prospective terms, a 'lengthening' of the productive structure, irrespective of whether techniques are shorter." Obviously there is something missing here.

Notably, Hayek recognized reswitching issues in his early works (as noted in Yeager 1979, p. 209; Huerta de Soto 2006, p. 573). First, he stated that processes of production are so complex that it is practically impossible to compare their length. There is no general answer to the question of which process is shorter and which longer, so we cannot make the comparison (Hayek 1941, p. 76). We may agree with this, but at the same time it sounds as if Hayek meant it is impossible to find a relationship between length and interest—hence it is impossible to do what Hayek himself tried in his graphs in *Prices and Production*, reproduced above. Hayek also repeated that the rate of investment cannot be reduced to a single time interval, or amount of "waiting." Different investment periods cannot be reduced to a common denominator, because various inputs are used (Hayek 1941, pp. 140–142). Again, the heterogeneity of capital (and Yeager's notion that the input of "waiting" is heterogeneous) makes it impossible.

For a long time, followers of Hayek and Jevons were not very disturbed by the reswitching challenge: they treated it as a somewhat obscure, narrow technical point in some unrealistic models. The reasons for this are perfectly understandable. The Hayekian perspective was not the main target in the Cambridge debate—neoclassical production functions were. Nobody attacked the trapezoid directly—only indirectly (through Samuelson)—which made ignoring the attack much more natural. Everything changed when the attack came from works within Hayek's tradition: Hülsmann (2010) and Fillieule (2007).

Both of those works' models attempted to explain the influence of the interest rate on the length of production by following the rigorous step-by-step procedure that Rothbard had adopted. They started with ceteris paribus assumptions and attempted to find a necessary relationship between interest and stages of production. One such assumption, as we have seen, had been omitted by Garrison: fixed monetary spending. Fixed monetary spending in Rothbard's framework comes with fixed money supply and stable demand for cash holdings (put differently, stable velocity of money). There are no monetary expansions, no contractions, and no pressures from money holders exerted on the price level in general (whether a result of higher overall spending or lower overall spending). Such a budgetary approach to the structure of production leads to very specific results about the interest rate and length of production. Let us start, in figure 2.10, with Hülsmann's graph (2010, p. 24).

In the graph, consumer expenditures are fixed. Money spending is also fixed. Producers spend in the stages preceding consumer spending, as usual. The only variable we manipulate is the interest rate. Assume we start from the middle line, with interest at 14.5 percent. If interest is lowered to 2 percent, then the structure is described by the upper line. Why? Simply because, as imputation theory teaches us, with a lowered interest rate, discounting falls. Hence, the prices of all factors of production used before creating consumer goods rise. If the prices rise, more money has to be spent to buy those factors. With an unchanged amount of money in the system, the budget for factors is used up faster because of the higher prices. The more we spend in the last stages, the less money is available to spend in the even-earlier stages.

Such is the economics of the graph. Naturally, there is a mathematical explanation. We could write a geometrical series. In a geometrical series with a fixed sum (namely, the money supply and the field below the line), if the ratio (interest) is getting lower, then the number of terms (number of stages) also has to fall. Some critics may immediately echo the famous question,

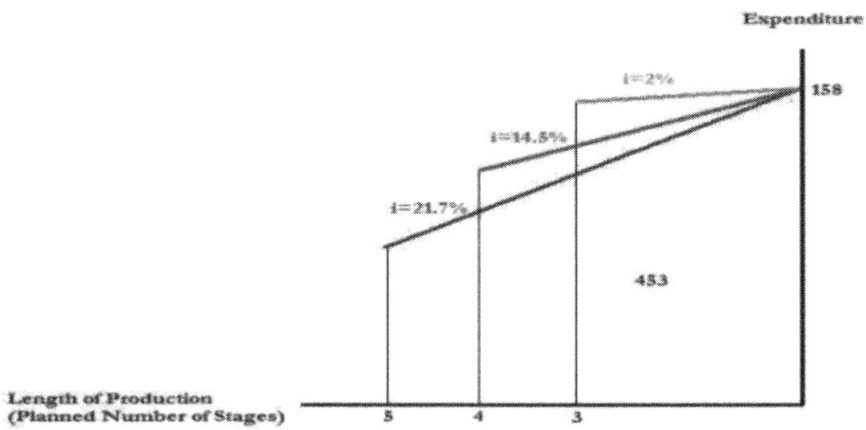

Figure 2.10 Hülsmann's Trapezoids

"But how is the interest rate to change without consumption going down?" It is certainly possible, as I plan to show in the next section. Yes, for interest to go down, the amount of saved money has to go up. But increased net savings in the system need not result in decreased total consumption. (Think of a simple case: Capitalists decrease their consumption by 100 units and save it for production. All the money is spent on the wages of workers, who in turn spend 100 units for consumption. Total consumption remains the same, while savings increase and interest falls. I discuss this example in the next section.)

But does Hülsmann's observation relate to reswitching? After all, he did not find reswitching, but (apparently) merely discovered a different relationship between the interest rate and the length of production. Lowered interest apparently leads to shorter processes of production (and counteracts the lengthening effect of higher savings). There is no reswitching here. That is true, but then the question becomes, how come the Jevonsian tradition for so many years did not see this inverse relationship? Because—says Hülsmann—it was obscured by a change to an additional variable in the equation: the pool of savings, which increases the length of production. The net effect of the two variables (i.e., interest and pool of savings) is indeterminate. Therefore, in a sense, reswitching is possible because other variables are prone to change too and to reverse the previously assumed relationship.

There is one problem with Hülsmann, however: he did not decompose productive spending in the production structure the way Rothbard did, between spending on intermediate goods and original factors of production. There are just total spending flows from the perspective of owners of money capital. To explain imputation in a changing productive structure, such decomposition is necessary—especially because the interest rate itself depends on it. Here is the partial answer to the problem of how interest can change without a change in total consumer spending. Unfortunately, Hülsmann's vision resembles Jevons's general trapezoid instead of Rothbard's detailed trapezoid.

Fillieule reached conclusions similar to Hülsmann but attempted to do the decomposition, though not to the full extent. Just like Hayek and Rothbard, he divided productive-capital spending into two categories: original factors of production and intermediate goods used up in production. Nevertheless, he decided to keep the relationship between the two as a fixed ratio across all stages. Figure 2.11 reproduces his illustration (Fillieule 2007, p. 198).

Final consumption is on the right axis. From the left, we start from earlier stages of production that accumulate value consecutively. Grey rectangles represent the value of capital goods in the production process. White rectangles represent original factors of production added on top of that. Each stage receives the same equilibrium rate of return, completely uniform through the whole structure. Total factor incomes (net) are also equal to final consumption. One very important and crucial assumption that Fillieule made—that the ratio between original factors and capital goods is the same at each stage of production—dictates how the model behaves. As we will see in the next section, this is vital for his observation concerning interest and the length of production.

What comes out of this model? I do not plan to repeat the whole mathematical argument. In fact, Fillieule did exactly the same thing as Hülsmann, but with more rigorous math and also by separating productive spending at each stage into original and produced factors. After the series of mathematical transformations, the formula is

$$\text{ʎ} = I(1 + i) / C$$

Here, ʎ represents the overall length of production, *I* investment spending, *C* consumption, and *i* the interest rate. It is not surprising that ʎ increases with higher investment spending, since increased spending goes into the productive structure and therefore extends it. Neither is it surprising that consumption spending is negatively correlated with ʎ, since higher spending on final goods means less spending is available in the productive structure (with a fixed amount of money supply and stable velocity of money). What comes as a theoretical—though not mathematical—surprise is that ʎ is positively related to the interest rate. That is, the higher the interest rate, the longer the process of production and the lower the interest rate, the shorter the process of

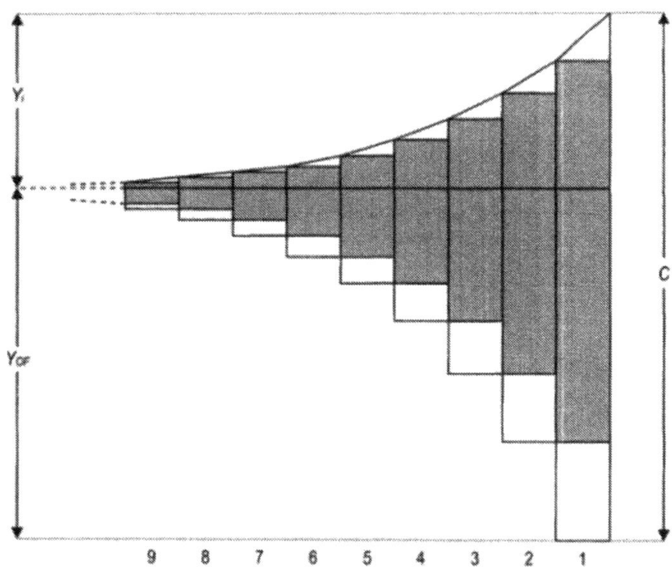

Figure 2.11 Fillieule's Diagram

production—ceteris paribus. What the ceteris paribus clause means here is a separate discussion. Yet, clearly under comparative statics we see a different relationship than the one found by Böhm-Bawerk and his forerunners. In the case of interest and roundaboutness, it appears to not only be "not a simple story," as Samuelson lamented. It appears to be a wrong story. The criticism within the Böhm-Bawerkian camp is even stronger than from the Cambridge academics. Interest is positively related to the length of production, and reswitching can happen once we change other variables.

To summarize, graphical expositions of the length of production were meant to illustrate fixed relationship between interest and roundaboutness of production. The progression came through a series of developments starting by presenting a negative relationship between the height of interest and the length of production and ending with recent developments finding that the relationship is positive. (Recent developments have made vital contributions to the reswitching debate, contributions that in general have been ignored by the followers of Jevons and Hayek.) There is no uniform and one-direction relationship between interest rates and the length of production. The relationship depends in Samuelson's example, as in Jevons's trapezoid, on the details. But they are tied together in a very fundamental way, as we will see below.

INTERTEMPORAL LABOR INTENSITY AND THE LENGTH OF PRODUCTION

To properly capture the relationship between all of the variables in the production structure, we have to start by specifying critical assumptions and therefore avoid some of the problems presented in the previous formulations. Let us begin with Rothbard's equilibrium, since it appears to be the least controversial picture of the productive structure and seems best by far.

Table 2.1 provides the data underlying the figure 2.12.

The total amount of money in the system consists of 300 units. At the same time, these are total revenues in the intertemporal circular flow. We have five hypothetical stages of production. At the first stage, a capitalist has twenty units of money, two of which are his income from previous expenditures and can therefore be spent on consumption. Eighteen units have to be productively invested. Therefore, they are spent on original (primary) factors of production. The factors may be either labor and land, or just labor. We need not specify which is the case here. Those eighteen units of productive spending create the value for the next stage: twenty units of money. Eighteen units of productive spending create the value of twenty units, of which two can be consumed. The process repeats itself (as the system is in equilibrium).

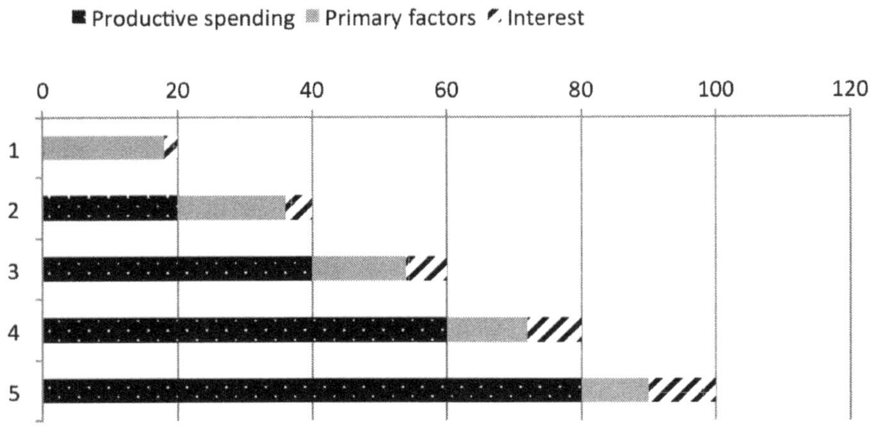

Figure 2.12 Rothbard's Trapezoid

Table 2.1 Spending Patterns for Figure 2.12

Stage of production	*1*	*2*	*3*	*4*	*5*	*Sum*
Capital-goods spending		20	40	60	80	200
Original noninterest factors	18	16	14	12	10	70
Interest payment	2	4	6	8	10	30
Total revenues	20	40	60	80	100	300

Rothbard classifies capitalist expenditures as either consumption or productive spending (savings in the classical sense). Money hoarding has no part in the above model, whether by the capitalists or the workers. Productive spending determines the whole structure of production, including wages and—in the form of total revenues and net income, or interest (Wray 1991, p. 956)—capitalists' earnings.

Now the intermediate good is purchased by the next capitalist. His total revenues from previous spending are forty units of money. Four units of that represent interest (or as some would say, profit on capital), which is spent on consumption. The remaining thirty-six units are spent on productive investments to create more advanced intermediate goods, or goods of the next-lower order. To do this, a less reshaped capital good with value of twenty is purchased from stage one. On top of that, original factors of production with a value of sixteen units are hired. A value of forty units is created and sold to the third stage of production. Productive spending of thirty-six generates the value of forty, where four units can be spent on consumption (they are interest income).

The whole process looks basically the same at all stages, though with different numbers. In the third stage, the capitalist buys the capital good for forty units, adds original factors of fourteen on top of that and resells the reshaped good of the lower order for sixty units, such that six units are his interest payment and used for consumption. Fifty-four units are then reinvested. The case is the same in the fourth stage, where the capitalist spends sixty units on the capital good, adds twelve units' worth of original factors, and resells the reshaped good of even-lower order for eighty units. Eighty units are spent by the last capitalist, who adds ten units to the capital good and sells it to the final consumer for 100 units. Ten units are his interest income, which he uses for consumption.

Naturally I narrated the production process of one good in the productive structure, but the picture should rather be treated in a macroeconomic manner: all stages added, as with consumption expenditures. If we treated this as only one process of production, we would reach slightly absurd conclusions (e.g., that the last capitalist earning ten units of interest spends them on his own product).

The benefits of Rothbard's analysis are very clear. He incorporated in this simple numerical example all necessary factor payments and created an equilibrium model that was not presented elsewhere. It is truly a masterpiece achievement supplemented by his detailed description of the imputation process throughout an industry. From the macroeconomic perspective, there is a complication with Say's law, which I will discuss in the third chapter. For now it is important to realize that Say's law is necessarily satisfied in the above diagram because there is no monetary disturbance (again, described later in the book). The money supply is fixed, and the preference to hold money is stable. All net incomes are spent on consumption. Total payments to original noninterest factors are seventy units. Total interest earnings are thirty units. Altogether this gives us 100 units of consumption. No new savings are formed, because we assume a balanced economy without growth, decline, or monetary reshuffling.

The interest rate in the example is roughly 11 percent—naturally, it is the same in each of the stages since the model is in equilibrium. Total aggregate demand driving the market process is 300 units.

As mentioned previously, monetary demand does not change. Actually, a good case against including money in the equilibrium framework at all can be made. Many theorists emphasize the inherent contradictions in most equilibrium models, especially with respect to money. Without the need to coordinate, without the need to perform transactions—since all factors are properly allocated—what is the need for money? There is no discoordination, so the need to use money to "keep track" of the transactions is questionable (Kuenne 1958, pp. 3–4).

It has even at times been argued that "money is a problem" because in most sophisticated general-equilibrium models, there is no room for it. Money in a sense does exist in the models, but only as a veil for barter or as sophisticated barter itself. If money was not included, not much would change, though

(Dillard 1988, pp. 299–300). I leave the issue of money aside until the following chapters. For now it is sufficient to notice that monetary constraints and budgetary considerations given fixed spending apply perfectly well not only to imaginary theorems but to the real world, where equilibrium does not hold and where there is "room for money" or perhaps even a need for money. To draw a street and describe its position on the city map, we do not need to capture all the people populating it.

The essential element in the productive structure is the primary role of productive expenditures—"investments" in the mainstream sense, "savings" in the classical sense. Such an approach makes Rothbard's intertemporal circular flow much more sensible than the typical circular flow in modern textbooks. Case commented lucidly on the typical (Knightian) circular flow:

> Not unrelated to the stock/flow confusion is the fact that many senior majors in economics cannot define capital. Not that the formal meaning of capital is simple or uncontroversial, but students must have "goods that are produced" in mind at bare minimum. They must understand that investment is the flow of capital goods that increases the capital stock and that depreciation is the obsolescence of capital goods. There is always a great deal of confusion about saving being the supply of capital. All of this can be cleared up by spending a couple of days on the circular flow, starting with product markets and turning to the labor market (which is straightforward) and finally to capital markets (which are not) (Case 2002, p. 454).

Decrease in the Interest Rate

Time to tackle the issue of interest and roundaboutness. Let us change the rate of interest in the model. The typical Böhm-Bawerkian description of the causation is the following: the interest rate goes down, which favors more-roundabout processes of production, since more funds are available for future-oriented projects. On the other hand, we hear reswitching challenges, muted in the Böhm-Bawerkian tradition and indirectly echoed by Fillieule and Hülsmann. Where is the truth, then? The answer is to be found by continuing where Rothbard left off. Let us take a step-by-step approach, as Garrison suggests, to explain the true process behind the interest rate change. The first question to be asked is why the interest rate should go down.

In Rothbard's model, the proper and main influence is assigned to productive spending by owners of money capital. They decide about reinvesting their revenues and decide not to increase what they consume. That is the only reason why the production structure can be sustained. Similar causes have to operate in the case of increasing thrift: owners of money capital decide to reduce their consumption further, increase their savings, and invest their savings in the structure. In figure 2.12, it means the striped rectangle has to be cut by some percentage, and the extra money from such additional savings can be transformed into more investment spending.

The central question, which incidentally helps to answer the reswitching challenge, is where the savings are spent in the structure. Notice that we did not yet settle what the level of the interest rate is. We start by reshaping productive spending first. The mechanics of the model basically allow for any change in t`he productive structure. To explain this, we can use the concept developed elsewhere of ILI: intertemporal labor intensity (Machaj 2015, p. 286). ILI indicates how much money is spent on original factors of production in the earlier stages of production relative to the later stages. When ILI goes up, it means labor is becoming a relatively higher-order good in the structure—relatively more is being spent on wages in earlier stages. When ILI goes down, it means labor is becoming a relatively lower-order good: more money is spent on hiring people closer to final consumption. Note that we do not mean the level of wages here, but aggregated spending on labor.

Hence, the additional money saved because of increased thrift can increase ILI, decrease ILI, or leave it at the same level. Let us discuss examples for each of the three cases. Before we proceed, it is important to distinguish between two different forces: one force has to do with increasing the savings rate, and another one with decreasing consumption. These two things are actually not the same, even though the Böhm-Bawerkian tradition often treated them as the same. Increased savings means owners of money capital are deciding to decrease their consumption spending in favor of investing the money in the productive structure. But capital owners can put 100 percent of the money spent in the production structure toward higher wages. If they do, then total consumption in the system will not be diminished and will stay at the same level. There is no way around that observation: once we accept that the driving force of the market is capitalist (entrepreneurial) spending, then this is how things are (workers are treated as pure consumers[16]). Do we have to assume consumption is fixed? Not really, but it will be useful to assume it to more clearly explain intertemporal labor intensity. After this, we can then assume increased savings, lowered interest, and lower consumption at the same time.

Going back to figure 2.12, let us assume that each capitalist decreases consumption by 75 percent so that their income is, respectively, in each stage 0.5, 1, 1.5, 2, and 2.5. Now (figure 2.13) assume that each capitalist spends their saved income on proportionally higher wages of all their workers, so that original noninterest factors start to earn more nominally.

Table 2.2 gives the numbers.

The interest rate is roughly 2.56 percent, significantly lower due to the increased savings rate. Nevertheless, in the above model all savings are being spent on workers' wages. Moreover, they are being spent everywhere to the

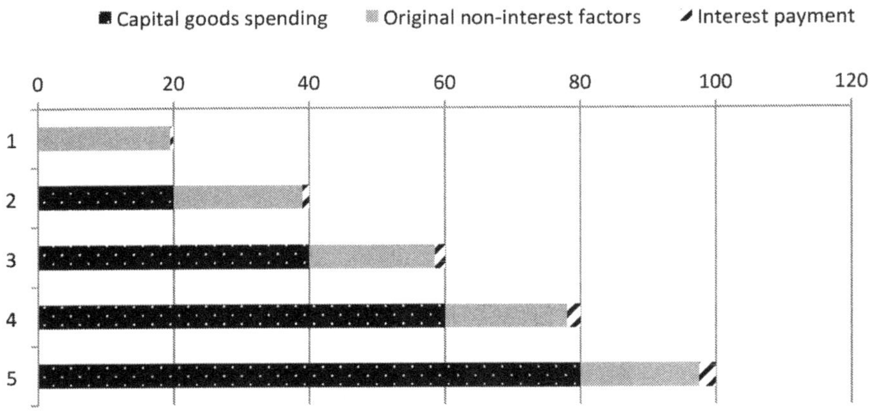

Figure 2.13 Lowered interest rate, same total consumption, and no change in the length of production

Table 2.2 Spending patterns for figure 2.13

Stage of production	*1*	*2*	*3*	*4*	*5*	*Sum*
Capital-goods spending		20	40	60	80	200
Original noninterest factors	19.5	19	18.5	18	17.5	92.5
Interest payment	0,5	1	1.5	2	2.5	7.5
Total revenues	20	40	60	80	100	300

Source: Author's (own) numerical example.

same extent. Everybody gets the same raise. Basically nothing changes in the real production structure. The number of stages of production remains the same. Hence, even though the interest rate has fallen dramatically from roughly 11 percent to almost 2.5 percent, the number of stages of production has not changed. The reason is because intertemporal labor intensity stayed the same: there was no movement of original factors toward lower or higher stages of production. Such an example, while theoretically possible, would hardly happen in practice. Bidding for factors is usually not a gift to its owners, but must have something to do with real changes. Wages can be bid up by productive spending, but most of the time because there are some allocation alterations happening.

The process starting with increased savings goes differently once we change the assumption that capital owners bid for wages proportionally without increasing their demand for capital goods. Let us assume additional savings by capitalists will be used to bid for original factors relatively closer to consumption. Using our terminology, this would lead to a decrease in intertemporal labor intensity: a higher nominal amount of spending will go to

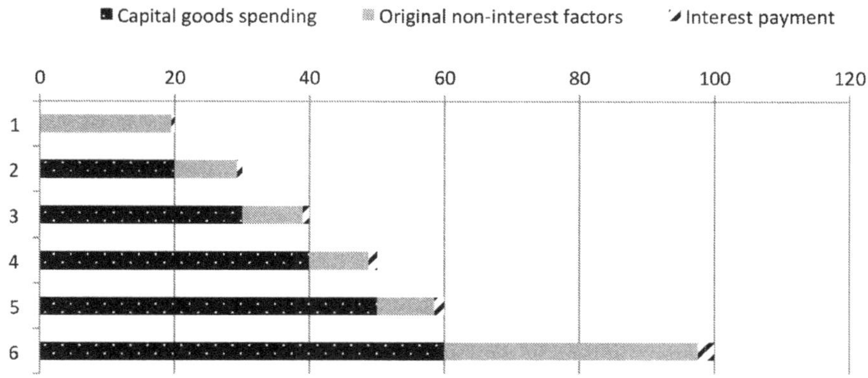

Figure 2.14 Lowered interest rate, same total consumption, and an increase in the length of production

Table 2.3 Spending patterns for figure 2.14

Stage of production	*1*	*2*	*3*	*4*	*5*	*6*	*Sum*
Capital-goods spending		20	30	40	50	60	200
Original noninterest factors	19.5	9.25	9	8.75	8.5	37.5	92.5
Interest payment	0.5	0.75	1	1.25	1.5	2.5	7.5
Total revenues	20	30	40	50	60	100	300

Source: Author's (own) numerical example

workers hired closer to consumption. How can we interpret the case empirically? Simply put, it means additional savings are mostly used up to bid for wages in sectors closer to consumption. More stages appear in the higher-order goods and more "technological" advancement throughout the industry. Also we would see more machines building machines, whereas people would work closer to the consumer sector, in services. The hypothetical structure of production could look like figure 2.14.

Table 2.3 provides numbers.

As in previous cases, interest payments are significantly lower. A higher amount of savings is used for capital spending (though not capital-goods spending). At the same time, total consumption is unaltered. Yet, the length of production evidently increases to six stages of production. Why? Because relatively more labor is hired at the very last stages of production. Relatively, much less is hired in producing the higher-order goods.

To complete the story of a decrease in the interest rate, we have a third example of higher savings, lowered interest, and total consumption remaining the same: a shorter production structure. In the hypothetical case, the first stage of production is very labor intensive. Most labor spending happens in

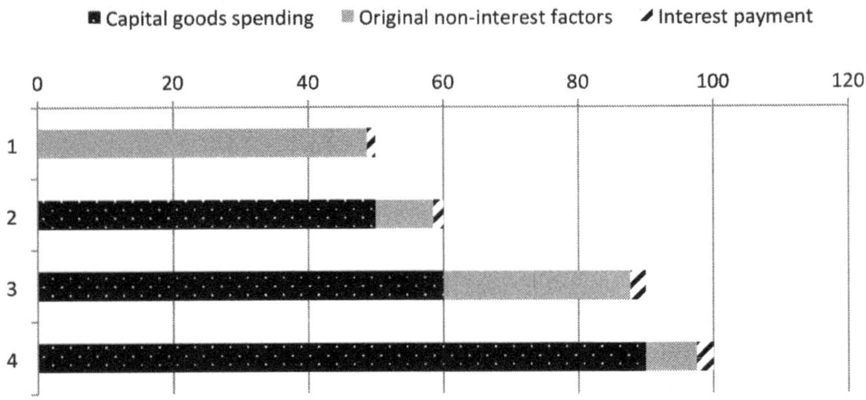

Figure 2.15 Lowered interest, same consumption, and a decrease in length of production

Table 2.4 Spending patterns for figure 2.15

Stage of production	*1*	*2*	*3*	*4*	*Sum*
Capital-goods spending		50	60	90	200
Original noninterest factors	48.75	8.5	27.75	7.5	92.5
Interest payment	1.25	1.5	2.25	2.5	7.5
Total revenues	50	60	90	100	300

Source: Author's (own) numerical example

the first stage—intertemporal labor intensity is very high—which means later stages of production are using mostly capital goods, whereas most labor is used very early on.

Table 2.4 offers the numbers for figure 2.15.

In reality, it is very hard to envision such a scenario, but perhaps possible to associate it with a very primitive economy with very few capital goods. The real-world economy is characterized by movements of labor associated with decreases in intertemporal labor intensity. Nevertheless, there is no a priori reason why this always has to be the case, as there is no a priori reason why reswitching cannot happen. It is quite possible. Most of the examples used in the reswitching debate are focused on two selected stages of production and then compared under static conditions. My aim was to incorporate such examples into a much broader framework with a complete macroeconomic picture and under true ceteris paribus conditions and budgetary constraints, namely, a fixed amount of money (and stable money velocity).

The important conclusion to be drawn is the one the exponents of the reswitching challenge gave us: the interest rate cannot be exclusively tied to either the amount of "waiting" or to the length of production precisely for the reason that length of production depends on intertemporal labor intensity.

One possible counterargument to the above could be that intertemporal labor intensity is dependent on interest rate and other factors. It could well be dependent. However, it would not be interest rate dependence but rather mutual dependence of productive spending and its composition at each stage of production. Once we start imagining an equilibrated production structure with given capital spending and intertemporal labor intensity, the interest rate becomes an end result. A similar observation could be made of interest rate formation in real markets—not the loanable-funds market, but from the market arising from productive spending of capitalists and entrepreneurs who choose the labor and capital composition of in their chosen modes of production. Individual decisions and price bidding cause the interest rate to be at a certain level, not the other way round. The interest rate itself does not cause individual decisions.

To summarize, the interest rate is an effect of savings and investments distributed across the factors in all the stages of production. Therefore, the question about the relationship between the interest rate and the length of production cannot really be settled because another more crucial factor plays a role. Hence, the reason for the reswitching debate and also the conflicts between typical Böhm-Bawerkian models and Fillieule and Hülsmann's expositions. One can draw various equilibriums with differing results, and those results are skewed in one direction or the other because of specific assumptions about the labor distribution along the investment horizon.

The interest rate cannot be causally and one-dimensionally linked with the length of production. In a similar manner, the height of the price for any specific good cannot be linked with the amount of sales contracted in the market. Does a higher price coincide with higher or lower sales? It of course depends on other underlying factors. Precisely the same answer has to be given to the question of whether higher interest rates increase or decrease the length of production. It depends: other factors are crucial.

Hayek, Rothbard, and others argued for an increase in the length of production after interest falls because they made two additional assumptions: more funds going into the production structure due to decreased consumption (a phenomenon I will analyze below), and a decrease in the intertemporal labor intensity. In the case of Hülsmann's exposition, he neglects to decompose productive spending (unlike Rothbard and to a lesser extent Hayek). His mathematical operations look as if all the spending on original factors happens at the very first stage of production. Such an assumption means the most extreme possible increase in intertemporal labor intensity: all original factors are employed in the first stage. Due to this assumption, any additional capital funds made available in the production structure move toward the early stages, which then causes the production structure to shorten. But it is precisely this reallocation that causes it to shrink, not the interest rate per se.

It is similar with Fillieule's model, where he assumed the organic composition of capital is fixed. His analysis has the advantage over Hülsmann's of decomposing productive spending into original factors and capital goods. Nevertheless, the composition is perfectly equilibrated at the same level everywhere—the ratio between original factors and capital is fixed. Although Fillieule cited Hayek positively for assuming fixed relation between capital and labor (Fillieule 2007, p. 195), I am not convinced. Why does the ratio have to be the same everywhere? Is it really necessary to assume the ratio of labor to machines is the same in the early stages of very mechanized industries (car production, mining, plastic, etc.) as in the later stages of production (car sales, insurance, supermarkets, the service sector, etc.)? If we want to stay faithful to empirical reality, we should drop this assumption (see below).

Even provided Fillieule's assumption is correct, it is this assumption that causes the length of production to shrink—not just the lowering of the interest rate. By assuming a fixed organic composition of capital, Fillieule assumed that with lowered interest, additional capital spending has to be invested more in labor placed relatively farther from consumer spending. Hence, intertemporal labor intensity needs to be increased (i.e., relatively more spending on original factors in the early stages of production).[17] Again, it is ILI that causes the structure to shorten, while the interest rate is an end result. Fillieule perhaps could argue that it is lowered interest that makes it necessary, but even from a purely mathematical perspective all inputs to the model "make it necessary." That is how this particular equilibrium is constructed, and the main role in it is played by spending on original factors distributed across the stages.

Decrease in Total Consumption Caused By A Decrease in Nominal Spending On Original Factors

Modeling the interest rate as a result as in Rothbard's model, we can also see how decreases in total consumption put pressure on the production structure to lengthen. In the above examples, we kept total consumption constant and decreased the interest rate. Now we can present the examples with a fixed interest rate and lowered total consumption. Let us go back to Rothbard's initial trapezoid (figure 2.12) and again start off with a decrease in consumption by the capitalist. Assume capitalists decide to decrease total consumption by, say, ten units, but by substituting labor with machinery (i.e., capital or intermediate goods) in terms of nominal spending.[18] Spending on original factors goes down to sixty units, whereas capitalist consumption stays at thirty units. Total consumption is ninety units.

Before going forward, let us note here an additional important consideration: we are assuming the same levels of capitalist consumption because we want to keep the interest rate at the same level. We can of course analyze the model also with lowered consumption by capitalists but not by original factors, but then the interest rate would also have to go down. *It is not possible to keep the interest rate at the same level while capitalist total consumption goes down.*

What is the effect of lowered consumption on the length of production? We again can assume various levels of the interest rate. Since in the examples above we assumed lowered interest and unchanged consumption, let us now reverse this (ceteris paribus): consumption goes down, but the interest rate does not change at all (and because of this we have to assume original factors' consumption goes down). How will the length of production be affected?

Figure 2.16 gives the example of the production structure with the same number of stages.

Table 2.5 provides just the numbers.

Now (figure 2.17) let us examine the case of lower total consumption with the same rate of interest but a longer production process (six stages).

Table 2.6 offers just the numbers.

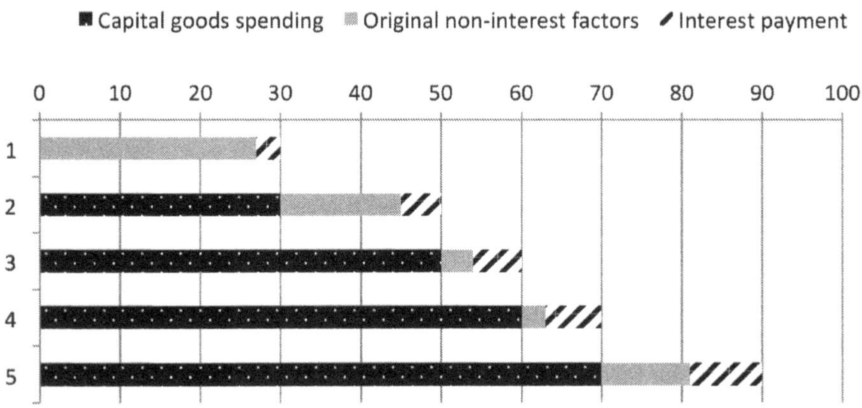

Figure 2.16 Lowered total consumption with the same interest and length of production

Table 2.5 Spending patterns for figure 2.16

Stage of production	*1*	*2*	*3*	*4*	*5*	*Sum*
Capital-goods spending		30	50	60	70	210
Original noninterest factors	27	15	4	3	11	60
Interest payment	3	5	6	7	9	30
Total revenues	30	50	60	70	90	300

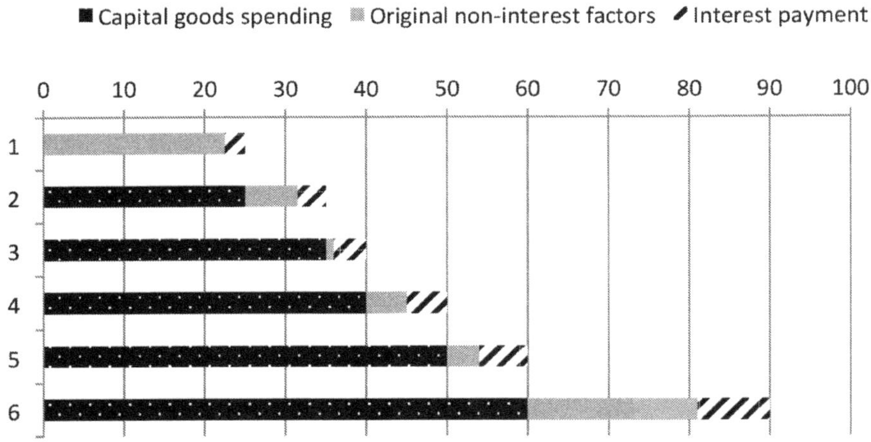

Figure 2.17 Lowered total consumption with the same rate of interest and an increase in the length of production

Table 2.6 Spending patterns for figure 2.17

Stage of production	*1*	*2*	*3*	*4*	*5*	*6*	*Sum*
Capital-goods spending		25	35	40	50	60	210
Original noninterest factors	22,5	6,5	1	5	4	21	60
Interest payment	2,5	3,5	4	5	6	9	30
Total revenues	25	35	40	50	60	90	300

Source: Author's (own) numerical example

As in the examples with the same consumption levels, the shift is caused by a decrease in the intertemporal labor intensity: relatively more original factors are being reallocated to the lower-order stages of production. Hence, productive spending is mostly used up in the structure to bid for capital goods and productive equipment, not to increase nominal spending on labor.

To complete the picture, the last example is with lowered total consumption and the same interest but a shorter production structure.

Table 2.7 gives the numbers for figure 2.18.

As in the figure 2.15, the funds saved from laying off workers are used to hire more of them in the earlier stages of production—a quite bizarre phenomenon, theoretically possible but very rare in practice, just as reswitching is known to be a very rare phenomenon.

The above analysis focused on decreased total consumption by laborers, along with no change in consumption by capitalists and therefore with no change in the interest rate. We could also construct another example of

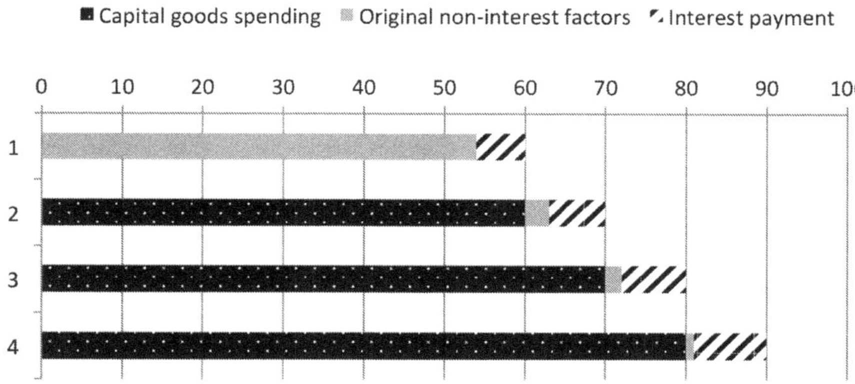

Figure 2.18 Lowered total consumption, same interest, and a decrease in the length of production

Table 2.7 Spending patterns for figure 2.18

Stage of production	*1*	*2*	*3*	*4*	*Sum*
Capital-goods spending		60	70	80	210
Original noninterest factors	54	3	2	1	60
Interest payment	6	7	8	9	30
Total revenues	60	70	80	90	300

Source: Author's (own) numerical example

decreased consumption, but on the part of capitalists, not original factors, or even on the part of both of them. It is not necessary, however, since we already established the main point: the length of production depends primarily on the intertemporal labor intensity. Here, at the end of our diagrammatic exposition, let us present just one more case: decreased consumption by capitalists and therefore a decreased rate of interest, but with no change in the length.

Table 2.8 provides hypothetical numbers (figure 2.19).

There is one notable thing about decreasing capitalists' consumption in favor of more productive spending that will not finance higher wages. Such a change does indeed lengthen the structure of production. Why? Because additional monetary units not used to bid for wages but rather to purchase more capital goods have to extend the length almost by necessity, since the trapezoid gets boosted on its capital-goods spending. By assuming that additional money is not bidding up wages but spent on capital goods, it has to contribute to lengthening the structure. Shifts in the intertemporal labor intensity can only mask such a force, provided it works in the other direction.

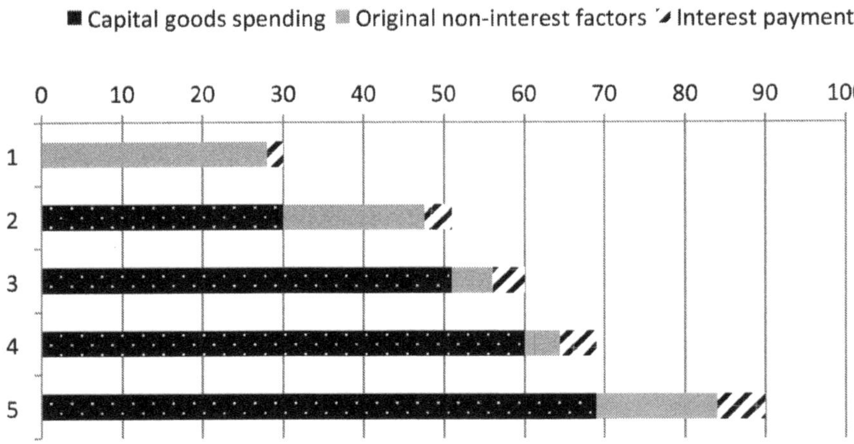

Figure 2.19 Lowered total consumption, lowered interest, and no change in the length of production

Table 2.8 Spending patterns for figure 2.19

Stage of production	*1*	*2*	*3*	*4*	*5*	*Sum*
Capital-goods spending		30	51	60	69	210
Original noninterest factors	28	17,6	5	4,4	15	70
Interest payment	2	3,4	4	4,6	6	20
Total revenues	30	51	60	69	90	300

Source: Author's (own) numerical example

Trapezoids and Empirical Surroundings

To sum up, what determines the length of production? Is it the interest rate? No, since the interest rate is a function of savings. Savings are always transforming the economy, and the result depends on changes in the spending pattern. Shifts in monetary allocation shift the allocation of labor. Depending on the direction of change in intertemporal labor intensity, the effect on the length of production can differ.

One question may be interesting to ask: what shapes intertemporal labor intensity? In our model, it is an aggregate element, resulting from the decisions of all entrepreneurs, who are not at all interested in it. They choose those methods of production that allow for highest productivity, cheap production, and high quality relative to other productive possibilities and consumer preferences. This can lead to either more capital-intensive or more labor-intensive processes. The solution cannot be determined a priori.

We do have some empirics concerning economic growth. The macroeconomic history of capitalism is the history of declining intertemporal labor intensity. Employment statistics and generalized models demonstrate such evolution. First, trade and production were based on primitive rural conditions, with labor being hired very early on. The industrial revolution led to an increase in spending on capital goods and to a structure in which values of capital goods became increasingly important (with relative shifts from pure interest returns). In twentieth-century history, industrial production deepened through more specialized, larger technological equipment with people being hired in lower-order stages, closer to consumption and machines being produced by machines. The further development of industry can be seen as "post-Fordism":

> Counterposed to neo-Fordism is flexible production, which includes everything ranging from flexible mass production to flexible specialization. . . . These are technologically dynamic production systems in which skilled workers use flexible capital equipment to produce a constantly changing variety of goods. Flexible specialisation typically occurs in smaller-scale industries with a greater variety of output than is possible in flexible mass production. . . . [I]ndividual firms use flexible and widely applicable technologies: general purpose machines rather than large, dedicated machine systems. Product innovation is not held back by massive capital investments in rigid technologies. (Storper 1989, pp. 73–74)

There is also one important limitation of the trapezoid analysis that we have not mentioned. We have assumed that capital goods are smoothly used up during the process of production. There is no sinking of money capital on them, which might have resulted in uncertain shifts in their value and therefore to capitalization of losses. Hayek noticed this while working on his version of the trapezoid:

> In the first instance it made it impossible to treat adequately the case of durable goods. It is impossible to assume that the potential services, embodied in a durable good and waiting for the moment when they will be utilized, change hands at regular intervals of time. This meant that so far as that particular illustration of the monetary mechanism was concerned *I had to leave durable goods simply out of account.* (Hayek 1933, pp. 194–195)

Rothbard did not think it poses a very serious issue, since we can think of durable goods (also known as fixed capital, as opposed to circulating capital) as service units (Rothbard 2004, p. 290). Each durable good is simply the embodiment of future rental services.[19] That is why the trapezoid progressively grows: it only incorporates the values just added by renting a durable good. In reality entrepreneurs often purchase particular durable goods of value higher than the year's total production only to economize on those durable goods through longer periods of time and to generate profits in the future (or even just minimal positive returns). To properly mimic reality, the trapezoid would have to be bumpy and chaotically increasing in value from time to time. Instead of doing this, we have assumed the value of a durable good is added to the reshaped intermediate goods sold for the next stage. Durable goods are not actually purchased. If they are, then we have a problem of sinking capital and all the vital aspects surrounding it that impose additional costs on the company—for example, time lags (Altuğ 1993, p. 301). Investment lags dramatically alter the price uncertainty of investments (Bar-Ilan and Strange 1996, p. 616).

The reason for omitting the notion of purchased durable goods is to engage in equilibrium analysis. Since we do not deal with industrial fluctuations in here, but comparative statics and steady paths, we do not have to study the notion of sinking money capital into particular goods. They can be rented as if they are partially produced in a particular year. Obviously this amounts to another great demonstration of the shortcomings of equilibrium analysis. It is also one of the reasons why the above trapezoids *cannot be used to illustrate the problems in the business cycle*: fluctuations have a lot to do with sinking capital into durable goods used over the long investment process. Equilibrium analysis of trapezoids is unsuitable for many things, but for one purpose it can be safely used: to show which factors the length of production depends on.

NOTES

1. Hence, the mentioned concepts are closer to John Bates Clark than Böhm-Bawerk, since the difference between capital and capital goods is actually blurred in favor of views in which the means of production are seen as the same entity as capital.
2. For more on the critique of Levhari see, for example, Garegnani (1966).
3. Notice that the example uses labor units as the basics of the calculation. That is questionable, yet does not change the essence of the argument, since it can be easily changed to monetary units. We make that change at the end of this subchapter.
4. Fundamentally, however, it was really Irving Fisher—with his concept of rate of return—who was under attack (Pasinetti 1969, p. 509).
5. Robinson's insights about capital nonmeasurability are so thoughtful and at the same time ironic that it is almost unbelievable that she proposed to reduce capital to labor units (Robinson 1953, p. 82). Such an approach suffers from similar flaws as using the mystical *K* variable but also has its own technical issues (see Champernowne 1953, pp. 112–113).
6. Although a successful measurement of capital would open the door at least for properly assessing capital accumulation adding productively to capital and for seeing how much is objectively worn and torn. It would also allow for cross-country comparisons (Robinson 1959, p. 158).
7. Samuelson attempted to construct a heterogeneous-capital-goods model based on linear programming, so that Clark's concept of aggregated capital for the whole

economy can be dropped in favor of more reasonable model (Samuelson 1962, p. 194). Nevertheless (as Sen emphasized), he did assume a specific fundamental-factor price frontier (Samuelson 1962, pp. 195, 198). In fact, after a while, Samuelson himself proposes to "suppose labor and a homogeneous capital jelly (physical not dollar jelly!) produce a flow of homogeneous net national product, which can consist of consumption goods or of net capital (i.e. jelly) formation, the two being infinitely substitutable (in the long run, or possibly even in the short run) on a one-for-one basis" (Samuelson 1962, p. 200). As Garegnani observes, Samuelson's surrogate function (apparently heterogeneous) is actually a regular homogeneous production function in disguise (Garegnani 1970, pp. 415–416).

8. It comes as no surprise—as Samuelson reports—that it was an absolute shock to Schumpeter that Douglas, while analyzing manufacturing between 1899 and 1922, assumed that no technical progress happened (Samuelson 1979, p. 924) (the increase in value could be ascribed to factor inputs).

9. Ironically Robinson admitted that factor allocations according to the neoclassical perfect-competition model are good for normative considerations of socialist central planning, rather than meant to be descriptive of a capitalist economy (1964, p. 410). This view resembles Lange's model of market socialism, which is to be built according to neoclassical principles. Apparently neoclassicism is not good for capitalism but was invented for socialism!

10. Wicksell never attempted to separate physical changes from price changes (Pasinetti 1978, p. 186).

11. There are some problems with classifying goods as "permanent" (see Weston 1951, pp. 130–131). For our considerations they can be put aside.

12. Why would there be such a classification? Technology is always introduced via entrepreneurial decisions about capital possessions, and human capital is simply a part of a developed labor market. Yet, in modeling we may want to emphasize that part of the entrepreneurial allocation of capital, which will be seen as a "technology" variable. It is similar with that part of the labor market in which knowledge is particularly valuable in workers' employment. One should remember, however, the case could become misleading, since "human capital" cannot be conceptually separated from labor in a way that, for example, capital can be separated from labor. Even if it resembles to some extent the development of a typical material capital good (as stated by Cochrane and Kiker [1970, p. 385]). The same is with technology that cannot exist outside of particular capital-goods and entrepreneurial decisions. Actually rather than speaking of technology, it would make more sense to talk about "information" as a factor of production (Berczi 1981, p. 15). The three reasons are that information is a much wider concept than technology, it already includes technology, and doing so also makes information more related to human action upon it.

13. Xu et al. go on to select six factors of production in a very entrepreneurial manner: labor forces, physical forces, financial forces, natural forces, transport forces, and time forces (Xu et al. 2009, p. 223). The classification seems little bit over the top, but in general demonstrates how creative we may be in teleological grouping of the factors of production. There is no strong reason to close forever the sets of classification, as those categories grew out as historical ideal-types.

14. At the same time, remembering all its shortcomings, especially the assumption that after the series of rounds we are "back where we started." Obviously, this can never be the case. So-called natural resources are not superabundant but used up all the time, and therefore, each next "round" of equilibrated process has to be altered in some way (even as we discover new resources, they are "new"). And there is an undeniable energy waste, due to entropy, which changes conditions in which humans live (Swaney 1985, p. 860).

15. In a second article, Garrison gives an excellent exposition of the reswitching issue, since he uses monetary prices instead of labor inputs from Samuelson's example (Garrison 2006, p. 7).

16. The same feature can be found in Kalecki's model discussed in chapter 3 in the spirit of Say's law. However far apart Kalecki was from Rothbard, they actually are similar in the case of spending analysis.

17. In one of the empirical analyses for United Kingdom it is noted: "The organic composition of capital generally followed an upward trend (see Table 3 and Figures 3A-3E). For total industry (including construction), this indicator stood 80% higher in 1981 than in 1959, while for total manufacturing, it was 44 percent higher. The sector showing the greatest increase was that of intermediate goods, where the level at the end of the period was more than two and a half times that at the beginning of the period" (Reati 1986, pp. 538–539).

18. A feature someone could call "Ricardo effect" in a general sense—when the adjustment in labor employment happens. Yet, the term "Ricardo effect" is usually associated with Hayek, who coined the term and meant substitution of machines for labor because of specific causes related to raising real wages (Gehrke 2003, p. 144). In Rothbard's framework, causality would rather be reversed: increased investments in capital goods and decreased consumption result in higher real wages of laborers.

19. Durables are the embodiment of future services during a good's lifetime. Time, of course, becomes a crucial factor for determining the good's present value (Rothbard 2004, p. 166).

Part II

MACROECONOMIC ASPECTS OF THE CAPITAL STRUCTURE

Chapter 3

Expenditures Equilibrium and Say's Law

Fixed Aggregate Spending versus Money-Market Dynamics

The essence of macroeconomic equilibrium is when aggregate demand equals aggregate supply, or differently put, when the conditions for Say's law have been met. Clower and Leijonhufvud named the case "Say's principles" and presented it as general equilibrium: when incomes paid out cover revenues necessary to establish equilibrium (Clower and Leijonhufvud 1973, p. 158). There is no dynamic money market, since cash is hoarded at a fixed level (or not hoarded at all), and no monetary inflation or contraction disequilibrating spending flows. All unconsumed income is transformed into investment spending. Additionally, Say's law is best presented with full general equilibrium, the case when the whole economic structure repeats itself without any changes within it (although that assumption may not be necessary).

Physiocracy and the *Tableau économique* appropriately come to mind: a complete and unified circular flow with no disturbances. At some level, Say's law can be seen as a version of the circular flow with equilibrated sales, expenditures, consumption, and production (Shoul 1957, p. 617). The debates on the role of consumption and savings have gone on since even before Thomas Malthus, Jean-Baptiste Say, and David Ricardo; and the times of the French Physiocrats were also full of claims about how consumption spending has to be encouraged in the quest for economic prosperity (Spengler 1945, p. 194). These types of statements have generated a vast amount of responses with explanations of how production and investments have to precede consumption. Properly, the main purpose has been to emphasize money holders' productive spending. Money holders' function can be seen in the diagrams in chapter 2 since they are the source of aggregate demand, in terms of both future consumption and expanding productive capacity. Say did not actually stand out that much from other thinkers, but followed Turgot, Say, and others (Skinner 1967, p. 154). The typical version of Say's law could be ascribed to

James Mill (Thweatt 1980, p. 469). Various traces of it can be found in most thinkers, including Adam Smith, Richard Cantillon, A. R. J. Turgot, Ricardo, and others (Van Allen 2001).

Hence, one of the main reasons why nobody called this approach a "law": it was not any particular proposition about how markets function.[1] It was a complete description of market production, a tool to reject various erroneous points raised by mercantilism and other beliefs surrounding it. Responses to those beliefs clustered around a few theorems associated with Say's law: money is not an end in itself, domestic savings are not a threat, an unfavorable balance of trade does not reduce domestic demand, savings are necessary for investments, investments are better than wasteful consumption spending, and technical change does not threaten growth (Baumol 1999, pp. 196–197). What has come to be known as "the law of markets" was very broadly related to several economic issues and developed through generations of classical economists (Baumol 1999, pp. 202–203).[2]

Since classical economists lived through shaky economic times and depressions, they did not assume full employment and did not imply that markets under any conditions can achieve perfect coordination. Such a utopian vision could not be defended by anyone. Rather the approach was to demonstrate a vital function of the price system and demonstrate that markets can work while issuing benign price signals (Johnson 2001, p. 46). Hutt restated the point that discoordination in various sectors of the economy is to be associated with withholding supplies, wrong price signals, and apparent refusals to sell at market-clearing prices (Hutt 1974, pp. 37–38). Nevertheless, this statement does not imply what the sources for such mistakes are, and most importantly, with which policies they could be rectified.

The unfortunate reality of the classical analysis is that it came to be treated by John Maynard Keynes, who threw classical analysis away with the unfair summary that those classical economists believed no serious economic crises can happen. "Supply creates its own demand," the famous quote goes, even though Say was actually talking about a particular supply creating demand for something other than initial production.[3] Summarizing in this manner, everything classical economics had to offer guaranteed spurring a "hopeless confusion about the history of economic thought" (Blaug 1997a, p. 231). An offer on the supply side potentially allows a seller to purchase other goods and services offered in exchange. Say's approach definitely has its shortcomings, but the flaws in Keynes's caricature are not among them. Careful study of Keynes's views on Say and of Keynes's views popularized by Oskar Lange (1942) show that they actually rarely mentioned Say (Keynes, for instance, mentioned Mill instead). Keynes did not quote him, and Lange just gave a mathematical treatment of Keynes. There is also just one footnote to Say in Lange (Johnson 2001, p. 26).

Say (just like Mill) had a theory of coordination failures and problems of effective demand, which for some reason stop real-world exchanges from happening (Jonsson 1995, pp. 148–149). At the same time, at the heart of the classical way of thinking are efficiency issues, which nowadays one could call microeconomic considerations. Output, employment, and expenditures do not have any values in themselves. What matters are sustainable output, employment, and rationalized expenditures. Wasteful expenditures are not to be encouraged, since they cannot generate wealth—that is the central message of Say and Mill (Kates 1997, p. 197). High levels of spending on anything do not constitute fundamentals of growth; the economy cannot prosper and thrive without adding to a country's overall production. The main reason why Keynes radically opposed Say was to reject such a line of thinking and market-oriented rhetoric (Kates 2010, p. 5).

One good offered for another good ties together the concepts of demand and supply. Under hypothetical barter, they are two sides of the same coin. Things change, however, when we allow ourselves to focus on a specific market: money. Barter models dealing with coordination problems have to fail because coordination happens in the nexus of contracts where money is acquired and disposed of later (Leijonhufvud 1988, p. 211[4]). In our framework of Jevonsian trapezoids, this means that there is fixed money supply and no hoarding or dishoarding of money. Under such assumptions, any changes in the pattern of spending have to happen in at least two places. The money being spent somewhere in the structure has to be accompanied by decreases in spending elsewhere. In this sense, Say's law also has to be met. No general overproduction is possible: some goods in various markets may be overproduced, but only if others in different markets are underproduced. In economic growth, this is usually the case, so older companies die out and pave the way for the newcomers who are more capable of gaining market share and increasing profits.

William Baumol wrote a famous piece discussing various meanings that could be attached to Say's law from softer to harder versions: (1) Society's purchasing power is limited by production. (2) Increases in output lead to higher expenditures. (3) Investment expenditures are more beneficial for the economy than consumption expenditures. (4) Increased output will eventually be sold. (5) Production is the source of demand. (6) Any overproduction of goods is always relative (there is underproduction in other markets). (7) Supply and demand always become equal due to fast-equilibrating market mechanism (Baumol 1977, pp. 147–159; compare also with the four meanings mentioned in Shoul 1957, pp. 615–616).

Is any item on the list what Say actually had in mind while referring to what is now known as the famous "law of markets"? Perhaps. There are so many interpretations of this theorem that one could devote a whole study to deal only with them. The same could be said about dozens of quotes from Say and Mill, and about further dozens of quotes about those quotes. The list could go on almost indefinitely. I would rather set aside this challenge. No matter what Say meant, the message was clearly addressed to the people in a crisis lamenting a "scarcity of money" (Say 1971, p. 132). While responding to this challenge, Say listed many important and crucial features of the monetary system, including the fact that the seller does not ultimately need money, but other products, and that money serves as a medium of exchange in order for sellers to get access to other markets. He also provided the essence of a picture of long-run growth by pointing out that more production opens possibilities for broader market demand and opportunities for exchange.

At the same time, Say prepared the way for quantity theorists' view of money as a veil:

> They will universally find the most extensive demand in those places, where the most of values are produced; because in no other places are the sole means of purchase created, that is, values. Money performs but a momentary function in this double exchange; and when the transaction is finally closed, it will always be found, that one kind of commodity has been exchanged for another. (Say 1971, p. 134)

Say's observations about the market process on the production side are well thought out and important for modern considerations of growth. Nevertheless, they are not complete because his analysis lacks monetary theory. Also, despite the correctness of his observations about demand and supply, they are not a sufficient critique of the notion of "scarcity of money." At best they amount to advice to pay attention to the supply side while analyzing the flow of money. They do not completely cover the absence of spending. Neglect of monetary considerations has led both classical and neoclassical economists to dichotomize the pricing process (Blaug 1997, p. 147). Economists have seen prices of goods and services as almost detached from cash balances and demand for money. In such a framework, it is indeed logically impossible for a global glut to appear. Such a view requires an unaltered money market (i.e., both demand and supply of money stay the same). It can therefore be seen as a "strong version of Say's identity" (Blaug 1997, p. 145).

What if people universally increase their demand for money and do not just spend it elsewhere in the production structure? With this question we are moving away from the equilibrated monetary model. Say's answer was insufficient: "Even when money is obtained with a view to hoard or bury it, the ultimate object is always to employ it in a purchase of some kind. The heir of the lucky finder uses it in that way, if the miser do not; for money, as money, has no other use than to buy with" (Say 1971, p. 133). To be sure, some money hoarded will be spent at some future point, but the timely process can potentially be burdensome and therefore deserves more of a special treatment than be given in just a footnote. Yet to do this one has to break away from equilibrium concepts (an attempt I undertake later in the book in chapters 5 and 6). Failing to do so was the main deficiency of classical economics. As Don Patinkin notes, money did not enter any utility function in Say's writings—he did not treat it as a special type of good that can be demanded (Patinkin 1948, p. 135). He treated money only as an accounting unit, or at least as a transaction unit—not as an asset to hold for the sole purpose of deriving utility from cash balances.

Patinkin and Oskar Lange (1942) may have been too harsh to the classical economists. They almost went so far as to suggest that the classical economists believed nobody would be interested in holding money.[5] There is a difference between claiming that ultimately money has no value of its own and saying that people will not be interested in purchasing money because of its exchange value. Also, the first claim does not imply the classical economists were unaware of the time lag between accepting money in a transaction and then spending it. The classical economists, however, did not see that normally money would be treated as a special asset to hold (Tsiang 1966, p. 343). Unfortunately, this led them to neglect to develop monetary theory enough. Despite their unwillingness to develop a comprehensive theory of demand for money Say's law appears to be something different from Walras's law. The latter takes the equilibrium concept to its extreme point: money is just a unit of account, a *numeraire*. Say's law in its various versions does not need to go that far. A monetary equilibrium with total aggregate spending unaltered is enough: the amount of money demanded does not change, but changes in relative prices are possible and do happen (Balassa 1959, p. 264). With this additional notion we can see that Walras's approach means no money is hoarded, whereas with Say hoarding money is sort of stable, despite changing prices in decentralized markets. It is not demand for money that is zero, but "excess" demand. The term "excess" refers in this context to the demand for money as an additional asset, not just a medium of exchange with its transactional value (Mishan 1963, p. 615). Some amount of money has to be held for it to perform its vital functions, so holding it cannot be completely excluded in considering monetary spending.

Naturally it was hard not to be aware that people demand cash balances and can simply refrain from spending money on anything. Nevertheless, in a manner typical for Say, he quickly summed up the notion then put it aside by saying that ultimately money will be spent somewhere. While this notion is certainly true, "ultimately somewhere" can take some time. Why does money deserve a special kind of attention? Because people can hoard the money or dishoard it. So aggregated spending can be boosted or curtailed, leading to macroeconomic adjustments and production structure reshufflings. While focusing on the money market, there are two sides to be described, the demand side just mentioned but also the supply of money, which can be expanding or shrinking. Just like changes in the demand for money, changes in the supply of money also have macroeconomic effects, which I consciously omitted discussing until now by assuming fixed money supply and fixed total spending. In the classical presentation of Say's law (such as the Jevonsian one that I reviewed in chapter 2), there is a Walrasian flavor with quantity of money equal to the demand for money (Lange 1942, p. 3). This negates the potential need for any monetary process, with the pricing process concentrated only on the "real" side, "real prices," seen separately from nominal cash balances and nominal prices.

Can a "general glut" happen? Naturally—when people increase their total willingness to hold money. And an upward shift in the demand for money affects all, or most, markets for goods and services (Blaug 1997a, pp. 231–232). One way to get away with this claim is to treat money like any other good that can be purchased in the market. Under such circumstances we could see underproduction of money as accompanied by overproduction of other goods and services. Those overproduced goods and services are consciously withheld from the market by the sellers. Such withholding can be a part of general demand in the market (sellers temporarily demanding their own products rather than accepting lower prices). Such was the approach by the great William Harold Hutt, who both argued that hoarded money delivers special utility (Hutt 1956) and exposed the view that withheld capacity is part of total demand for products (Hutt 1963, pp. 391–392). Hutt was in most respects quite correct; however, it may be doubtful that this is exactly what Say and others had in mind while discussing a market framework for crises and depressions. Following Hutt's line of thinking it would be perfectly sensible to build a Keynesian model of depressions while at the same time accepting the basic notions and concepts of the classical school, so that Keynes becomes a great champion of Say's law (Hutt 1979, pp. 65–66)![6]

Due to the importance and size of the literature on "idle resources," it would be more appropriate to associate it with "Hutt's Say's law," rather than just "Say's law." Moreover Hutt's works do not reach the heart of the problem: terminological confusion in the overall macroeconomic literature about the essence of savings and cash balances.

SAVINGS MARKET VERSUS MONEY MARKET

Say's law entered into economic controversies in part because of terminological muddling, especially associated with the term "savings." While analyzing the history of macroeconomics and the Keynesian shift, one can often find dubious statements that Say assumed an efficient loanable-funds market in which any unconsumed income is transformed into investment spending. In this view of Say, savings are unconsumed income, which depends on the interest rate via the law of supply (lower interest decreases savings, higher increases them). Any such additional money finds its way back into the economy through the loanable-funds market. People decrease consumption and save their income, which is then somehow transformed into investment (Snowdon and Vane 2005, pp. 47–48). The social advantages of being thrifty could not have been presented in a more compelling and universal manner. The interest rate as a price in the loanable-funds market could balance society's will to save for the future—represented in the supply-of-savings curve—with the existing market conditions hidden in the investment-demand curve. Not only are savings and investment balanced, but the whole financial market appears to be in a healthy condition (Kent 2005, p. 64).

Such a presentation can allow for further Keynesian reasoning: decreases in spending on consumption lead to decreases in total spending. Due to this shift expenditures fall, revenues fall and incomes fall, and so does output along with employment. The "paradox of thrift" means economic potential is curtailed due to the disappointing attempt to save more (Snowdon and Vane 2005, p. 48).

However, even assuming such reasoning is correct; it is not about savings really, but about cash balances. The way we understand savings and the way Say understood them are radically different. As Henry Hazlitt explained it, in order to save one also has to spend—on stocks, bonds, or various types of instruments that capitalize companies directly (Hazlitt 1959, p. 42). Savings is not really (or at least not just) hoarding, or even if it is, it deserves to be recognized with special terminology. Saving in cash balances is miles apart from saving and investing. Those two types of saving lead to differing macroeconomic results. Unfortunately, many debates about Keynesianism do not help to sort this out. Keynesians lament that savings is a leakage and investment is a source of growth. Most of the confusion stems from lack of clarity about this. Moreover, this confusion has led theorists to create the notion of a multiplier mechanism, where consumption is seen as adding to overall aggregate demand, while savings are a leakage from the system creating slumps in output and production (Ahiakpor 2001, p. 747). Richard Kahn, one of the creators of the multiplier concept (before Keynes) stated in his classic article that increasing investments means reducing savings (Kahn 1931, p. 182). Such a presentation can make sense only if saving is treated as money withdrawn from circulation. But one could counterargue that that is not the way classical economists understood savings.[7]

The reason for this terminological confusion and also for Keynes's caricature of Say's law lie probably in Keynes's attempt to radically change the concept of interest rate formation in the loanable-funds market. Hence, the reason why many books and articles on the history of thought often mention Say's law in relation to the loanable-funds market, where the interest rate is the mechanism for balancing savings preferences with investment opportunities. Say's law has to hold planned investments equal to planned savings under the "loanable-funds theory of interest" (Gerrard 1995, p. 448). Keynes, on the other hand, believed the interest rate to be a balancing force in the money market with varying levels of demand for money (Lydall 1961, p. 74)—a perspective that corresponds well with the redefinition of savings as cash balances leaking out of the macroeconomic system, where savings directly cause falling incomes, with output and employment problems following. The relationship appears to contrast with the classical view because it apparently reverses the relationship between expenditures and incomes. Investment expenditures determine income, which then balances savings with investments (Lydall 1961, p. 72). The whole concept and its anticlassical character rely on rhetoric, however: investment spending is somehow not treated as savings but as a separate form of spending.

The reality is that nonconsumption of income has actually three alternative forms: saving in cash balances, saving and investing directly in companies, and saving and indirectly investing in companies. Problems about savings discussed after Keynes are not really about savings but about either cash balances or about indirect investments in companies. The latter case comes to our attention when intermediation in the financial market fails: when people save their money and the financial institutions do not lend it further. Yet, even this is not really a savings issue but an issue of broken intermediation. Therefore, the supposed savings problems are not really about saving but more about the demand for money and possible problems in the banking and financial sector, which deserve a more specific treatment. The apparent failure of increased savings has to do not with savings per se but with the failure of the banking system or the monetary system in general. What needs to be explained in the face of the crises is how banking intermediation may be broken and why people's willingness to hold on to liquidity would suddenly and tremendously rise. That normally does not happen: something has to trigger it. Usually it is a failure of monetary and credit institutions in general.

KALECKI'S EQUATION AND THE ACCOUNTING IDENTITY

The equilibrated structure in terms of expenditures is demonstrated by Kalecki's equation. The assumptions Michal Kalecki used are in accordance with Say's law and can also be fully integrated with its nonmonetary framework. Naturally the money market is equilibrated, so there are neither changes in cash holdings nor any changes in the money supply. Additionally, we are abstracting from budget deficits and foreign trade, therefore focusing on a laissez-faire closed economy (Kalecki 1942, p. 258).

Kalecki went on to establish the following equation:

> Gross capitalist revenues (fixed capital and working capital) + wages = workers' consumption + capitalists' consumption + investments. (Kalecki 1942, p. 259)

Both sides of the equation are equal under typical monetary equilibrium, where total money spending is constant. The left side represents total gross earnings, which consist of workers' wages and capitalists' gross revenues. The right side illustrates how the money is spent. It is either spent on consumption or on investments. If it is spent on consumption, then how we classify it depends on the source of the income. Hence, consumption can be divided into two economic categories based on the individual's role in capitalist production: workers' consumption is different from capitalists' consumption. Expenditures are equal to the money earned in the form of factor payments. The equilibrium holds since there is no money hoarding or any other monetary disturbance on the supply side.

The equation should be supplemented by the additional condition that workers' wages are naturally equal to workers' consumption. The reason is not that workers are in some way obliged to consume. In reality workers could save part of their money and invest it in various avenues. The theoretical approach is, however, to treat them in a model as pure consumers. The argument is for simplification, since it keeps the model concise and helps to avoid unnecessarily obscuring the facts (Kalecki 1937, p. 77). Relaxing this assumption in empirical findings in no way alters the essence of the equation, which demonstrates how various income and expenditure streams are formed. It also demonstrates how to capture the influence of those streams upon productive decisions.

One could ask what Kalecki's equation has to do with Say's law. As I have mentioned, Say formulated his law of markets in order to point to the influence of supply on future consumer demand. It can either be seen as sales of one product creating room for demand for another product or as a movement of money. Income streams filter down into the hands of market participants, who are then ready to spend the full amount on consumption and investments. Where does Kalecki come in the production structure picture? The equation illustrates the importance of capital spending on capital dynamics. Capitalist spending is also a main factor in the business cycle (Kalecki 1949, p. 61). Actually it is gross accumulation that equals the production of capital goods and increment of various stocks (Kalecki 1935, p. 328).

The second issue is that increased wages are not a way to boost profits or overall aggregated business revenues. When Say responded to underconsumption theories, he was at the same time responding to the notion that consumer stimulus is not a way to make business conditions better (since according to him consumption is a way of "destroying" things). In the above equation, it is quite evident. Higher consumer spending by workers can lead to increases in the revenues in some sectors but from an accounting perspective it has to be financed through higher wages. Therefore, any potential increase in the form of higher flows on the right side has to be accompanied by increases on the left side. In the case of workers, this means higher wages, which are a cost to capitalists and entrepreneurs. Therefore, a business seeking higher revenues through boosting wages is like a snake eating its own tail:

> Gross capitalist revenues (fixed capital and working capital) + wages + *1000 units in additional wages* = workers' consumption + capitalists' consumption + investments + *1000 units in additional consumption spending.*

The added items on both sides have to be equal, since workers are treated as pure consumers. Even if revenues could be boosted on the right side, it could not result in higher profits or capital formation out of those profits because exactly the same amount has to be counted as economic and accounting cost of paying higher wages to workers. Aggregated profits equal spending on investments and consumption by capitalists (Kalecki 1937, p. 445). Therefore, they cannot be increased by increasing workers' consumption. The observation coincides well with another observation: overall capitalist spending determines short-run macroeconomic equilibrium (1937a, p. 79)[8]. Higher wages will not and cannot cause higher profits.

This does not mean Kalecki believed the laissez-faire economy to be completely efficient. He favored deficit public spending in order to increase business revenues (Kalecki 1945, p. 89). His reasoning was based on the assumption that deficit spending can add to overall business revenues. At the same time, the equation confirms that private entrepreneurs cannot boost their profit margins by artificially bidding for higher wages.

A natural accounting truth to be inferred from Kalecki's equation is, famously, that capitalists earn what they spend, whereas workers spend what they earn. The statement is not necessarily true but a consequence of choices related to earning income. Workers can become capitalists once they choose to save their money and invest it to receive future interest payments. In any case, gross profits are determined by gross private investments and capitalists' consumption (Kalecki 1942, p. 259). Hence, for business to flourish and for business profits to rise, the economy needs more capital accumulation in the form of direct investment spending by capitalists, directly into the production structure. The last thing it needs is artificially high wages at the expense of reducing capital formation and investment. That is the conclusion at least from Kalecki's equations of profits.

NOTES

1. The term "Say's law" was probably invented by Fred Taylor in 1925 publication (Kates 1995, p. 75).
2. For an excellent treatment with concrete examples of the pre-Keynesian literature about classical components—often related to Say's law—see Kates 2010, pp. 12–24. See also Gordon 1965 for the views in British periodicals in the nineteenth century.
3. An interesting aspect is that "supply creates its own demand" is a twentieth century invention that did not appear in the writings of the classical economists. Keynes is famous for using it, but he has borrowed it from Harlan Linneus McCracken while reading his *Value Theory and Business Cycles* (Kates 2008, pp. 40–41). The letter from Keynes to McCracken proves that Malthus was a direct inspiration for Keynes. Kates even argues that McCracken may be highly underrated economist in the twentieth century, at least in terms of influence on the history of thought. Another possible inspiration for using the term could be James Bonar (Kates 2007, p. 34).
4. Leijonhufvud famously develops his arguments that Keynes's message was more sophisticated than his watered down rhetoric against Say.
5. The further flaw is to construct Say's law concept on the idea of general price level. See on this an illuminating analysis in Salerno 2006, pp. 144–145.
6. Such is indeed the case of works of Clower and Leijonhufvud.
7. There were also huge differences in the meaning of "savings" even before Keynesian revolution. A good example was a Böm-Bawerkian revolution. In classical economics, savings were often understood as stockpiling of various goods for future uses (that was also something on which Keynes ironically commented that overproduction of consumer goods has to be a beneficial glut). Böhm-Bawerk, on the other hand, diverted the focus from consumer goods to the production structure. Savings need not be understood as a surplus of consumer goods, but as a conscious decision to be more future oriented, for example, to reallocate factors of production to more remote processes in order to increase consumption in the future. On this important point, see Bresciani-Turroni 1936, p. 9.
8. Here Kalecki goes along the lines of traditional Keynesianism, where investment spending is not being seen as a form of spending *saved income*. Rather it is treated as another form of spending and representing demand. This usage of words further deepens artificial conflicts in Say's law interpretations as mentioned in the last section (confusion between cash balances and savings).

Chapter 4

Potential Output versus Intertemporal Equilibrium

Common Sense of Potential Output

Potential output is the pillar of macroeconomic theorizing, or most economic theorizing. It hides behind the production-possibilities frontier in microeconomics, and behind any policy proposal in macroeconomics and any consideration of business cycles. Intuitively, it means reaching the maximum potential of an economy, when all significant factors of production are employed in sustainable economic projects. Focusing on factors, another expression suggesting the idea of potential output is full employment. Potential output means "how much an economy can produce at full employment" (Okun 1962, p. 1).[1] Related, Okun's law—stating unemployment higher by 1 percent lowers economy's potential by 2–3 percent—was invoked all too commonly for many years (Gordon and Clark 1984, p. 538).

The meaning of "potential output" and "full employment" seems almost self-evident, for most economic concepts have a common sense meaning—almost to the same extent as the concept of equilibrium (and in fact, an economy with full employment is an equilibrium case). Potential output becomes a standard for assessing any current economic conditions, since it concerns the overall production potential of the economy (Kuttner 1992, p. 2). When we theorize about a bigger or smaller downturn, we usually assume that real production is lagging behind what it could be (real business cycle theory, mentioned below, may be an exception). When we talk about the economy being below full employment, we mean the unemployment rate is higher than it needs to be.

Similar, though a bit more complicated, is the case of employment reaching higher levels than "full employment" and production going beyond "potential output." How can we hire more people than when we fully utilize resources? How can we produce beyond our limits? Apparently, overemployment and overproduction have to be temporary and not sustainable in the longer run. In the microeconomic framework, the production-possibilities frontier seems to be a physical limit that cannot be exceeded. The frontier moves outward only due to some technological progress and capital accumulation making older production methods obsolete. Without such capital and innovation accumulations not much can happen. Movement is possible only along the frontier. In the microeconomic framework, it is not possible for actual production to exceed potential production.

Macroeconomic thinking, however, often concerns sustainability, and therefore, macroeconomists have theorized that actual production can be higher than potential production, although such theorizing clearly contradicts the technological-microeconomic approach. In any case, the challenge is to properly differentiate between, let us say, "natural" movements of actual production—movements related to fundamental microeconomic efficiency—and movements that diverge from the economy's potential production (Basu and Fernald 2009, p. 187). Applying the challenge to economic downturns, the central question is whether real output is falling below potential output, or whether the economy's potential is falling.

Among the competing macroeconomic schools of thought, we can identify three theoretical approaches—at least on a purely common sense level. The first one, a purely microeconomic view of the production-possibilities frontier, says potential output can never be lower than real output. The economy can only fall short of its potential; it can never exceed its potential. Likewise is the relatively old purely Keynesian model positing that policy can only stimulate the economy. Similar too are the relatively old monetarist models, such as Milton Friedman's plucking model of depressions. In such perspectives, potential output depends only on "supply-side" factors understood in a narrow way: capital goods, labor, and technology (Kuttner 1992, p. 2).

The second approach, a typical modern macroeconomic one, holds that real output can lag behind potential output, but can also exceed it at times. Excessive actual output could imply some unsustainability. One can interpret it to mean employment is higher than the "natural rate" in the monetarist sense, or infer the economy is in a bubble in the Minskian sense, or see the economy through the lens of Hayekian malinvestment theory.[2] In any of these interpretations, and unlike the neoclassical view of the production-possibilities frontier, production is not higher than potential output. It only masquerades as being higher; hence, it involves some unavoidable mistakes in the business sector. The second approach deems a correction, recession, depression, or any other adjustment as necessary and inevitable. Alternatively one could see it as the form resembling the first type, since in the end real production is not exceeding potential output. In the alternative, microeconomic view, increased actual production would in reality imply the economy has reached a new, higher potential output.

One should note here the unfortunate imprecision of macroeconomic language. The second approach, which speaks of "real output higher than potential output," should really speak of "an illusion of real output being higher than potential output." A correct understanding should acknowledge the first, neoclassical understanding of potential output: we can never exceed it, but can only create the impression that we are exceeding it. The confusion may be exemplified by the Congressional Budget Office (CBO), responsible for estimating potential output in the United States. Its own definitions suggest that "maximum output . . . can be achieved over a prolonged period without straining productive capacity and thus increasing the risk that inflation will rise above the Federal Reserve's goal" (CBO 2015, p. 1). Obviously, understanding the economy's "exceeding" of potential output as only leading to inflationary pressures comes up short because if that is the case, then it is hard to explain why simple indexation of prices cannot solve possible inflationary problems.

Finally, another approach sees potential output as always equal to real output. The view is somewhat theological: economically, the existing world is the best of all possible worlds. Economic data (prices, employment) convey not only existing benefits but also all frictions, mistakes, disequilibrating tendencies, and costs associated with unavoidable and natural downturns. Such a view interprets current recessions as a necessary cost of previous economic growth. Yet the cost is seen as unavoidable, nevertheless, a price for the previous benefit. The clearest examples of such an approach are equilibrium business cycle theories, real business cycle theories in particular (Lucas 1976, pp. 1113–1114). Increasing unemployment is a necessary adjustment but does not signify wrong choices. It makes no sense to distinguish between real-world unemployment and potential employment (Kuttner 1992, p. 3). The choices made are the best possible ones, even if the outcome is painful. In a way a decision to stay unemployed is therefore a conscious adaptation to very unpleasant circumstances. Perhaps it would be best to summarize the real business cycle approach as simply getting rid of the potential-output notion as unnecessary to analyze business cycles in the real world.

Given the above breadth of views, I understand the notion of potential output as constituting a very broad spectrum that relates to real production. Potential output should remain in the theoretical toolbox as a helpful concept without being amenable to clear empirical measurement. The above perspectives should be seen as ordinal, as is the case with illustrations and graphs. The notion of potential output is ordinal just as utility is ordinal in consumer theory. To simplify perhaps too much, the notion of potential output summarizes social and economic conditions as they could be: better, worse, or not very different than they actually are. It is as far as we can get with a general theoretical ordinal notion of potential output and output gap: a hypothetical divergence of real output from potential production.

Things become different once we start to treat potential output as something cardinal and quantitatively related to real-world macroeconomic policy.

REAL-WORLD POLICY: POTENTIAL OUTPUT AND OUTPUT GAPS

As in most controversial aspects of economic science, in discussing the production gap, a debate has developed concerning differences between the theoretical and the practical dimensions. Most thinkers probably accept potential output as understood in a common sense way. Potential output as something actually present in reality is an entirely different story. In macroeconomic policymaking, potential output is not an ordinal variable but a cardinal one: a concrete index of possible production. Afterward the creation index is confronted with real-world production, real output, so that an output gap can be inferred from the two. The notion of an output gap becomes crucial for macroeconomic policies: as with any gap, it apparently needs to be filled. By determining the size of the output gap, policymakers are at the same time authorizing the bodies to provide monetary stimulus (Gavin 2012, p. 1).

One needs to take two steps to arrive at output-gap estimations. The first one is to measure real production. We have known how to do so in the many years since Simon Kuznets's work on national income. Real output is called gross domestic product, an index that can be measured with some acceptable degree of accuracy (although, as we have seen in chapter 2, it does not properly capture investment expenditures). The second step, a much more difficult one, is to attempt to measure something immeasurable and nonexistent (outside of economists' minds): output that could have been; output sustainable and compatible with "full employment" and perfect "utilization of resources" with no idle capacities; a value of output that cannot be measured with reasonable accuracy, since it simply does not exist (Kliesen 2004).

Macroeconomics faces inherent and fundamental problems with either of the steps. I defer one key problem till the next section: neither real output nor potential output can be an index referring to equilibrium in the capital structure, as I discussed elsewhere in the book. There are other issues, though. The first one has to do with the data being incomplete. Any data gathered by the bureaus are subject to revision. Real-time data are not the same as revised data. The fact is especially salient in estimating real output—gross domestic product—which analysts significantly adjust after a few months because not all the statistics it depends on are immediately available. Aside from the issue of real-time versus revised estimates, sometimes data are path dependent: we often understand our position in the business cycle only once we experience subsequent phases. The third point related to the practice of macroeconomic modeling is that new experiences adjust the model—that is, they change the variables and coefficients—and hence also adjust the potential output itself (Orphanides and Norden 2002, p. 569).

As more information comes in, the data are revised. Orphanides and Norden further note that estimations are unreliable (Orphanides and Norden 2001, p. 582). The sizes of measurement errors are comparable to the sizes of the variables themselves. Armchair assessments of potential output and the output gap are quite uncertain, and revisions are perpetual, especially during recessions (Grigoli et al. 2015, p. 29).[3] It should not be surprising, since recessions are when the trend breaks down. At those times the adjustments are especially stark.

How much do economists adjust their estimations of potential output? The answer depends on overall economic conditions: When conditions are stable, one should not expect huge differences. Everything changes once we reach crisis conditions. Let us take the example of the recent Great Recession as viewed by the Congressional Budget Office by looking at graphs in Figure 4.1.

The lighter dashed line in figure 2 represents a 2007 estimation of projected potential output. Since 2007 and particularly the crisis of 2008, potential output has been systematically adjusted downward, closer to actual output. The above graphs present just two years' revisions, 2011 and 2014, when the estimations closed the gap. Why such a big adjustment? What changed? The answer is paradoxical: falling real output dragged down potential-output estimates. It sounds implausible and completely against common sense logic about potential-output estimates as indicating the true potential of the economy to produce goods and services. Potential output is supposed to be the benchmark against which to compare what is happening in reality. Here

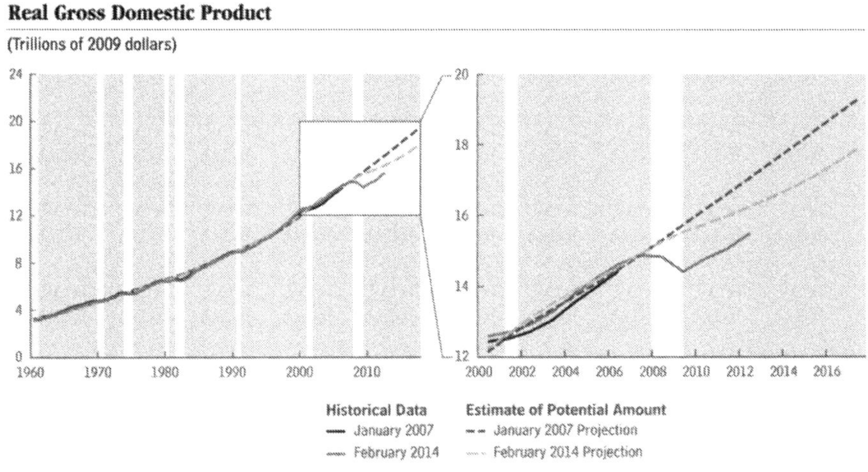

Figure 4.1 Potential output 2007 vs. 2014 CBO estimation

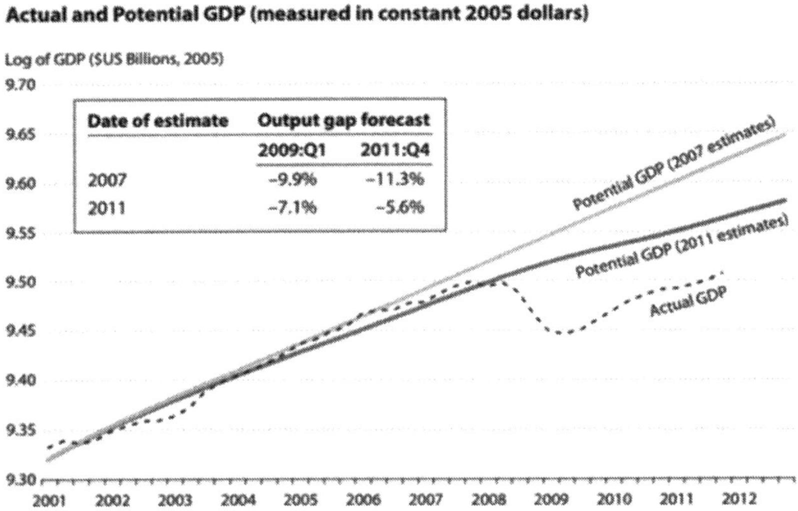

Figure 4.2 Potential-output revision after 2008: 2007 vs. 2011

things are reversed: apparently real output is determining potential output. James Bullard's expression of this view, commenting on the Great Recession, is worth quoting at length:

> I want to now turn to argue that the large output gap view may be conceptually inappropriate in the current situation. We may do better to replace it with the notion of a permanent, one-time shock to wealth. The key to the large output gap story is the use of the fourth quarter of 2007 as a benchmark for where we expect the economy to be today. The idea is to take that level of real output, assume the real GDP growth rate that prevailed in the years prior to 2007, and project out where the "potential" output of the U.S. should be. By that type of calculation, we are indeed stunningly far below where we should be, perhaps 5.5 percent below, using data through the fourth quarter of 2011. . . . Most analysts seem to agree that the middle part of the 2000s was characterized by a "bubble" in the housing sector. Housing prices were high and rising fast compared to nominal GDP. It is not prudent to extrapolate a bubble into the indefinite future and claim that such a calculation provides a good benchmark. Yet, that is what we are doing when we extrapolate fourth quarter 2007 real GDP. . . . When I put the case this starkly, I think many would agree that establishing a benchmark by extrapolating from the previous peak of a variable, when that variable was clearly influenced by a bubble, is a mistake. It gives a distorted view of the situation. (Bullard 2012)[4]

Bullard admits that potential output to some extent derives from real output. Such a macroeconomic phenomenon in fact goes against a common sense understanding of potential output. If potential output is to be used as a standard to assess existing real output, then how can we derive potential output from real output? To suggest that a one-time shock to wealth decreased potential output strongly confirms the view. How can a shock to wealth have anything to do with productive capacity and the hidden potential of existing idle and employed factors of production?[5] There are of course other, more sophisticated and detailed answers, related to general uncertainty, credit squeezes, financial intermediation, volatility in commodity prices, and more (Basu and Fernald 2009, pp. 203–204). In any case, Bullard's approach seems to be state of the art. Since the 1980s, economic studies stopped portraying twentieth-century growth as a deterministic trend. Aggregate output consists of both a nonstationary growth component and a stationary cyclical component, so growth itself appears as a nonstationary stochastic process (Nelson and Plosser 1982, p. 160).[6]

Bullard is also keen to note that we can construct estimates of potential output from competing extrapolations. Hence, it is not only that real output determines potential output, but how we tell the story is arbitrary: We can extrapolate real variables, but what trend should we extrapolate from? Should we just focus on the data until 2007 and arrive at much higher estimations of the output gap, or perhaps include the worsening conditions after 2008? The choice is purely arbitrary when it comes to narrating the story of the crisis. And if, as Bullard believes, the story of a bubble and mistakes in the real estate sector is true, then why was the potential-output line adjusted downward strongly after 2008 (and mildly after 2004)? If the bubble story is correct, then the potential output before 2008 should have been lower, since increased real output before 2008 had to have been only an illusion created by mistaken investments.[7]

More generally, estimates of potential output can be squeezed out of the data in three not necessarily distinct ways: (1) trend estimations, (2) the production-function approach, and (3) econometric techniques that mix statistical methods and are loosely based on economic theories.[8] All those methods are based on choices that are to some extent arbitrary since the parameters, variables, or estimation techniques have to be chosen ad hoc (Morrow and Roeger 2001, p. 5).

Trend estimations are a clear example of squeezing potential output from actual output. The detrending methods include deterministic-trends and unobserved-components models such as the Hodrick-Prescott filter[9] or the Phillips curve (Orphanides and Norden 2002, p. 570). In the first method, we identify the deterministic trend by cleaning up actual data by using the filters (such as H-P filter). The Hodrick-Prescott filter is effectively equivalent to a moving average. Obviously, then it is merely an average of real gross domestic product that uses some smoothing parameter to make it more "end-point biased," since otherwise the last few observations would be disproportionately emphasized (Morrow and Roeger 2001, p. 119).[10] In any case, such details cannot conceal the reversal of economic reasoning: actual output determines potential output. Because of its emphasis on past variables potential output works best in exercises in economic history (Plosser and Schwert 1979, p. 185). We can additionally criticize trend estimations because they smoothen the movement of potential output. Yet, why should we see potential output as nonfluctuating? We do not have either firm macroeconomic theories or empirical proofs for viewing potential output as a smooth series (Basu and Fernald 2009, p. 187). After all, after many years the essence of Schumpeterian wisdom about growth seems to have become universally accepted: creative destruction is part of the market process. The economy is growing and developing in a nonsmooth series. Importantly, this is not to say that all nonsmoothness of actual growth is the result of huge potential-output changes: much of it is surely caused by disturbing policy factors. However, it does not follow that potential output itself is universally straight and stable. Shocks on the so-called supply side that lead to long-term changes in productivity do not generate perfectly smooth changes in output (see Rotemberg 2002, p. 34).

The second attempt to squeeze potential output from real output, the production-function approach, is based on the aggregative neoclassical production theory, which calls for various inputs (capital stock,[11] labor force, and technological knowledge) to be measured. Inputs then are put into a functional form that intends to create a correspondence between the available inputs and the production potentially achieved by employing them. Since the approach is neoclassical, the production function is a variant of the Cobb-Douglass function with defined inputs—total factor productivity, employment levels, and the capital stock (aggregative and relative to total output—again, as if the reswitching debate never happened)—all summarized in coefficients: labor is expressed as the number of laborers, and capital is measured by spending on structure and equipment (Morrow and Roeger 2001, pp. 22–23). We have therefore a classic reversal of economic reasoning: pricing happens before production. Monetary prices in the market are used to represent capital, even though the description of productive potential should be detached from monetary and financial variables (at least in the basic form).

On top of the problem of aggregation, the production-function approach makes simplifying assumptions of constant returns to scale and constant factor shares, assumptions usually represented in the Cobb-Douglas function. The assumptions are quite standard, but clearly the assumption of known and fixed shares is in tension with economic intuition. The reality of economic dynamics is that factor shares change and reshuffle with each new production process, and even within the existing ones (Arnold 2009, p. 277). Additionally, the approach uses statistical filters—for example, to discover the trends in the labor-participation rate and also to arrive at the nonaccelerating inflation rate of unemployment and structural concepts of unemployment—so that not all unemployment seen in the data appears inefficient. Total factor productivity is of course the Solow residual, which is not at all observable but contributes to making observations and functions tautological (Giorno et al. 1995, pp. 172–173). Hence, in this approach, output growth is simply backed by growth in inputs and a residual, so the uncertainty in measuring potential output is reduced to uncertainty about measuring inputs, which is definitely not easy (Cahn and Saint-Guilhem 2009, pp. 221–222).

The last approach to mention is dynamic stochastic general equilibrium (DSGE) models, which are inspired by the production-function approach but include much more (e.g., they can be backed by econometrics using Bayesian or other methods). At the same time, the underlying assumptions are based on some equilibrium theorems. Maximizing agents, rational expectations, and market clearing then can be used to demonstrate nominal rigidities, expectations-augmented Phillips curve, and so forth (Fernández-Villaverde 2010, p. 4). Yet, as Robert Solow noticed, the fundamental flaw is similar to that in previous cases: DSGE modeling treats the economy as if it was a single person with a rationally designed long-term plan, even if the models include various frictions and real-world imperfections (Solow 2010, p. 2). Perhaps the Nobel Prize winner overstates the case. Nevertheless, DSGE models, despite their sophistication, basically average out all past economic tendencies as if everything happened according to predesigned and internally consistent sets of equations. For this reason, DSGE models, as well as other methods of measuring potential output, are not useful in the most important case: serious crises.

To summarize both statistical and economic methods of measuring potential output, they are all based on decomposing the time series of the variables that are not directly observable. Therefore, modelers make a number of categorizing assumptions about functional forms, stochastic properties, and various correlations (Morrow and Roeger 2001, p. 9). Because of these elements, estimations are uncertain and differ to a huge extent. Even the results of using the same method are not strictly the same, since the results of the method already selected are adjusted and revised significantly. Therefore, methods not only compete with each other but also within themselves. Even choosing just one method leads to various results over time. Many admit the problems in measuring the potential output and the output gap, though they often express hopes for "better techniques" (Cotis et al. 2004, p. 16). These methods also suffer from one fundamental flaw that relates to the capital structure: whichever way we measure potential output, it cannot capture the notion of intertemporal equilibrium in a capital structure. The critique concerns all three methods. Someone may argue it is better to have flawed measurements than none, and that is surely the case, but one should remember their limitations.

INTERTEMPORAL CAPITAL EQUILIBRIUM AND THE STRUCTURE OF PRODUCTION

In the end, all potential-output measurements are directed at finding an imagined number related to gross domestic product. Real product is measured in money—as is imagined potential output (indexed for inflation, naturally). The output gap can be seen as a percentage gap between the two. If real GDP is 3 percent lower than potential GDP, it means that some form of policy could step in and fill the gap. The obvious problem with such a view is that the gap is one number, as if the problem of macroeconomic disequilibrium could be captured in one macroeconomic number (and then solved, for instance, by lowering the interest rates).

As we have seen in the chapters about the stages of production, the question of finding equilibrium within the capital structure is not a question of reaching the potential level of aggregate production in toto. It is a question of reaching the right balance among different stages of production. Capital has a disaggregated microeconomic structure. Each successive stage has its unique position in overall production. That is not to say there are no attempts at disaggregation in macroeconomic modeling. For example, the Congressional Budget Office's approach to US potential output divides the economy into a few sectors and lays out seven different types of capital (Arnold 2009, p. 277). After noticing this little bit of disaggregation Arnold points at the same time to a deficiency almost in a manner seen in the capital reswitching debate (see also Lachmann's quote below):

> [The] disadvantage of using a growth model to estimate potential output is that including the capital stock introduces measurement error. Most economic variables are subject to measurement error, but the problem is particularly acute for capital, for two basic reasons. First, measuring the stock of any particular type of capital is difficult because depreciation is hard to define or measure. Purchases of plant and equipment can be tallied to produce a historical series for investment, but no corresponding source of data exists for depreciation. Second, even if accurate estimates of individual stocks were available, aggregating them into a single index would be difficult because capital is heterogeneous, differing with respect to characteristics such as durability and productivity. (Arnold 2009, p. 277)

If the concept of capital cannot be modeled using known functions, how can we understand the concept of equilibrium, then? We cannot reduce it to one index number—potential output—indirectly measurable by empirical data because the capital structure's performance cannot be measured cardinally. We can assess it in the already-mentioned common sense way described by general economic theory, where potential output is understood as an ordinal concept. F. A. Hayek had doubts that the concept of equilibrium could be meaningfully applied to the economic system as a whole (Hayek 1941, p. 20). At the same time he suggested that an equilibrium point would require a balanced production structure: the interval between adjustments of more mobile factors of production and adjustments of the more rigid elements of the structure would be negligible. That is, we would not see a prolonged period of significant underemployment of factors devoted to already-unprofitable processes. Such an inquiry is of course a matter of degree but so are many cases in the social sciences.

A negligible interval between misallocation and renewed successful allocation of factors basically means that any unemployment is "frictional." The emphasis here is on a broader definition of factors, so we are talking about not only the labor market but also the market for factors in general, which includes factories, intermediate goods, and other complementary capital goods used up in production. In this sense, equilibrium could also be seen as a point in time at which various plans among individuals are "mutually compatible" (Hayek 1937, p. 41).[12] Notice that it does not unavoidably imply no mistakes are made. It does not assume that projects planned in the beginning are being executed as initially planned. Such an attitude would make the concept completely unempirical, since practically all business plans are constantly readjusted and re-formed. To be exact, the whole notion of a business plan is an a priori empty concept both in economics and management. A much better term has been invented, "business canvas": a general outline for future actions that starts from the assumption that future adjustments (even unforeseen ones) are not only required in the plan but are actually desirable responses to changing consumer preferences and competitors' actions. Plans are good for Soviet planners (see on this, e.g., Blank 2013).

Hence, to adjust the Hayekian concept and make it at least more amenable to shifting market conditions: we can envision an equilibrium construct implying mutual compatibility of individual canvases instead of plans. Plans are constantly adjusted to ever-changing conditions. For any economic agent the main aim is to not let the canvas completely break down, so that extreme capital waste can be avoided. Substituting a canvas for a plan at least allows us to some extent to break away from the concept of "exact coordination"—that is, when ex ante expectations are in full accordance with ex post events (O'Discroll and Rizzo 1996, p. 80).

A more relaxed, canvas approach to equilibrium is brightly illustrated in a metaphor of Roger Garrison's:

> A Newtonian extremist with a comparative-statics bent of mind might insist that the tight-rope walker is in equilibrium only in the just-barely-conceivable case in which he is balanced motionlessly atop the rope such that a line drawn from his center of gravity to the center of the earth passes exactly and continuously through the center of the rope. . . . The tight-rope walker might be genuinely concerned about "losing his equilibrium"—but only if this term is understood in the moderate sense. His concern would not be lessened by pedantic instruction from the first extremist to the effect that he was unlikely ever actually to achieve equilibrium and therefore need not worry about losing it or by equally irrelevant instruction from the second extremist to the effect that losing equilibrium is definitionally impossible since any eventuality can be described in the language of equilibrium. The tight-rope walker is not worried about losing something he could never have or having something he could never lose; he is worried that he might fall off the rope. (Garrison 1995)

Exact coordination is simply a chimera, since it can never happen, as is true of any ceteris paribus clause. New projects cannot be separated from new uses of existing assets that change their current valuations. As Ludwig Lachmann vividly notes, "*cetera* are no longer *paria*" (Lachmann 1948, p. 129). Existing capital resources are diverted from their existing employments to some other projects. The result is a complete break between the value of capital assets and their costs of production. Therefore, it is simply impossible to talk about a given quantity of capital. New decisions about a change in the capital structure create economic value in one place and destroy it in another. The value of existing capital equipment cannot be settled on the basis of historical costs of production. Many rare-metal elements used right now in digital equipment (phones, batteries, etc.) were considered almost waste in the twentieth century with production oriented around iron and other metals rich in supply. Right now most innovative parts of the economy are based on rare metals used in electronic and computer devices (Abraham 2015, pp. 9–10). They have huge economic values not seen before, as additional productive processes have developed.

While dealing with economic functions elsewhere Lachmann notes:

> [A] capital structure in our sense can only exist in equilibrium, where all plans are consistent with each other, and the network of plans displays the firm outline of a clear and distinguishable pattern. But in dynamic reality this structure is in a state of continuous transformation. As production plans prove inconsistent and fail, the outline of our pattern becomes inevitably blurred. Plans have to be revised, new combinations formed, old combinations disintegrate, even those which persist have to undergo an often drastic modification of their factorial composition. In reality the coefficients of production are ever changing. Every day the network of production plans it torn, every day it is mended anew. Under these circumstances we shall find some, at least temporarily, unutilized capital

> resources while others are scarce. In any case, in the world of our daily experience all unexpected change entails more or less extensive capital regrouping. (Lachmann 1948, p. 204)

Oskar Morgenstern referred to such cases in his famous paradox about Sherlock Holmes and Professor Moriarty (Morgenstern 1935, pp. 173–174). One anticipating the other's actions means that the other one cannot anticipate successfully. A contest between the two can only create one winner, the other being left as a loser. Such conflicts are not as extreme in the real marketplace (they are also not violent like Moriarty's character). Nevertheless, to some degree some of the sellers and producers compete for consumers—especially when we consider sectors with a higher degree of innovation and therefore with a huge amount of capital reshuffling. Morgenstern's criticism of equilibrium constructs was so strong that Hayek's essay mentioned above could be seen as a partial response to him (Innnocenti and Zappia 2005, pp. 65–66; see also Ingrao 1998, pp. 86–87),[13] even though Morgenstern was actually criticizing John Hicks, who assumed all variables held constant through time and price changes could not be anticipated (Young et al. 2004, pp. 5–6). Morgenstern's criticism is so strong that even with changes, complete anticipation seems almost impossible.

And so we can notice the shortcomings of any equilibrium analysis. Yet, the question remains of where we go from here in thinking about potential output. How does the analysis relate to our discussion about proper balance in the theory of the capital structure? At least it tells us one thing: capital cannot be measured and firmly placed in any aggregate production functions; therefore, finding potential output through the production-function approach will not do the work to find the right equilibrium balance in the economy. Therefore, potential output remains an invented variable, and aggregating monetary prices of capital has no relevance to an equilibrated structure of production—one that could at least be theoretically imagined under sustainable growth.

Here we should stop at the concept called "intertemporal equilibrium," which can be found in the works of Erik Lindahl, Hayek, and Hicks (Kurtz and Salvadori 2003, pp. 226–227). The term itself originated probably in Hayek rather than in Hicks (Milgate 1979, p. 4). The words appear in many different places in the literature but actually can mean profoundly dissimilar things. In the neoclassical (Arrow-Debreu) tradition, it means mutual determination of "*nt* market clearing prices (for *n* commodities over *t* 'elementary time periods')" (ibid., p. 1; see also Araujo and Maldonado 2003, p. 58). In the above portion, I mean something quite different. Rather than a mathematical model abstracting from real time I see intertemporal equilibrium as a general complacency (canvas type) of stages within the productive structure. Intertemporal equilibrium may also mean something else in the typical macroeconomic approach: creating a fully consistent balance. This meaning incorporates both short-run fluctuations and long-run growth within one framework (e.g., Woodford 2009, p. 269). We see it in the new neoclassical synthesis—hence, I stress again that consistency in designed models is something different than real-world canvas coordination.

The notion of capital in (intertemporal) equilibrium as we discussed it above goes back to Knut Wicksell's natural rates, where demand for capital meets supply of capital (Wicksell 1962, p. 103). The fundamental problem, also seen by Wicksell himself, is interpreting supply and demand of capital, since they pose dimensional problems. Wicksell's contributions are of course acknowledged also in modern equilibrium analysis, like the analysis associated with DSGE models. Nevertheless, we believe they do not answer the central macroeconomic problem of how intertemporal coordination, understood as a Hayekian reinterpretation in terms of canvas coordination, happens.

Can measuring potential output help us solve the puzzle? Not really, because each of the methods for measuring potential output suffers from its own problems. Even putting aside the question of which method is best and the question of revised versus real-time data, estimating trends and using statistical techniques means projecting the future from the past. They are past oriented, and they extrapolate into the future. The case of estimating potential output in 2007 versus 2014 clearly confirms this. The second method, the production-function approach, is flawed because it does not reflect the lessons from the capital debates. The method treats capital as a simple homogenous stock that can be measured as if no underlying misallocations were possible.

I am not suggesting that equilibrium is a construct that can be met in reality, or that it has to be used to analyze fluctuations. The real economy is always out of equilibrium, but the question is how far out it is. A common sense canvas-equilibrium concept says production processes can go awry but not catastrophically. Such a theoretical entity cannot be embodied in one index number and compared to real gross domestic product. Therefore, using measures of potential output based on real-world data as a panacea for correcting macroeconomic disequilibrium fails and cannot live up to its promises.

NOTES

1. Here it is important to note that in empirical macroeconomic research potential output achievement is sometimes understood from a narrow technical perspective, in which there is no downward or upward pressure on inflation (for example, see recent analysis of the output gap in the United States: Alichi 2015, p. 4; central banks while performing a monetary policy also tend to rely on a definition related to inflationary

pressure, see for example Barnett et al. 2009, p. 248). Such approach is just one very narrow understanding of potential output, which simplifies the issue to mismatching between "aggregate demand" and "aggregate supply" almost in the spirit of the short-run Phillips Curve: AD>AS means inflation (and overemployment), AD<AS mean deflation (and underemployment). Economic reality is, however, something more. Real output can be much lower than its potential even with positive inflation. See below.

2. Such schools would rather be seen as contrarian. In the typical central banking macroeconomic research, real output is higher than potential output, when inflationary pressures step in; and actually "just" that; at least in the simple usage of the models. It is not clear in such typical macroeconomics how higher inflationary pressure may cause serious problems (and contrarian approaches offer exactly this explanation).

3. Authors further note, "Output gap data and revisions can be used to construct confidence intervals around any initial or revised output gap estimate. The width of the confidence interval will vary by country, and by the vintage of the revision, with a wider confidence interval for an initial estimate than for a revised estimate. We find that, at the time of the initial estimate confidence intervals are usually so large as to span positive and negative values for the output gap. In other words, only in rare cases is there a high degree of certainty about whether policy should be contractionary, neutral, or expansionary." Ertz and Smets in 2001 register for the euro area the standard deviation of potential output at one third and note that even with continuous updates, hence no ex ante errors, the ex post misperception of the potential output is substantial (Ertz and Smets 2001, pp. 26–27). The results from this are a series of correlated errors on part of the central bank, which is focused on the potential output estimation. See also Delle Chiaie 2009, p. 11.

4. We are not discussing here this particular position, but only use it as an example to point to potential output problems. There are dissenting views about the Great Recession itself. Fernald, for example, takes the position that the Great Recession cannot explain potential output slowdown, and searches for causes elsewhere (Fernald 2014, p. 39).

5. Paul Krugman in one of his blog posts (2012) seemed very much confused by Bullard's description, since he reacted with a neoclassical sensibility: potential output stems from technological productive capabilities; hence, it cannot be shifted by changes in spending or allocation patterns. Yet, the post presents precisely everything that is wrong with the concept—at common sense level everyone seems to assume it is indeed some underlying technological potential in the style of production-possibilities frontier. Despite such, the reality of potential output estimations is totally opposite, since it is based on ambiguous filtering of real output data.

6. Less popular Blanchard and Quah, on the other hand, try to differentiate between supply and demand shocks, so that trends and cycles are seen as independent phenomenon.

7. On the analysis of the cycle 2001–2008 from the perspective of monetary rules see Taylor 2007. For partially critical approach, see Machaj 2016.

8. Although the econometric approach is seen as leading to estimation problems, particularly because of determining coefficients due to statistical approach and problematic correlations between capital and the error term in regression; also, capital

input would have to be adjusted based on how intensively is the capital stock used (CBO 2001, p. 10). Despite those reservations being genuine, they are not applied to full extent, since production function approach also suffers from serious problems because of capital measurements.

9. Naturally the procedure of smoothening the time series is described in Hodrick and Prescott 1997. The reasons for its overall acceptance may stem from its correlation results (Morrow and Roeger 2001, p. 20). With regard to the comparison between Hodrick-Prescott filter and the other ones (like band-pas, moving average and first difference), see Baxter and King 1999, pp. 583–588. For Kalman filter, see Morrow and Roeger 2001, p. 13. Examples of less used but more sophisticated methods could be Blanchard and Quah, where two disturbances in the GDP are presented (Blanchard and Quah 1989, p. 656); and Beveridge and Nelson (1981, p. 154), where again permanent and transitory elements are separated. Differences between all those filters are not significant for the content of our discussion. In essence they rely on a similar methodology.

10. End point bias can be corrected with Box-Jenkins series such as ARIMA models (autoregressive integrated moving average)—where mechanical projections into the future are used so that last observations are not overemphasized (Morrow and Roeger 2001, p. 122)—or by extended multivariate filters (St-Amant and van Norden 1997, pp. 23–24). Naturally it is a detailed technical problem, which is not the subject of our discussion. Nevertheless, it is quite symptomatic of how the approach of potential output measurement is undertaken—the variable is to be again squeezed out from the real data, and the projections to be used are based on purely stationary conditions, that is as if nothing really changes in the underlying variables. Under such assumption, the estimation always works . . . as long as things are stationary, hence as long as there isn't any correction in the underlying data.

11. Almost as if the reswitching debate was completely irrelevant.

12. A very similar (and quite careful) approach to general-equilibrium analysis has been developed by Hülsmann, who points out that it is necessary to focus on actions in terms of failures and successes (Hülsmann 2000, p. 7). Also, as Salerno argues, coordination should be understood in the pricing framework (Salerno 1991, p. 182).

13. It is worth noting that a few years before publishing "Economics and Knowledge" Hayek (writing in German) considered equilibrium almost in terms of perfect foresight; see on this Hülsmann 2000, p. 30.

Chapter 5

Non-Neutrality of Monetary Flows for the Structure of Production

Quantity Theory of Money and Non-Neutrality of Money

The quantity theory of money used to be the cornerstone of economic theorizing, and in a way it separated charlatans from economists (despite its unclearness). For a long time it was seen as a test for distinguishing a monetary crank from a person grasping the essential features of money. The fundamental conclusion of the quantity theory of money was that in the long run one cannot enrich any nation by simply increasing money in circulation, for the end result after a possible short-term boom would be price inflation with no effects on the real variables. Nowadays, the influence of the quantity theory of money has significantly decreased. One of the many reasons lies in the inadequacy of measuring the money supply. It is not that we cannot obtain necessary statistics to measure the money supply, but that it is debatable which of the monetary aggregates can be meaningfully tied to the price indices that react to them. Another reason is the theory's tautological aspect: the way it is defined, it simply holds true as an accounting identity.

Despite the decreasing popularity of the quantity theory of money, especially among central banking policy makers, it is important for macroeconomic reasoning and monetary policy in general (the latter to be discussed in the next chapter). The quantity theory of money is very useful in explaining how growth (or a fall) in the money supply could *theoretically* be neutral to the economy. Through this demonstration it becomes possible to reveal why money growth in reality can hardly ever be neutral, and how various schools of macroeconomic thinking see monetary disturbances as the source of macroeconomic problems.[1] Paradoxically then, the quantity theory describes the concept of neutrality of money in order to illustrate that neutrality is a fantasy.

David Hume was one of the most prominent theorists in the eighteenth century, especially in the field of monetary theory. It is quite safe to say that if economics started in the eighteenth century, then the quantity theory of money started with Hume's famous analysis of specie flow. Additionally, he seems to have been responsible for the first "helicopter" model of monetary expansion and its theoretical analysis. He was one of the first to emphasize that real wealth does not stem from nominal money capital, since the real value of money capital depends on its purchasing power. He starts off from the idea that suddenly by some miracle every single person in the economy has more money in their pockets. If the money supply doubled in these circumstances, it appears that not much would change: all prices would simply double since absolutely nothing should change in terms of preferences, technology, capital goods, consumer goods, and so on.[2] Here is Hume:

> Where coin is in greater plenty; as a greater quantity of it is then required to represent the same quantity of goods; it can have no effect, either good or bad, taking a nation within itself: no more than it would make any alteration on a merchant's books. (Hume 1742)

Hume's early model has some shortcomings, but we can easily fix them. To demonstrate a purely nominal adjustment we need to start off with three assumptions:

1. An increase of the money supply is proportional.
2. There is full information about the process.
3. Information has to "go back in time."

Only under those circumstances will increases of the money supply become neutral for the economy, so that real variables will not be affected by monetary disturbances. What is hidden behind each of the assumptions?

Proportionality of an increase of the money supply would mean that under, say, a doubling of the money supply, money doubles everywhere in the economy. Following Friedman one could call this a "helicopter" effect (Friedman 1969, p. 4). The cash balances of everyone—be they the owner of a company, someone consuming the money out of their retirement fund, or someone inheriting the money—have to be increased to the same extent, by 100 percent. Hence, the composition of money also does not matter. Whether it is cash or bank deposits, the balance is doubled. If the money supply is doubled, but not proportionally—some people receive more of the money than others—then the change will not be neutral: monetary expansion will have redistribution effects and favor those receiving the money first.

Yet the assumption of proportionality in increases is necessary but not sufficient to ensure neutrality of money. We also need full information. Information does not have to be perfect: one does not have to assume omnipotence or perfect rationality of economic agents. We only have to assume that people understand such a simple and obvious process of monetary expansion.

Everyone should know that the money supply doubled and that it doubled in each place at the same time. Also everyone should know that everyone else knows about this process. This assumption means there is no possibility to exploit extra knowledge about the development. For example, assume some of the sellers did not know about the change. Then they would not immediately raise their prices. In that case, some knowledgeable buyers could take advantage of the sellers' ignorance and purchase the product before the prices adjust. The assumption of full information takes care of that problem.

Still, the two assumptions are not fully sufficient. They eliminate the possibility of redistribution effects through disproportionate increases and partial market information, but there is another possibility allowing real effects to happen. We could assume that money is proportionally increased and assume that people know about this process. Nevertheless, because of path dependency, even such unrealistic assumptions are not going to make monetary change neutral for real variables. Some people already made plans about future investments, and they formed their strategies based on the expectation that the money supply would not suddenly increase. For example, they signed contracts for future sales, and those contracts set prices for exchanges. Someone may have signed a long-term contract for renting their apartment. When the money supply doubles, the owner would probably prefer to increase the price. The renter, however, would definitely take advantage of the circumstance and argue that the contract is valid. Apparently it was the owner's risk to accept fixed prices for the future.

Here is the reason why we need a third assumption: information has to go back in time, which amounts to adjusting all past contracts so they account for the prospect of a future monetary disturbance.[3] The first and second assumptions make sure future prices are adjusted on transactions taking place after the monetary disturbance. But for the money to remain neutral all future prices would have to adjust. This would have to include future prices for transactions that took place before the monetary disturbance. Such an important issue lies behind the idea of information going backward in time. We have to envision that market actors signing contracts in the past knew exactly what monetary disturbance would happen and therefore included such a fact in their business calculations.

All three assumptions complete the Humean model and allow for a thought experiment in which a monetary disturbance would become virtually neutral. Doubling the money supply would merely result in doubling all nominal prices. Relative prices would remain the same, allocation decisions would not be affected, and consumer spending would remain unchanged. Inflation in the money supply would transform itself immediately into price inflation in the exact same proportion. In this sense, money expansion would become truly neutral for real variables.

It is also worth noting that neutrality does not matter only in the case of money expansions. Neutrality can also appear in the case of monetary contractions, or deflation in the money supply. If the money supply deflated proportionally by the same amount everywhere, if there was full information about the process, and if information went back in time, then monetary deflation also would result only in nominal changes, price deflation in this case. The real side of the economy would remain unaltered.[4]

The reason why changes in the money supply are never neutral is that those three assumptions are almost never met in reality. For above-mentioned reasons, it is virtually impossible to give an empirical example of neutrality of money. Nevertheless, we know of cases in which we can observe something close to perfect neutrality of money: the currency exchanges that happened in many countries after hyperinflationary periods. The usual approach is to "cross out a couple of zeros" from the old currency and introduce a new one. The case is seen nominally as introducing new money, but from a certain theoretical perspective it may be seen as a form of monetary disturbance done in a purely neutral way (Fisher 1912, pp. 29–30). In the real world, it is of course never the case precisely because the above assumptions are not met. If they were, however, then there would be virtually no difference between introducing new money and a purely mathematical adjustment of the existing nominal values.

Let us take the case of multiplying the denomination of the old currency by 10,000 and then eliminating zeros on bank notes (as was done, for example, in Poland in 1995). Can this be seen as a neutral money shock? Yes, indeed. Let us confront the case with the assumptions of a modified Humean model: all the money in circulation is decreased proportionally everywhere in the economy 10,000 times. Every 10,000 is changed to 1, 100,000 is changed to 10, every 1 million is changed into 100, and so on. The procedure includes every single monetary instrument and every single individual owning some amount of money. The proportionality criterion is met.[5]

At the same time, the process is public and arranged officially by the government. Everyone is well aware of it taking place: there are even campaigns addressed to elderly people to make sure they are capable of grasping it. All buyers and sellers are aware the money supply will be hugely deflated. The full-information assumption has been met.

Yet that is not all that is needed for the monetary transition to be neutral. There are past contracts, credits, mortgages, and other instruments that have been signed in the past with expectations that such a huge monetary deflation will not happen. Therefore, for the monetary change to stay neutral, the information about monetary deflation would have to go back in time: it would have to be included in the contracts signed at that earlier time, so there will be no sudden shift in the purchasing power.[6] The monetary exchange is done by state decree—and all contracts immediately adjust. If in 1993 someone promised to pay back 1 million zlotys in 1996, he would know he would have to pay 100 zlotys.

The example is a bit exaggerated, but it serves to demonstrate two inquiries about money. The first one is the quantity theory of money: money supply is always related to its purchasing power, and the purchasing power has a tendency to respond to monetary changes. The second one is that monetary disturbances in either direction do not automatically and always entail positive or negative effects. Monetary adjustments lead to real consequences for the economy—that is, changes in the money supply can never be neutral—because of the three mentioned assumptions that have never been met in reality. But how exactly monetary changes lead to real changes depends on specific factors—especially how new money reshapes the capital structure and factor prices. Therefore, it is virtually impossible for prices to mechanically and uniformly respond to changes in the money supply. Such a feature of money as a medium of exchange was recognized as early as when the quantity theory was formed. None of the three assumptions in the quantity theory of money are ever met in reality, so different schools of thought focus on each of them.

The first aspect of monetary expansion is its disproportionate character. Newly created money by the banks appears in different sectors. Therefore, it affects various industries to dissimilar extents. Some businesses are stimulated by the extra money, while others do not experience booms, since the money is boosting economic activity elsewhere. Usually in the modern banking system, monetary increases are translated into bursts of credit expansion. Commercial banks create money by creating liabilities in the form of credit. The banking sector, therefore, along with its beneficiaries benefits by increases in the money supply at the expense of late money receivers. It is worth quoting Friedman, who recognizes the effects but downplays them at the same time:

> We can now drop the assumption that each individual happened to pick up an amount of cash equal to the amount he had to begin with. Let the amount each individual picks up be purely a chance matter. This will introduce initial distribution effects. During the transition, some men will have net gains in consumption, others net losses in consumption. But the ultimate position will be the same, not only for the aggregate, but for each individual separately. After picking up the cash, each individual is in position that he could have attained earlier, if he had wished to. But he preferred the position he had attained prior to the arrival of the helicopter. Nothing has occurred to change the ultimate alternatives open to him. Hence he will eventually return to this former position. The distributional effects vanish when equilibrium is re-attained. (Friedman 1969, p. 6)

Surely there is some kernel of truth to it, but the systematic impact of monetary expansions can be prolonged and introduce permanent, institutionalized redistribution effects. At another instance, Friedman confirms that newly generated money is an incentive to search for new returns in the market:

> Potential creators of assets now more in demand are induced to react to the better terms on which they can be sold, including business enterprises wishing to engage in capital expansion, house builders or prospective homeowners, consumers—who are potential purchasers of durable consumer goods—and so on and on; this, the initially redundant money balances concentrated in the hands of those first affected . . . become spread throughout the economy. . . .
>
> The monetary stimulus is, in this way, spread from the financial markets to the markets for goods and services. (Friedman 1963, pp. 230–231)

Long-run injection effects and the disproportionality of monetary increases are present in various models, but the most famous ones are associated with the modern Austrian school of economics and are inspired primarily by the work of Nobel Prize winner Friedrich August von Hayek (briefly discussed in chapter 6). Hayek got his prize for extensive publications on business cycle theory. According to him, it is a monetary impulse that causes the business cycle: credit expansion is triggered by the commercial banks and usually orchestrated in some way by the central bank. New money created by the banking sector appears in the form of credit and therefore leads to additional investments, which usually turn out to be malinvestments. The structure of production is permanently altered. In the literature, the phenomenon is often referred to as a "Cantillon effect"—after Richard Cantillon (Cantillon [1755] 2010, pp. 147–148; Thornton 2006, p. 46), the first economist to present monetary injection effects in an economic treatise.

The second aspect of monetary expansion has to do with lags in expectations and information incompleteness. Models to depict it usually comparatively analyze two separated markets (Lucas 1972, pp. 103–104). Not everyone is well aware of the credit expansion taking place, and not everyone can satisfactorily foresee its effects. Information incompleteness gets more important when the increase in the money supply becomes more disproportional. Therefore, gaps in information can be seen as effects of the credit expansion. The more disproportional the expansion, the greater the potential incompleteness of information. Consider the unrealistic example of a perfectly proportionate increase in the money supply with lack of complete information. Even if there are some people without knowledge of the process, the absence of change in their usual economic behavior should not lead to serious effects. If, however, the increases of the money supply are disproportionate, their ignorance would mean not spotting potential changes, bubbles, and significant redistribution effects not present under proportionate increases.

The third aspect of monetary expansion is investment mistakes caused by not anticipating the credit expansion. Some of the mistakes come from what are called "rigidities," when issues arise because contracts cannot be easily settled (see for example Gunter et. al. 2007, p. 2440). Such perfect cases would exist only if a completely unrealistic scenario arose of perfect equilibration but not just present equilibration (adjustment of present prices). It would have to be backward equilibration: fixing contracts in order to anticipate monetary expansion, something that could probably be done only with a time machine, which shows how absurd the assumption is.

All three aspects are distinct to some extent, but the last two have a strong real effect on the economy only because of the first one. If the increase in the money supply was proportionate, then the two additional elements would be less consequential. At the same time, it is worth noting that the element of surprise is always crucial:

> Anticipated inflations or deflations produce no transfers from debtors to creditors which raise questions of equity; the interest rate on claims valued in nominal terms adjusts to allow for the anticipated rate of inflation. Anticipated inflations or deflations need involve no frictions in adjusting to changing prices. Every individual can take the anticipated change in the price level into account in setting prices for future trades. (Friedman 1969, p. 45)

Additionally, Friedman notices the importance of existing regimes and their influence upon expectations. When we live in a world where only positive inflation rates are anticipated, then an additional rigidity arises precisely for that reason.

The quantity theory of money remains an important tool for presenting the fundamental aspects of monetary economics, despite its disappearance in central banking practice. Paradoxically the quantity theory was built on the idea that money does not matter for the real sector only to realize that it does.

TAXONOMY OF MONETARY REGIMES AND MONEY STOCK

Spending flows (of existing and newly created money) depend on monetary regimes. Regimes can be classified according to three different features: (1) the role of government in money production, (2) the character of base-money production, and (3) the role of the banking system in monetary creation and financial intermediation. The table below summarizes all the possible concepts.

The first feature is the extent of government intervention into the monetary framework of the economy. Economists have proposed alternative regimes that differ about government's role, and it is not surprising that this part of monetary theory is the most discussed. The government can play a role either in producing base money or in producing bank money. It can either produce both or regulate both. It can also abstain from one, the other, or both. Government regimes are all based on visions about legal aspects of money production: banking regulations, and contract oversights. Overall, the *general* distinction at least seems quite simple: on one side of the debate there is complete monetary freedom and a laissez-faire monetary system; on the other side, there is nationalized money production and complete monetary planning, including in the banking sector (as in socialist systems—e.g. Bałtowski 2009, pp. 145–147). In between are numerous middle-ground proposals. Despite the simplicity at the general level, the practical implications of these views become puzzling when we get into the specifics of various monetary systems and once we start to ask such questions as what a government intervention really means (an example of such a puzzle is the debate about fractional reserves). Before we do that, let us focus on the following two clearer distinctions in monetary regimes.

Base money can be called "outside" money because it is the money that "circulates" in the economy outside of the banking system and outside any liability framework. In other words, it is the ultimate means of payment in the economy and does not have to be backed by anything (see on this Lagos 2006). There are two extreme regimes we could envisage from this perspective. The first one is commodity money, the other one is fiat money. Commodity money is money produced with the use of scarce resources—resources that have costs of production. Therefore, producing commodity money is constrained because resources are physically scarce and valuable. The perfect historical examples of commodity money are specie moneys. Production of gold and silver coins depended on producing specie and on the amount of specie in the economy. Consequently, a physical constraint checked any increases in the money stock. Had the costs of production fallen dramatically, commodity money would have quickly lost its value because of the supply effect. Under unusual circumstances any commodity can become money, as witness cigarettes in POW camps (Burdett et al. 2001, p. 118).

Fiat money, on the other hand, is, as its Latin meaning indicates, money produced by an act of will. To be clear, this "will" is the ultimate constraint in producing money (Hoppe 1994, p. 49). Obviously commodity money is also produced by an act of will; meanwhile, fiat money is produced with some scarce factors (paper or electricity). The main difference is that in the case of commodity money, its relative scarcity is a result of the physical scarcity of particular resources: commodity money has to be produced with the use of real resources, and the costs of additional supply set the limits on the value of money. In the case of fiat money, costs of production play almost no role

Table 5.1 Taxonomy of Monetary Regimes

Type of monetary regime	*Role of government*	*Production of base (outside) money*	*Fractional reserve banking (inside money)*
Government fiat money with 100% reserves	Imposes standards of money production and credit creation	Produced by the government	Nonexistent; banks as warehouses
Government fiat money with fractional reserves	Imposes standards of money production and regulates credit creation	Produced by the government	Essential part of monetary creation; the mechanism used for inflation targeting (monetary policy)
Government commodity money with 100% reserves	Imposes the standard	Produced partially either by the market or by the government	Nonexistent; banks as warehouses
Government commodity money with fractional reserves	Imposes standards of money production and regulates credit creation	Produced by the market with privileges from the government	Essential part of monetary creation; also usually a part of monetary policy
Market commodity money with 100% reserves	Debatable role of the legal system	Produced freely by the market	Formally nonexistent, but potential substitutes could develop
Market commodity money with fractional reserves	Debatable role of the legal system	Produced freely by the market	Present and completely unsettled by the legal system
Market fiat money with 100% reserves	No role for the government	Produced freely by the market (cryptocurrencies)	Nonexistent
Market fiat money with fractional reserves	No role for the government	Produced freely by the market (cryptocurrencies)	Depends on the currency issuer

Source: Author's classification.

(when they do, it is during hyperinflation, when the value of paper is higher than the money's nominal value). An example of fiat money is paper money produced by the government: the nominal value of a banknote has no relation to the costs of paper and ink used for production. Another example is Bitcoin and other cryptocurrencies. Bitcoin's supply is constrained by the rules chosen by the money producer (we may see it as a third category between fiat and commodity money: Yermack 2013, p. 4). Government-produced money is also to some extent constrained by the rules. The main difference is that government's rules are imposed on society, whereas Bitcoin's are chosen voluntarily (also the pace of monetary expansion differs radically—particularly because of the involuntary nature of government money). Importantly, there is also a difference between introducing a money and sustaining it. As the case of Somalia proves, government fiat money can exist in circulation even after a state collapses (see Luther and White 2011). Hence, even though the government may be necessary to introduce fiat money, later on, compulsory legal tender laws may not be necessary for it to stay in place.

It is usually implicitly assumed that the distinction between fiat money and commodity money relates to the extent of government influence on it. Statistically and historically it does indeed seem correct, with economists favoring commodity money usually against government intervention and supporters of fiat money usually strongly in favor of government intervention. Yet this need not be the case. Some economists favor government intervention and are favorable to commodity money, while other economists oppose intervention yet believe fiat money should be produced by private entities. The distinction has been dissolved even further by the rise of the Internet and privately issued cryptocurrencies. In any case, fiat money needs some form of "credibility" (Ritter 1995, p. 134). In the case of market fiat money, credibility is established by programming rules that are virtually impossible to evade (as in the Bitcoin case). With government fiat money, credibility can be imposed by simply outlawing the alternatives (Hülsmann 2004, pp. 35–36).

The third characteristic of the monetary system concerns the banking sector, in which "inside money" is produced. Inside money is the means of payment issued by the banks (which therefore bear the money as liabilities) that is also a generally accepted medium of exchange. This money can be produced in two fundamentally different ways. Banks can either produce "pure money substitutes" or "fiduciary media." Pure money substitutes are certificates (in the form of paper, open accounts, electronic devices, etc.) that are fully backed by the outside money. For any money substitute issued by the bank there is a corresponding amount of the outside money, which is taken out of circulation by increasing reserves and providing proper backing. Acting exclusively this way, banks would be on 100 percent reserves: base money would fully cover all money deposits or notes that substitute for deposits. Banks would act as if they were monetary warehouses that keep the money safely stored and offer services to their customers (safekeeping, quick transfers to other parties, etc.). Naturally they could still provide additional services such as making money in other geographical areas instantly available or making it transferable to other banks and owners. They could also engage in credit transactions, but the transactions would have to be financed via voluntary disposal of money possessed by the depositor. Deposits could not be created to expand credit. The deposited base money could cover only deposits and notes payable instantly on demand. It could not be used to fund somebody else's projects without the explicit approval of and ownership transfer from the initial owner. In those circumstances, banks would have to charge fees for acting in this way as warehouses (Rothbard 2008, pp. 86–87).

Fiduciary media are special money certificates different from pure money substitutes, since they are not covered by base money—that is, by bank reserves (Selgin and White 1996, pp. 83–84). They are a promise to redeem uncovered money substitutes on demand even though all promises cannot be kept at the same time. Fiduciary media are the basis of a fractional-reserve system, where banks are capable of creating inside money and therefore significantly increasing the money stock. In a fractional-reserve system, banks are capable of doing this without going bankrupt because not all depositors show up at the same time to redeem all the outside money, which is supposed to cover the inside money. Banks should act prudently enough in this manner and try to foresee how often their customers are interested in redeeming money. Under this system, banks are also active money creators engaged in a sophisticated form of financial intermediation. They are in a position to arbitrage away money not spent by customers (and kept as demand deposits) in order to finance credit expansion and additional illiquid investment opportunities (Boot 2000, p. 9). The role of government, again, becomes crucial for this regime. It is debatable to what extent free banking is possible under such a regime and what role the government should play in regulating the sector.[7]

Based on these three features it is possible to envision at least nine different monetary regimes. Some have been defended wholeheartedly by many economists, some have never really existed, and some may seem paradoxical or self-defeating. Let us briefly identify the nine systems in order to notify the money supply creation in each of them. It is relevant for describing how shifts in total spending affect the production structure.

Government fiat money with 100 percent reserves is the first hypothetical system that never existed. Despite its ahistorical nature, the benefits of that system were favorably discussed by James Tobin (1985), the late Irving Fisher (1936), Maurice Allais (1987), Merton and Bodie (1993), and at one point Milton Friedman (1960). Even though those economists came from different traditions, they favored that regime because it allowed an almost-perfect control of the money supply by the government. Monetary policy could be pursued smoothly and according to designed rules. Monetary creation would not be in the hands of any private entities. Government would produce money by decrees (fiat). The financial institutions would be allowed to accept that money in the form of deposits. They could not, however, issue more deposits than fiat money warehoused as reserves.[8] Uncovered money substitutes would not exist. It would be impossible to back inside money by anything other than outside money (e.g., long-term credit contracts). The extreme case of maturity mismatching (issuing deposits to finance credit expansion) would be outlawed.

The money stock in circulation would of course consist only of the outside assets produced by the government (banknotes, coins). Some inside money could exist and be accepted as means of payment, but it would be perfect money substitutes: it would correspond exactly to 100 percent reserves kept in banks' vaults. Hence, even though inside money could contribute to the amount of money stock in circulation, it would only be in exactly the same proportion in which outside money was stored and not spent. Monetary expansion would be possible, and would definitely happen, since it would allow the government to receive extra revenues without the obstacles the financial market presents it in the current system. Such an expansion would happen through fiscal policy. Therefore, increases in the money supply would result in a much bigger public sector. Hence, the capital structure would most likely shrink, since government spending is directed toward present consumption (Garrison 2001, pp. 91–96). It would even be questionable to speak of a financial market under such a regime.

Government fiat money with fractional reserves is a second type of system, one that is present in most countries nowadays. It allows the commercial banks to create additional inside money without backing it with outside money. Credit creation happens along with the monetary creation. The details of the system and modern monetary policy are discussed in the sixth chapter of the book. For now it is sufficient to mention that there is a form of money creation by banks, and it also reshapes the existing structure of production.

Market commodity money with 100 percent reserves is a system where base money is produced only by market participants (on this, see for instance, Rothbard 1991; Salerno 1983; Hoppe et al. 1998; Huerta de Soto 1998; Hülsmann 1996; Skousen 1988). Ideally a fully laissez-faire, 100 percent commodity system would mean that each step of money production is owned by private entities and free of any regulations—from the mining industry (which in many countries is nationalized or partially nationalized) to the minting of coins and the issuance of money to the public. No particular commodity would be enforced as a general market standard, so it could well be a system with a few commodities (historically silver and gold circulated together). Money would naturally expand with additional specie supplies produced by market participants. Commodity production would depend on profitability and hence would crucially depend on the money's purchasing power and on technological constraints. With systematic growth a unit of money supply would gain in value, and therefore, most costs of production would go down and make gold and silver discovery cheaper and hence more profitable. With a huge technological game changer we can imagine that specie would be driven out of circulation. If such technical progress appeared—for example, if gold could be cheaply produced from other elements—then the supply effect could potentially make money inflationary. Although now it seems very unlikely, we cannot be sure what the future holds. Under current circumstances we know that a market commodity standard with full reserves would result in systematic slow increases in the money supply, around 2–3 percent per year. The monetary expansion would happen through the mining industry. The potential for money expansion would already be factored into the profitability of the industry (pricing of stocks, etc.).

Assuming 100 percent reserves, under such a system, banks would be obliged to hold full reserves on deposit accounts. Credit intermediation would be a conscious transfer of already-existing money (or full money substitutes) from savers. Creating fiduciary media would be outlawed. Such a feature of the system sparks theoretical controversy over the nature of such a ban. Proponents of free banking argue that the ban constitutes an intervention in the market. Some of the ban's defenders (though not all) argue that it is not intervention but contract enforcement. Under such a view, fiduciary media and fiduciary property titles violate the rules of the competitive market. I am not inclined to resolve the legal debate (see footnote 7). For now it is sufficient to say that a system of 100 percent reserves with a market commodity requires a specific legal system as backing. Whether it requires government action or "correct" interpretations of property rights is beside the point, since it is a normative assessment. In such a system, no monetary expansion by banks is possible. Newly created money is reserve money slowly and physically produced by market participants.

Government commodity money with 100 percent reserves would differ from market commodity money with 100 percent reserves largely because of outside-money production. Mines could be nationalized, monopolized, or highly regulated, and so could the mints. Additionally, the government could impose a monetary standard and forbid any currency competing with the main commodity (e.g., silver against gold). At the same time, banks would not be allowed to create money (just as in the case of market commodity money with full reserves). There is somewhat of a paradox in such a hypothetical system, however. When the government monopolizes money production and minting, it does so to generate additional revenues. Such circumstances create an obvious incentive not to stop at this point. Why not debase the coins or actually substitute for them paper promises, which could be the basis for fiduciary-media creation? And indeed the history of government's approach to money production proves the point (Hülsmann 2008, pp. 193–236). Hence, although a government commodity money with full reserves is theoretically possible, it is highly unlikely because of contradictions among the goals stated by such a government. To the best of my knowledge, there is no economist who has supported such a system. Neither has it existed in reality, although perhaps Peel's Act may be seen as a step based on the general idea.

Government commodity money with fractional reserves, on the other hand, would have a bigger role for the state. Government would be involved in standardizing, regulating, and monopolizing commodity money, at the same time allowing the banks to create additional deposits. Such a partial commodity system would involve the state engaging in some sort of manipulation of the price of reserves. Examples of such a system have been given by Heilperin (1936), Laffer (1980), Wanniski (1978), and Mundell (1997). The system would probably evolve, as history demonstrates, into government fiat money with fractional reserves—a system known today. Again, as with hypothetical government commodity money with full reserves, it is hard to imagine why the government would have an incentive to stay on any standard if the government itself is in a position to decide what the standard is.

Market commodity money with fractional reserves would naturally share all the features of market commodity money with 100 percent reserves in terms of base money. Monetary expansion could and would happen through producing coins and discovering specie. The crucial difference would be in the banking sector, since with fractional reserves the banks could create credit along with deposits. Probably banks would be the main sources of monetary creation, more important than commodity discoveries. The forces driving such monetary creation would influence the productive structure and change the structure of spending on capital goods. For an analysis of such a free banking system see, among others, Horwitz (2000), Sechrest (1993), Selgin (1987), Selgin (1988), Selgin and White (1994), White (1984), and White (1989).

Market fiat money is the last and most exotic regime, either with or without fractional reserves. It is the most exotic not only because it has never existed historically but also because up until recent times very few people believed it could happen. The main reason is that people disbelieved that something produced by will could be very highly valued in the way of government fiat money. The existence of government fiat money is a result of historical links to commodity money and compulsory measures introduced to abolish it. Hence, even though fiat money can exist, it has to be introduced somehow. Various economists believed it cannot be introduced through market transactions because it lacks preexisting purchasing power (e.g., Polleit 2015, p. 75), in turn mostly because of lack of trust: an issuer of the currency could easily hyperinflate it if not constrained by the real costs of production. Although it is considered impossible to introduce the money, few economists discussed the functioning of such a system. See, for example, Klein (1974), Hayek (1976), Taub (1985), and Edwards (1980). For a new money to appear, publicly observable information is needed in order to assess the money's credibility (Ferris 2003, p. 15).

Everything changed with cryptocurrencies, where under an open-source system all rules are transparently laid out. Leaving aside whether the first bitcoins had a purchasing power, one thing is clear: market-produced fiat money—money whose value is detached from its costs of production—is possible. It is perfectly imaginable that Bitcoin will become a universal world currency, as there are no unavoidable obstacles to that outcome (Luther and White 2014, p. 6). It could be Bitcoin or some other currency with a different set of rules. Bitcoin is currently the winner because it was one of the first cryptocurrencies, but it also mimics the gold standard—something holders of money appreciate. Supply is limited, creation of new bitcoins is costly, and eventually there will be no new supply (as money growth decelerates). Hence, the purchasing power can steadily increase with economic growth and as production of goods increases.

Under Bitcoin's rules, we can also speak of 100 percent reserves. Bitcoins are used directly by their owners. Additionally, not only do Bitcoin holders not finance fractional-reserve banks. They also do not finance banks as warehouses. It is not necessary to open any accounts to pay other parties through bank transfers and other intermediate means of payment. Bitcoins can be transferred directly from one holder to another without any significant costs, even when holders are thousands of miles apart and in different countries with completely separated currency systems. That is a real game changer for the whole banking system because banking becomes unnecessary in many fields. Naturally one is free to offer fractional-reserve Bitcoin banking, but it is hardly imaginable why anyone would have an incentive to use it. The serious technological obstacle for now is that confirming transactions takes some time. Here banks and intermediaries could play a potential role, though it would certainly diminish as the system becomes capable of confirming transactions without intermediation.

A leading defender of the free-banking system with fractional reserves, George Selgin, is a little (in his words) "depressed" that market participants may in a purely competitive market choose a currency that does not allow for fiduciary media to be created (Selgin 2014, p. 11). Selgin arrives at market-failure arguments on how individual rationality conflicts with what is good for the economy, when people prefer to think about their wallets instead of about the economy (Selgin 2014, p. 10).

Nevertheless, since there are some alternative cryptocurrencies, one can envision at least hypothetically that one allows for fractional reserves to be created on top of it—although as I mentioned, it is hard to see why anyone would patronize such a business.

DEMAND FOR MONEY AND THE PRODUCTION STRUCTURE

Friedman believed that the quantity theory of money is actually a theory of the demand for money (Friedman 1956, p. 52). While discussing the effects of changes in the money supply, it is impossible to neglect market participants' preference to hold money. Participants are confronted with the choice of hoarding, spending on consumption, or spending on investments (Rothbard 2000, p. 38). Let us start from the example of equilibrium from chapter 2 and describe a simple scenario of decreased consumption spending leading to increased demand for money, in turn immediately affecting the consumption sector.

The squared bar in equilibrium corresponds to consumption of 100 units of money. Since the system is in equilibrium, 100 units are sufficient to cover all three types of incomes: capital-goods spending, the wage fund, and the interest return. Now the earners from all other sectors decide to decrease their consumer spending without altering their capital-goods spending. In the above example, consumer spending is reduced by seventeen units, which for the consumer goods sector means an economic loss of seventeen units, whereas the returns in the capital-goods sector are initially unaltered. Such an imbalance cannot last and results in dynamic adjustments. The capitalists in the consumer sector are unable to refinance their capital-goods purchases, hire laborers, and secure interest returns. The consumer sector suffers.

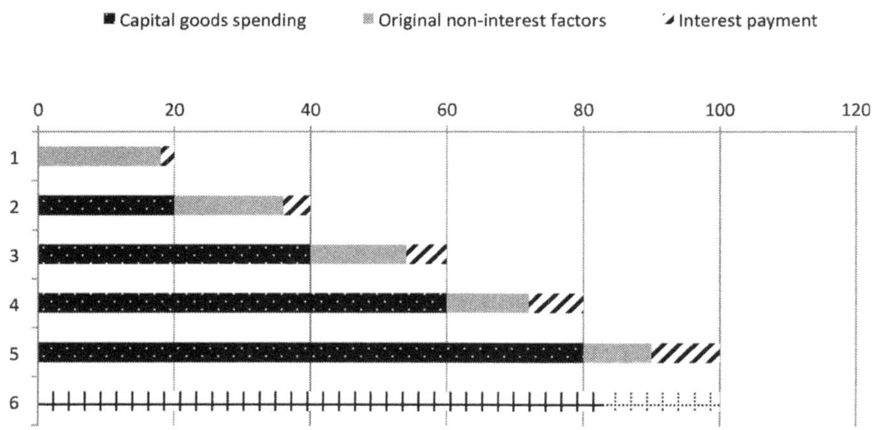

Figure 5.1 Increased hoarding at the expense of consumption

In the picture, the consumer sector is completely aggregated. In reality, some subsectors would stay completely unchanged in terms of their returns, and some would suffer more than others. In any case, the negative return in some of those subsectors causes capital to move and creates an incentive to search for higher returns elsewhere; hence, the movements toward higher returns. Capital moves into more profitable consumer subsectors, and also moves into the capital-goods sector. With such adjustments triggered, smaller returns in some of the consumer industries are imputed into related capital-goods industries. Downward pressure on some prices begins. In some cases, capital movements lead to upward price pressures, especially in the industries unaltered by the decreased consumer demand. Nevertheless, such an upward influence is smaller than the initial downward force, for the simple reason that total nominal spending is decreased (due to higher money demand).

One question that can be immediately raised is about imputing the lowered returns in consumer industries. Do lower returns mostly affect capital-goods spending, labor spending, or interest returns? What happens to the length of production and the interest rate? Inquiries made so far in the book have suggested that if the effect of higher monetary demand at the expense of consumption falls on the capitalists, then the interest rate will be lowered because both capital-goods spending in total and labor spending in total are not changed. How will this in turn affect the capital-goods–labor distribution and the length of production? Again various answers are possible because it depends on the intertemporal labor intensity. How exactly the industries will adjust to decreased returns depends on entrepreneurs' ability to react sooner than others. Profit opportunities may appear in different markets and for different ways of producing. The same applies for labor and capital-goods prices. Prices of capital goods would probably hurt more since capital goods are at most times more specific than labor and hence it is harder to find new employments for them.

How would the structure look? Just as the exercises in the second chapter showed, multiple equilibriums are possible. There is no reason for us to repeat some of those exercises, since they would be fully analogous, though with a smaller total budget. Before the change, interest to capital was 30 units compared to 300 in total spending with initial spending at 270. Therefore, interest was around 11 percent. If the decline in consumption mostly falls on capitalists after monetary demand increases, then interest should be lower. Say interest income has fallen to 20 units. Then interest would be 20 out of 270, or around 7.4 percent. With this effect, an increased demand for money should stimulate additional capital accumulation through changes in the price system favoring capital-goods industries. Hence, effectively there is higher capital accumulation due to decreased consumption, even though nominally savings have not increased. This is how higher money demand might actually lead to more growth, even if it does not entail more spending (Mises 1966, p. 420).

Now consider a second scenario of increased demand for money, with the increase not coming at the expense of consumption spending but at the expense of capital-goods spending (which can only fall on some of the capitalists in the trapezoid model). In such an adjustment, the interest rate would be increased because productive capital spending is reduced—while consumption stays the same, interest returns become a bigger percentage of overall productive spending. The higher returns are especially visible in the consumer sector, since spending was not reduced there. Lower returns appear in the capital-goods industries, stages away from consumption. This creates an incentive to reallocate capital, again into more profitable venues. This time capital shifts into the consumer sector so that returns would be equalized in all stages. In any case, the final result would be higher interest as interest income in total would become a bigger part of (reduced) capital spending.

And the final thing to consider: could nothing happen to interest, length, and structure when money demand increases? Hardly, for it would require all the market participants to partake of exactly the same increase in demand for money, making money effectively neutral to the economy. Yet, people increase the demand for money in order to make a difference. Their spending is not affected in the same way. They do not decline to spend the money just for its own sake, but because they prefer to reduce their spending *on something*—in other words, to alter their relative-spending pattern. Even for individuals, neutrality is hard to imagine, so for the whole economy it becomes virtually impossible. Increased demand for money affects the spending structure and spending configurations of the market participants. Hence, additional differences in the rates of return appear throughout the production structure but also within industries themselves. Not only do returns between the stages of production diverge, but also returns within the stages themselves. Increased demand for money can hardly be neutral, just as with increases in the money supply.

MONEY SUPPLY AND STRUCTURE

The above comparative statics of monetary demand shows that the relationship between the interest rate and money demand is not one-directional. How the process of increased demand plays out depends on additional considerations. The same can be said about increases in the money supply, which happen differently in each of the previously described monetary regimes. Increases in the money supply can happen through various channels depending on supplementing factors. Just as shifts in money demand alter spending patterns and productive structure, the same can be said about changing the money supply, both increasing it and decreasing it. There is no reason for us to go through each of the examples of increases in money supply, since it can be easily visualized with the above examples of shifts in money demand with reference to spending as described in chapter 2. There is, however, one important difference: with increased money supply, there is no corresponding decrease elsewhere in the system. Therefore, under increased money supply, factors of production are not released to be reallocated. Such a feature of increases of the money supply will be discussed in the sixth chapter on monetary policy.

For now it is sufficient to notice that neutrality of money, through changes in either money demand or money supply, is a chimera. As we have seen earlier, total capital spending and consumer spending do not fully determine the productive structure. They determine aggregate interest rate levels but not how interest is spread across the stages of production. Hence, even with no nominal change in capital spending and consumer spending, the productive structure can radically shift. When money demand increases proportionally both in the consumer and capital sector, the adjustment may still cause shifts in the Jevonsian structure. The story is no different with increases in the money supply, and even with the increases in exact correspondence with increased demand for money.

Let us hypothesize about possible increases in the demand for money and corresponding increases in the money supply. Assume that from the money supply of 1,000 units, 300 are spent on consumption, 450 are spent on investments, and 250 are hoarded. Now assume that an additional 250 units are hoarded as some spending on consumption and investments falls. Consumption is now 100 units, and productive spending is at 400 units. Such a fall in the consumption/investment ratio will favor capitalized industries and productive investments at the expense of the consumer sector. The shift will start to play out through capital reshufflings, changes in the composition of employment, and also the pricing of various factors.

At the same time, the banking system—in any regime—may respond by increasing the money supply in response to the increased demand for money. For simplicity assume that corresponding to the 250 units hoarded (as demand deposits, of course, not outside money), the banking system generates exactly the same amount for the purpose of expanding business credit. The key macroeconomic question is how that creation of 250 units will influence the production structure. Can the structure remain intact?

The immediate, completely a priori answer is that theoretically it is possible. In practice, it is very unlikely because monetary creation is based on intermediation—the holders of newly demanded money do not receive the additionally generated money. For this reason, Huerta de Soto points out properly that additionally created money will alter the structure as newly created money does not reach the sources of increased demand for money (Huerta de Soto 2006, p. 691). It is highly unlikely that it could.

Actually the argument can be further strengthened: there is every reason to believe additionally created money *cannot* reach the sectors that are the sources of higher monetary demand. Consider the following simple sketch of the Jevonsian trapezoids.

The graph does not disaggregate productive spending into production factors, but introduces another form of disaggregation that was not present in all the previous installments: division into industries. We start off with a simple equilibrium where interest return is uniform for all the stages and for all the industries shown in the six subgraphs. Suddenly demand for money increases (dotted bars). The sources for that demand vary. In the first and sixth industries, the source is primarily the consumer sector. In the second and fifth industries, the demand comes from very late stages of production. In the fourth one, the monetary demand comes at the expense of the middle stages, and in the third one, it is mainly at the expense of very early stages. The sources vary, although mostly later stages would suffer from the reshuffling of spending.

The market process would immediately generate negative returns in the sectors that lost spending and make the others relatively more profitable. Some of the less specific factors of production would immediately gain employment in the more profitable sectors, whereas more specific ones could suffer from idleness. Once the banking system begins to create money, the money will not reach the industries where spending declined as they are unprofitable from the market perspective. It is the other stages that remain profitable, and so they would benefit from money creation. Hence, a monetary expansion

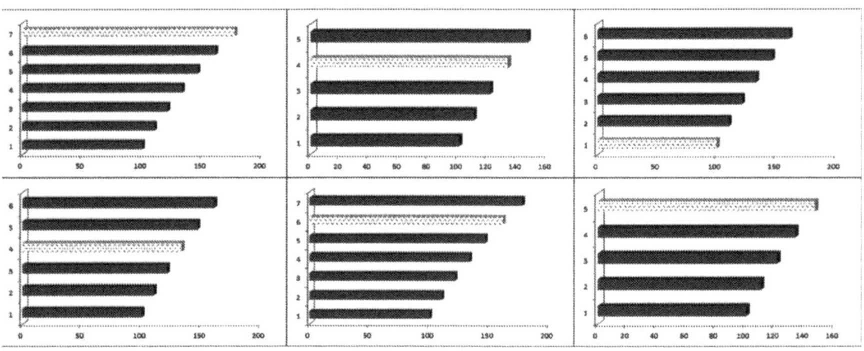

Figure 5.2 An economy consisting of six different processes of production with different changes in the demand for money

does not really respond to the causes of increased demand for money—it adds an additional force on top of that demand. It also does not exaggerate existing forces, but delivers extra purchasing power to those industries that are more profitable—exactly the opposite of the ones that suffer from higher monetary demand. Money would not reach the stages that appear as dotted bars in the figure. It would move into other stages.

It is not that there will not be an additional expansion due to monetary creation. There will be, but in other sectors, the opaque bars in the picture. More companies in those sectors will expand than would otherwise have been the case. The marginal investments invited by the credit expansion to be undertaken will be in more promising sectors with higher potential returns. Those marginal investments will be the riskier ones—the ones that could not raise capital from other, noncredit venues. The consequences for this increase in the money supply are discussed in chapter 6, on the works on the monetary transmission mechanism and the channels of money creation.

Even though the aggregate spending in the capital structure may not be changed, and even though the interest rates can stay the same, the capital structure virtually has to adjust because of changes in monetary demand and supply. How exactly the whole process works itself out is a topic to be further studied. For now it is sufficient to conclude that money is always a fluttering veil, never neutral. Any change in money demand irreversibly affects the economy. And so too is the case with any change in the money supply.

NOTES

1. Yet at the same time, the quantity theory of money helps us to understand why real magnitudes are the most important factors for long-run growth and overall living standards. The quantity of money influences them, but it is not the single most important macroeconomic variable (Friedman 1964, p. 278).

2. Hume is often portrayed as a pioneer of the quantity theory. In reality he also emphasized non-neutrality aspects of money increases.

3. "Information going back in time" is different from "perfect foresight," as the former means adjusting past contracts to present and expected future conditions in present. Perfect foresight, on the other hand, refers to foreseeing the future from now. One could of course suggest, then, that we need to have perfect foresight going back in time (even before an increase in the money supply), but that assumption is much narrower and more strict than simply saying that "information about money increases goes back in time." Therefore, it is unnecessary.

4. Naturally not all price deflation is caused by falling money supply. See the excellent treatment of the issue in Salerno (2003).

5. Although some argue that redenominating currency may also have real effects because it signifies the government's will to take its lower inflation promise as binding

(Žídek and Chribik 2015, p. 914; compare to the most sophisticated analysis in Mosley 2005). Yet the case is not obvious, since eliminating zeros can well be used to boost inflation to higher levels again. One thing is for sure: eliminating zeros makes using currency more convenient, and therefore there is some real effect involved even with such a change. Hence, even under such a reform the quantity theory does not fully apply. Otherwise no one would ever really do it, if it was 100% neutral!

6. Aside from those cases there are also menu costs, which at times of monetary changes are generally negligible.

7. See the descriptive representations of both sides in, for example, Selgin (2000) and Hülsmann (2000a).

8. The 100 percent government fiat money supporters often treat government debt as also a possibility for reserves on deposits. Naturally such a possibility offers a tremendous moral hazard since even in the current system (with some limitations on the use of debt) public debts are skyrocketing.

Chapter 6

Monetary Policy as an Interest Policy

Interest in the Neoclassical Synthesis and the New Neoclassical Synthesis

"The neoclassical synthesis" designates the integration of neoclassical microeconomics and a modern (a sort of Keynesian) macroeconomics. Modern macroeconomics can be seen as everything that came after the Keynesian revolution and the introduction of the Hicksian IS-LM model. It cannot be doubted that modern macroeconomic schools have very differing opinions on the workings of modern macroeconomic systems. Nevertheless, there is a common feature in most of them, one that can be traced back to Keynes's contribution: aggregative analysis.

Macroeconomic science can be rightly seen as the science of indexes. The topics are usually focused around aggregations such as gross domestic product, the inflation rate, and the unemployment rate (Friedman 1968, p. 95). Therefore, most potential problems are articulated in terms of averages. Such a tradition can be seen as a consequence of the Keynesian turn. As Coddington points out, before Keynes economics was framed by the concepts of individual choice and market interaction (Coddington 1976, p. 1258). Coddington calls the pre-Keynesian tradition "reductionism," but a more appropriate name would be "methodological individualism." Right now the state of the art is that macroeconomics requires microeconomic explanations (even without succumbing to reductionism). One cannot fully comprehend macroeconomic development (both in the long run and short run) without at least a basic apprehension of such concepts as capital, labor, and production (Taylor 2000, p. 93).

Yet no doubt a troublesome potential conflict arose between the macroeconomic and microeconomic spheres of economic theory. In microeconomics, a truly Walrasian approach persisted: prices were parameters that were constantly and instantaneously resolving mismatches between demand and supply. In macroeconomics the price mechanism apparently failed miserably because markets are not all powerful and cannot solve all the problems of mankind, including the problems caused by failures of government. The choice is, then, either to extend the Walrasian presumption into the macroeconomic sphere or to drop it. In the first case, this would require an equilibrium-always argument: even recessions and high unemployment would have to be seen as a "natural" part of economic evolution. In the second case, some modification of microeconomics would be necessary (Romer 1993, p. 6).

In macroeconomic development, there need not be any inherent conflict between macroeconomics and microeconomics. The proponents of Keynesian macroeconomics especially saw no such conflict. The evolution of mainstream thinking, which includes Keynes's contributions to understanding economic behavior discussed above, can be seen in Paul Samuelson's *Foundations of Economic Analysis*. Keynesian statements about stimulating aggregate demand are mathematically compatible with general-equilibrium constructs in which households and firms solve equations to maximize within a given set of parameters (Lucas 1980, p. 701). Samuelson also included the idea of unbalanced markets with excess demands, which would in turn influence the dynamics of price adjustments. In any case, such an approach opened the possibility that microeconomics could be made compatible with Keynesian econometrics (ibid., p. 702). A model in equilibrium behaved in the neoclassical way (i.e., clearing markets), but under shock could result in disequilibrated conditions. Consistency is not really the problem of modern modeling—content is.

The neoclassical synthesis was a way to combine specific theories with policy recommendations. As Paul Samuelson admitted openly:

> The "neoclassical synthesis" was no more and no less than a matter of-fact statement that there are alternative mixes of central bank money/credit configurations and fiscal expenditure/tax configurations that are compatible with full employment and price-level stability. (Samuelson 1997, p. 155)

Any moves away from equilibrium were seen as gaps that could be filled by a proper government intervention. No specific theory of market failure was needed to do so because fluctuations by definition meant diverging from an equilibrium potential output, or at least any equilibrium path. The promise that government would move the economy back to its equilibrium path meant the prospect of immediate progress and the possibility of arriving at full employment (Lucas 1980, p. 703).

After the neoclassical synthesis, the new neoclassical synthesis came, although at heart it was no different from the previous one. Macroeconomics needed certain "microfoundations." What lay behind this term was simply mathematical modeling of individual agents maximizing certain functions within a set of given constraints. The debate in the economics profession centered around "new classical" and "new Keynesian" sets of assumptions. But the framework and method was already chosen. Including "representative agents"—households and producers—in general-equilibrium theory was supposed to allow for slightly more thought-out microfoundations (McCombie and Pike 2013, p. 505).

The new neoclassical synthesis combined both Keynesian and classical elements, motivated especially by the rational-expectations and monetarist revolutions (Goodfriend and King 1997, p. 232). What differs between the older synthesis and the newer one is the notion of "intertemporal optimization," which deals with choices between consumers' consumption and investment (Blanchard 1997, p. 289; McGrattan 1997, p. 283). The existence of preferences subject to certain constraints allows for the proper optimization, all of which constitute microelements of macroeconomic theories (Mankiw 2006, p. 39). The key point of the newer synthesis is to continue the quest for justifying a specific monetary policy designed by the central bank, this time looking at various monetary rules within the rational-expectations framework. Due to rational expectations, the synthesis called for monetary policy to be transparent and neutral. Neutral is seen as implying "stable prices" along with no "output gap" (Goodfriend and King 1997, p. 232).

Why is there a concern about "microfoundations"? There are two reasons. The first has to do with Lucas's already-mentioned critique of macroeconomic models in which market expectations are not changing. Second, as a consequence of the Lucas critique, economics involves evaluating alternative policies in terms of the preferences of private individuals (Woodford 2003, pp. 10–11). The first rationale accompanies the obvious advantage of acknowledging rational expectations and allowing them to firmly ground macroeconomic modeling. The second rationale is more subtle and explains the whole notion of so-called microfoundations. Basically it is all about underlying the "structure relations" of one's model with some versions of private agents' utility functions (Woodford 2003, p. 12). In other words, on paper it is about integrating some microeconomic equations with bigger, macroeconomic models—just as with the older neoclassical synthesis, so too with the new synthesis. Basic utility functions, present also in the theory of public finance, can be applied to a priori models of monetary policy. Even though such an approach is known as building microfoundations, it merely extends already-assumed a priori models of macroeconomics with undesirable nominal rigidities. Once the rigidities are assumed in the macroeconomic framework, adding a utility function ("microfoundation") of an individual agent is just a further mathematical exercise in adjusting something already assumed. Such an approach of course demonstrates potential welfare losses stemming from nominal rigidities. Yet, to reiterate, the inefficient rigidities are assumed.

Therefore, one major aspect missing in both the neoclassical and new neoclassical syntheses could contribute to sound microfoundations: integrating the microeconomic theory of interest and the macroeconomic practice of interest. Microeconomically interest arises from consumer preferences and intertemporal allocation. Similar preferences and choices can comprise the basics of any macroeconomic model, synthesizing microeconomics with macroeconomics. At the same time, macroeconomic policy of interest almost entirely reduces interest to a lever: a force to use to play with bigger magnitudes detached from equilibrating microeconomic features (such as ones discussed in chapter 2). Interest is the mechanism for running a monetary policy and improving macroeconomic indexes and aggregates through the monetary transmission mechanism. Yes, consumer adaptation and parts of intertemporal choices fit well in this story, as in various applications of Ramsey-like models of consumer behavior under intertemporal budget constraints (e.g., Albanesi and Armenter 2012, pp. 1274–1275). What is missing is a story of intertemporal allocation of resources among the stages of production in a specific capital structure chosen with a given intertemporal labor intensity.

Macroeconomics was born as a discipline focused on a specific type of engineering rather than on carefully analyzed theoretical models. As Greg Mankiw noted macroeconomists used to see themselves as "problem solvers" who tried to deal with widespread unemployment (Mankiw 2006, p. 30). Later developments of microfoundations, therefore, do not seem to have served the purpose of truly solving the tensions between macroeconomics with microeconomics; rather, they have extended the assumptions in macroeconomic models to microeconomic utility functions.

AN APPARENT NEED FOR MONETARY POLICY

Most research on monetary policy is about how to conduct it. Much less time is devoted to studying why to conduct it. The prime reason is probably the existence of monopsonistic conditions in the market for monetary-policy research: most of it is acquired by the policy-making body itself (White 2005, pp. 325–326). That is not to say there is some inherent vice in such a state of affairs. Nevertheless, it can explain the skew in the topics of research, and also why the question of "why?" is very seldom raised as compared to the question of "how?"

Once raised, the issue of "why" is usually worked out a priori in macroeconomic models, much less in qualitative aspects of monetary-policy history.[1] How has the need for monetary policy been justified? As we have seen in the chapter on the quantity theory of money, there has to be an argument centering on market expectations, uneven distribution of new money, or prices not being completely responsive to monetary impulses. Otherwise changes in the money supply would remain neutral to the economy. Woodford properly notices that "monetary policy can have only small effects on the equilibrium allocation of resources in an environment with perfect wage and price flexibility"; therefore, the macroeconomic model of justifiable monetary policy should "allow for delays in the adjustment of prices and/or wages to changing aggregate conditions. In this way I allow for nontrivial real effects of monetary policy" (Woodford 2003, p. 139). Additionally, if the inflationary expectations are not immediately adjusted to the changes in the nominal rates of the central bank, real interest rates change, and so we have a stimulus increasing the utilization of resources. Since the problem is to fight negative aspects of nominal rigidity, the optimal level of inflation is zero at all dates and all states (Schmitt-Grohe and Uribe 2004, p. 199). Zero is just sufficient: anything more would require a much different justification (ironically policy makers rarely see the optimum as zero).

Hence, we have an essence of the need for monetary policy: it all starts with nominal rigidities in the model. Prices do not perfectly adjust to new conditions. Modern streams of monetary-policy analysis are actually historically reversed from what they were years ago around the time of the monetarist counterrevolution. The central banks were seen as preparing "surprises" on the supply side. Market agents did not expect inflation, so higher inflation could boost output and demand by surprising them. Right now surprises are not seen as effective anymore, and the role has been taken over by nominal rigidities alongside good communication on part of central bankers (Dixon 2001a, p. 17).

Blanchard argues that if we imagined a perfectly adjusting economy, each price would be set continuously, so relative increases in prices could not happen (Blanchard 2000, p. 1389). All prices would smoothly and immediately adjust to any nominal changes in the quantity of money. Demand and output would reach their natural levels, and monetary policy would be just as neutral as money. The reality would resemble a simple real-business-cycle model. Actually the evolution of models of dynamic stochastic general equilibrium demonstrates a true departure from the way of thinking in the new-classical models with no rigidities: nominal frictions create the basis for evaluating monetary policy (Clarida et al. 1999, p. 1662).

Zimmerman repeats the same argument:

> Why does money affect output in the short run? What is the cause of nominal rigidities and what role do they play in this process . . . ? These are the two key questions of modern macroeconomics. There is a consensus about what happens after an exogenous increase in nominal money supply: Given nominal prices, the increase of the nominal money supply leads to a decrease of the nominal

> interest rate and, due to nominal price rigidities, to a decrease of the real interest rate. This decrease in real interest rates induces a rise in aggregate demand and in the demand of every single good, given nominal (and therefore relative) prices. Higher capacity utilization leads to higher marginal costs. Hence, the increase in demand for each good gives price-setters an incentive to increase their relative prices. If prices were set continuously, the attempt of each price-setter to increase his relative price would fail. All prices, and therefore the aggregate price level too, would rise until the aggregate price level is adjusted proportionally to the increase in nominal money supply. Aggregate demand and output would adopt their initial values. Hence, money would be neutral even in the short run. (Zimmerman 2003, p. 63)

Here is where all simplified theories of inflationary benefits come from. Mild inflation is to work as motor oil for the economy to keep it working smoothly. Apparently, market participants are not eager to adjust their prices efficiently. Moreover, their situation is dramatic, since they do adjust them, but in a sluggish and ineffective way with Mandevillean fate: Microeconomic rationality says to adjust the prices sluggishly because it is most efficient. All participants do that, and the economy arrives at macroeconomic inefficiency. The new Keynesian literature attempts to explain this enigma, which resembles to some extent the paradox of thrift: microeconomic rationality at odds with macroeconomic rationality. The theory of monopolistic competition actually combines elements of nominal rigidity setting the stage for not only beneficial monetary policy but also the benefits of the fiscal multiplier (see, e.g., Dixon 2001, p. 24).[2]

Modeling nominal rigidities also demonstrates what it means in practice to build so-called microfoundations for macroeconomic models. A typical and perhaps the most often used example is the Calvo function of staggering prices with utility-maximizing behavior.[3] The vital starting points are that prices are not subjected to constant revisions (and therefore can be rigid for some time) and that once made, the revisions are not synchronized among the agents. The changes are assumed to start off at random, and then signals are to be transmitted with a certain geometric distribution (Calvo 1983, p. 383).[4] As mentioned above, then, microfoundations are in reality a way to a mathematical model already-implied and already-assumed macroeconomic statements. In another, more recent analysis, Christiano, Eichenbaum, and Evans justify the Calvo function by arguing there is no need for "explicitly tracking the distribution of prices across firms" (Christiano, Eichenbaum and Evans 2005, p. 10). Instead, one should assume a probability that the firm will need to adjust its nominal price. Rather than microeconomics starting from the fundamentals it sounds more like microeconomics practiced at random.[5] In the end, the conclusions in the mathematical model depend on the assumed parameters and conditions. Khan et al. use typical monetary-policy models to demonstrate the desirability of deflation (Khan et al. 2003, pp. 848–849). That is why a priori modeling as such remains an exercise in pure math, not pure economics.[6]

My aim is not to analyze all elements of the new synthesis's approach to modern monetary policy, but rather to confront it with the theory of capital structure. Nevertheless, two comments must be made on the existing state of the art on the issues of permanent non-neutrality and inducing nominal rigidities. First, even when assuming continuous price-setting alongside highly elastic expectations about the future, monetary policy could not remain neutral, because of the distribution effect of monetary expansion (Hülsmann 2003, p. 74). Hence, even with perfect prices, monetary impulses always lead to real-world consequences for allocation decisions. Under perfect adaptation and elasticity, prices are ready to immediately reflect underlying conditions, yet one cannot deny that those conditions change because of monetary expansion in one part of an economy at the expense of the other.

To illustrate the point, imagine an economy consisting of only eBay-like transactions, where all prices are set at auctions and ready to reflect conditions changing in the real time. All budgets of buyers sum up to total spending and total money supply in the eBay-like microeconomy. Now, let us imagine we double the spending, but we do it in an uneven way: we direct all the new money to people buying only cars. Assuming continuous pricing and bidding, the prices can adjust instantaneously and reflect new conditions. The end result would be higher prices for cars, not only nominally but also in real terms. The change would not be only nominal even if all prices smoothly increased at one stroke because the new prices would reflect the change in the distribution toward car buyers. Even with prices fully reflecting such a shift, a change by no means would be neutral. Changes in allocation would follow (I discuss this issue a little more in the upcoming sections). Some of the research based on nominal rigidities suggests that prices would have to be very, very rigid (e.g., lasting for three years) for monetary shocks to cause significant business fluctuations (Chari et al. 1996, p. 22). Such rigidity is very implausible and perhaps suggests another aspect of monetary expansion deserves an inquiry. Beside nominal rigidities, real rigidities have to be introduced into the explanation (Jeanne 1997, p. 2).[7]

Second, nominal rigidities are themselves shaped by the surrounding conditions, since ultimately the market participants set them based on their visions of the future. Expectations can be rigid, but do not need to be. There can be a self-fulfilling prophecy in performing monetary policy. Because market participants expect the monetary policy to be inflationary, they choose their pricing policy, both current and future, based on assuming future prices will be significantly higher than present prices. The paradox is that monetary policy itself can bring into existence something it is meant to fight. Market participants can easily expect prices to fall, as is the case with hi-tech industries, causing absolutely no harm to this constantly developing sector. There is no a priori reason to believe such pricing policies could not be made in other sectors. Therefore, there is no a priori reason to assume that nominal rigidities are like forces of nature. They are results of choices of market participants trying to predict what will happen in the market. Knowing that central banks are conducting inflationary monetary policy reshapes their attitude about future prices and possibly makes prices more rigid (the policy may justify granting more credit collateralized by expected asset-price increases). For example, if market actors expect the policy to be antideflationary, they may downplay deflationary scenarios and choose more rigid contracts. Furthermore, the elasticity of various markets also depends on the surrounding economy. Dickens et al. (2006, p. 28) point to huge differences in terms of real and nominal rigidity in various countries. For example, in Ireland and Denmark, a relatively negligible fraction of workers is affected by the rigidities, especially when we compare them to the other side of spectrum: Portugal and Sweden.

In any case, rigidities need not be very strong to start with. As Hanes and James sum up their analysis:

> We find no evidence of downward nominal wage rigidity in the historical data, especially when they include the various monetary regimes of the 1860's and 1870's. . . . Unlike fundamental preferences, social norms can change with the economic environment. . . . Of course, the apparent absence of downward nominal wage rigidity in the nineteenth-century United States does not rule out the possibility that a wage floor would persist in a future noninflationary regime. There have been many changes in American labor markets since the nineteenth century which might tend to preserve downward nominal wage rigidity, such as the spread of long-term employment contracts in the union sector and a possible decline in turnover. The role of these developments in the advent of postwar downward wage rigidity, apart from the change in the monetary regime, is a subject for further research. It seems safe to conclude, however, that U.S. historical experience fails to support the proposition that downward nominal wage rigidity is a fundamental feature of employment that prevails under any circumstances. (Hanes and James 2003, p. 1423)

Moreover, even studies of the twentieth-century labor market do not support the idea that wages are not at all flexible (see McLaughlin 1994, pp. 407–408). Therefore, for example, "the possibility that institutional and legal changes, which had their roots in the Great Depression, led to wage rigidity should not be overlooked" (Mitchell 1985, p. 278).

MONETARY TRANSMISSION MECHANISM: A ROCKY ROAD TO PRICE STABILITY?

In the previous section, we discussed an apparent need for monetary policy, a need that is assumed in the macroeconomic models used by central banks and also has some basis in empirical reality since prices are never perfectly flexible. The theory of central banking, however, does not stop at just apparent needs and justifications for monetary action. We need to describe the workings of monetary policy and its causal effects. That is the job for the so-called monetary transmission mechanism (MTM), which helps to deal with nominal rigidities. The central bank regulates its short-term interest rates. If the interest rate is lowered, then with some nominal rigidities, it means the lowering of real interest rates, which in turn change output and employment. By raising nominal interest rates given some amount of nominal rigidities, the opposite effects follow. Even though there is significant general agreement about monetary policy's influence on the real economy, we are far away from agreeing on how exactly this influence is exerted and what the consequences are. The MTM is the name for the mechanism of influence, but the transmission remains a black box (Bernanke and Gertler 1995, p. 27).

The simple reason for the mystery can be seen in a challenging question: how can so much depend on so little? Monetary-policy decisions are (in ordinary times) negligible compared to the size of the financial market. Despite central banks' relatively small share of the decisions about overnight rates, decisions to spend a few billion dollars in open-market operations have large effects (Lown and Morgan 2002, p. 217). Monetary-policy decisions must be triggering some sequences of events that permanently affect the economy. The transmission mechanism is debated vigorously for this reason.

Monetary policy for a long time was associated with regulating the money supply. Even today there are many macroeconomic textbooks that focus on monetary-policy tools such as reserve requirements, discount rates, and open-market operations (buying and selling assets). Such textbooks suppose that all three tools are used to regulate the money supply, hence influencing nominal income and other macroeconomic variables. The reality of monetary policy is, however, quite different. Since recent financial innovations and the breakdown of the simple relationship between defined monetary aggregates and output, it is no longer possible to approach policy from a purely monetarist perspective. We simply do not know which of the monetary aggregates to choose as an efficient way to manage economic activities. We could rightly question whether that was ever not the case. Yet even setting aside discussion about various monetary rules, it is clear they do not work for modern times given that the velocity of money is always changing and correlations between monetary aggregates and macroeconomic variables are unclear.

With such changes, money supply has been dropped from theorizing about monetary policy (although not completely—the biggest holdouts are macroeconomics textbooks in their chapters on banking). Instead, the main tool is the short-term nominal interest rate set by the central bank. Monetary policy is often designed without money. Nominal interest rates are targeted, which because of price rigidities means the real interest rate is affected, and so the monetary transmission mechanism can work its way in the economy. Notice that this policy perspective does not validate or invalidate the quantity theory of money; it merely stipulates that one does not have to pay attention directly to monetary aggregates (Beck and Wieland 2007, p. 527).

Below I spell out each of the channels mentioned in the literature on the transmission process. I should note that none of them is necessarily always the strongest, and even if strong at one point in time, it may not be the case most of the time. In analyzing the effects of each channel, one should also remember there is nothing mechanical, determinate, or unavoidable about monetary paths. Monetary impulses change current prices and anticipated prices in the various asset markets to different extents (Meltzer 1995, p. 51). How the process plays itself out depends on the particular circumstances.

The MTM is described both in the massive amount of communications of various central banks and in sophisticated theories. The transmission happens through different channels. Boivin et al. divide them into two groups in accordance with general economic theory: neoclassical channels and non-neoclassical ones. Among the neoclassical, we have investment channels, consumption channels, and international-trade channels (Boivin et al. 2010, p. 5). They work similarly: a monetary impulse from the central banks increases spending and prices. Before we proceed with the classifications, it is important to remember two things. First, channels are interrelated and hard to fully separate. Second, the strength of each channel can actually evolve over time since the channel is influenced by various institutional factors (Miron et al. 1993, pp. 1–2).

Among investment channels, the most obvious one is the direct interest rate channel: lower interest lowers the cost of capital and allows for a bigger pool of funding for investment goods (including real estate—a market also affected on the consumption side). Short-term rates affect overall spending on investment goods, which in turn affects output and overall prices (Brinkmeyer 2015, p. 8). Naturally the process is bounded by both interest rate elasticity and the term structure of interest rates. For investment goods, especially real estate, long-term rates are more important than short-term rates. In "normal" times, short-term rates affect long-term rates, putting downward pressure on long-term rates if short-term rates are lower. An explanation of the usual linkage lies in the expectations-based term structure of interest rates (Taylor 1995, pp. 17–18). The yield curve, however, need not behave in such a way all the time, and also the investment spending need not react automatically to interest rate decreases. The channels of monetary transmission can break down and become inefficient, even from the typical central banking perspective. The period after 2008 is a series of such events demonstrating some of the limits.

Another form of the investment channel is Tobin's *q*: the market value of the company divided by the replacement cost of capital (see Tobin 1969, pp. 21–23). It may be seen as an indirect channel as compared to direct investment's interest rate elasticity. In good times, the market values of companies traded in the stock market are going up relative to the cost of capital needed to replace existing assets of the company. With the interest rate going down, the *q* factor is going up, which then makes stocks a valuable place to invest money. The result is an increase in purchases of stocks, a sort of integrated move with the cost of capital directly benefiting firms.

The consumption channel of transmission rests on wealth effects and intertemporal-substitution effects. The wealth effect is the consumer response in the spirit of Modigliani's life-cycle hypothesis or Friedman's consumption function and is very similar to investment responses via the direct interest effect (Mishkin 1995, p. 6). Stocks, real estate, and assets become the prime targets for purchases even for the consumers because of broader access to a bigger pool of funding. Higher purchases are driving up the prices of such assets. At the same time as wealth effects and higher spending on assets there is also an increase in current consumption, related to intertemporal-substitution effects. Future consumption is limited in favor of current consumption. There may be an apparent tension between those two consumer effects, but once we realize that monetary expansion is key, the paradox disappears. Both spending on assets and spending on consumption rise. Those two effects lead to inflationary pressures.

The international channel of transmission is based on the exchange rate movements affecting net exports (Taylor 1995, p. 15). The forces accompanying currency depreciation make imported goods more expensive (inflationary pressure) and the profitability of exports initially higher because of higher revenues. In the end, the weakening of the domestic currency apparently affects output and prices both through higher export production adding to aggregate supply and through the higher prices of imports (Mishkin 1996, p. 5). Even though the international channel has long been recognized, scholars have limited its application to net exports and the exchange rate. Below we discuss channels related to the so-called credit view. The view can extend the international channel: monetary policy can be "exported" to other countries, as may also be the case with bank lending (for an example of recent analysis, see Takáts and Vela 2014).[8]

The neoclassical consumer and investment channels are also strengthened through agents' expectations, which in some of the schematic descriptions may be seen as a side channel for transmission. In the end, all investment and consumption decisions are based on some forecasts of the future conditions stemming from underlying factors in the present—including monetary policy, not just mechanically through the levels of interest rates but by overall policy decisions and the climate of opinion about future decisions (Grenville 1995, p. 23). We do not mean here to overemphasize the independent role of expectations, since they can quickly be disappointed, yet they have (at least) an initial influence on market participants. Articulating this channel can introduce us to the explanation of how short-term rates can have serious effects in the long run (see below).

The alternative to neoclassical channels is called the credit view and is sometimes associated with "market imperfections" or government interference. The most general case concerns the disequilibrating nature of credit expansion. Markets are not perfect in the neoclassical sense, and therefore the financial and banking sector does not immediately take into account the expansion of the money supply. The sector does not adjust instantaneously, and the expansion becomes a process extended across markets and time. Such non-neoclassical channels are usually not included in core policy models or models of dynamic stochastic general equilibrium. Hence, a crucial part of credit expansion is omitted in typical monetary-policy modeling.[9] Instead of assuming the frictions away, one can take a more "bank-centric" approach to credit expansion (Stein 1998, p. 483).

One of the reasons for separating the credit view from the typical neoclassical channels is the clash between the short run and the long run. The central bank can influence nominal interest rates in the short run to attempt to fight nominal rigidities, which disappear after some time. Provided the banking and financial sector works smoothly and generally accords with the efficient-market hypothesis, it is difficult to explain why the short-term nominal interest rate should influence long-term real interest rates at all. Why should the short-term-oriented monetary policy affect the yield curve always and in every respect? Unsurprisingly it does not, since the lowering of the interest rate can have negligible effects. Yet it does affect the yield curve often, especially in the normal times during which lowering short-term nominal rates affects assets—stocks, bonds, real estate, and so forth—in the long run. Something has to explain how the short run becomes the long run. The problem has been recognized for some time, but with little attention devoted to it:

> Beyond the problem of weak cost-of-capital effects in estimated spending equations, there is a presumption that monetary policy should have its stronger influence on short-term interest rates. For example, the federal funds rate, the most closely controlled interest rate, is an overnight rate. Conversely, monetary policy should have a relatively weaker impact on long-term rates, especially

> real long-term rates. It is puzzling, therefore, that monetary policy apparently has large effects on purchases of long-lived assets, such as housing or production equipment, which—to the extent that they are sensitive to interest rates at all—should be responsive primary to real long-term rates. (Bernanke and Gertler 1995, p. 28)

Such an inquiry has led to some developments in our understanding of the monetary transmission mechanism—in particular, the recognition that we need to separate the credit view from other channels in order to understand how the short-term nominal rate can influence longer-term investment projects. To be precise it is not a totally separate channel at all, since it relates to investment and consumer choices. Rather it is a parallel channel (Bernanke and Gertler 1995, p. 28). Additionally, the short-term–long-term interest dichotomy poses problems for the primary approach, concerning nominal rigidities, since the rigidities almost by definition disappear in the longer run.

The credit view centers around the banking and balance sheet channels. In the case of banking, we can speak of the banks' lending channel and banks' capital (Romer and Romer 1991, pp. 150–151). The lending channel (just as in the case of the interest rate) is an obvious notion: bank lending allows many companies to access funding that was not already available in the credit and financial market. Bank credit expansion channels additional funds especially to riskier firms, which otherwise would not get funds (Boivin et al. 2010, p. 18).

The banks' capital channel describes the transmission from the perspective of banks' portfolios. The state of financial institutions' balance sheets is one of the central features of an expansionary system, where rising asset prices are key for credit decisions, thus in consequence for spending and output. In the case of a crisis, prices of banks' assets are falling, the value of capital goods shrinking. It becomes more costly to continue adding new credit. Credit may even shrink. Having less capital means more expensive external financing, which cuts the amount of banking credit. Such an unraveling has come to be known as deleveraging, present especially in the post-2008 recession. The focus has turned to the channel of transmission via banks' capital in light of the development of institutional economics and regulation in banking. The Basel Accords and other legal elements are shaping the consequences of monetary-policy decisions (Van den Heuvel 2002, p. 261). A perfect example could be the decision by the regulator in the Eurozone to make the commercial banks increase their capital-adequacy ratio, which either meant raising more capital—hardly doable during recession—or switching to less risky assets as defined by the regulator: government bonds (including bonds of governments involved in the sovereign-debt crisis). The result was to direct monetary creation into the fiscal channel.

The second pillar of a credit view is the balance sheet channel, quite similar to the bank-capital channel, but it works in the rest of the market (Bernanke and Gertler 1995, pp. 35–36). Part of financing during credit booms relies heavily on the spectrum of collateral offered by debtors. In booming times, many assets gaining in value (especially due to monetary policy) can become collateral, and allow for the new funding. During the bust, the prices of collateral assets drop and a "shortage" of backing assets arises. Market creditors become more risk averse, especially in light of declining market value of securities. The net worth of companies goes down, spending goes down, and so does aggregated output. Interest rates affect disposable income, cash flows, and collateral value—vital elements in creditworthiness and therefore in banking decisions about supplying more (or less) credit (ECB 2008, p. 87).

The balance sheet channel also works with consumers, who use real estate for their leverage during the boom times. Even increases of value in already-purchased houses channel credit since they allow banks to offer more mortgages to households by serving as good collateral. Similarly, in a declining market, contraction results, though the previous boom in the banking and financial markets created bigger cushions for real estate during the contraction (Ryding 1990, p. 55).

Bernanke and Gertler insightfully point to a strong correlation between the federal-funds rate and the coverage ratio (Bernanke and Gertler 1995, p. 37). The coverage ratio (as they understand it) is the ratio of interest payments by companies divided by the sum of interest payments and profits (which is actually the opposite of how the term is understood by some others). In other words, it represents how much firms are struggling with getting financing through credit channels versus equity channels. The authors find that the lower the federal-funds rate, the lower the coverage ratio—another illustration of how this seemingly unimportant (because it is short term) nominal rate targeted by the central bank can actually play a big role in overall financing for all market agents including financing devoted to long-term investment plans.

Various banking- and capital-market developments create specific new ways of channeling extra funds into different investment venues. A suitable example is securitization, which allows agents to translate additional liquidity into loans, which then in turn can be placed off the balance sheet of the investing institution. The new institutional developments in the banking system not only confirm the necessity for new channels, but also demonstrate that despite older teachings, deposits are not driving the modern banking system and loan activity. As the older multiplier model is flawed, the availability of deposits does not constrain lending (Disyatat 2011, p. 712).

The process of expanding credit much more than deposit expansion, which flourished in the first years on the twenty-first century, had been almost completely ignored until the financial collapse after 2008, when suddenly all attention turned to it (Adrian and Shin 2009, p. 601). Now it is firmly understood that securitization allows for two important effects. First, due to liquidity management it allows debtors to convert illiquid loans into much more liquid securities, thereby affecting overall credit policy. Second, it reduces dependence of bank portfolios on more traditional ways of funding (or actually backing) loans—for example, through deposits or interbank markets (Loutskina 2011, p. 682).[10]

The balance sheet channel, securitization, and leverage together create a rather clear procyclical mechanism for boosting asset prices. With asset prices going up, and nothing else changed, leverage actually would go down as stable own equity must be matched by corresponding increases in the value of assets. The empirical evidence proves there is instead of this additional price rises lead to active asset management (Adrian and Shin 2010, p. 420). With assets increasing in value, the incentive for taking on more debt appears. The shift is amplified naturally by an active monetary policy with low interest rates—even just the short-term rates, because the short-term debt is getting cheaper and can be used against the long-term assets. As with any other leverage, it is a double-edged sword and creates the potential for a run on repo markets (Gorton and Metric 2012).

An important element in the leveraging part of the credit view is the risk perception by the lenders and borrowers. Naturally, lowered interest rates in general invite more creditors to receive additional funding, a feature enhanced by increased values of collateral (Sieroń 2015, p. 252). Yet during the times of expansionary monetary policy a risk-taking accelerator effect may appear, which goes well beyond just the influence of policy on asset values. Also, expectations are formed in a different manner, and so the actions curtailed previously by risk aversion may be induced. For example, lower interest rates crowd out safe assets and make them less profitable. The banks may search for financial intermediation in the short-term markets. In the world of banks' agency problems such monetary policy may trigger more risk-taking by banks (Jiménez et al. 2014, pp. 464–465). An analysis of Spanish banks based on credit records available in the documents of the regulator, Banco de España, describes the process impeccably:

> Our estimates suggest that a lower monetary policy rate spurs bank risk-taking and hence that monetary policy affects the composition of the supply of credit beyond the well documented effects of both the bank and firm balance-sheet channels. Consistent with "excessive" risk-taking are our findings that especially banks with less capital "in the game," that is, those afflicted more by agency problems, grant more loan applications and resultant credit to ex ante risky firms, that these banks require less collateral requirements from these firms, and that these banks face more default on their granted loans in the future—all bank actions that accord with risk-shifting. (Jiménez et al. 2014, p. 467)[11]

Borio and Zhu propose to select a separate risk-taking channel in monetary policy since both theoretical knowledge and empirical data support the notion that risk-taking on the part of banks should be included in macroeconomic considerations (Borio and Zhu 2012, p. 242), particularly when the shadow-banking system is subject to the "central bank's put" policy (Farhi and Tirole 2009, p. 589). As in other cases, the risk channel is not a completely separate channel, but integrated with three other economic factors. First, higher income, higher valuation, and higher cash flow (due to lowered interest) may add tremendously to risk perception. Even though the "financial accelerator" was already included in the previous channels, agents were seen as risk neutral or risk averse even with fundamental financial variables changing. Second, there is a "sticky" element (not to be confused with sticky prices) in the targeted rates of return by banks. Lowering interest rates lowers profitability. If the bank is to target the previous strategic profit levels, it has to either revise the plan or search for riskier venues. Third, consistency in communication policies lowers the risk premium, especially when the central bank provides assurance in the system (Borio and Zhu 2012, pp. 243–244).[12]

Looking at the first ten years of the twenty-first century, Altunbas el al. researched a wide-ranging database of risk measures and balance sheets of the banks operating in the European Union and United States. While holding other factors constant as much as possible (such as microeconomic aspects of banking and macroeconomic conditions of economies), the result is that low short-term interest rates for a prolonged period lead to an increase in risk-taking (Altunbas el al. 2010, p. 5). Bruno and Shin (2013) analyze the risk channel in the international context since globalization has profound effects on the worldwide banking system. It comes as no surprise, then, that the notion of "risk" of lower interest rates is appearing more often in the official statements of central banks.

Importantly, the banking sector is not an island separated from the rest of the market. Lowered interest rates by the central bank affect the banks and eventually overall rates of return. The policy affects other market participants. Rajan offers two examples. First, insurance companies have fixed interest rate commitments: when interest on their safest assets falls, they may default due to lack of necessary capital. Therefore, paradoxically, a safe strategy may threaten their existence. It may simply be necessary to take more risk. Second, hedge funds are also engaged in "risk-shifting" because lower rates mean they will not reach minimum targeted returns (also, lower rates allow for higher leverage) (Rajan 2006, pp. 517–518).

Here we reach the actual challenge for monetary policy and the pitfalls of the tools to reach stated goals. Monetary policy is aimed at stabilizing prices or stabilizing a particular consumer price index. The stabilization itself

Table 6.1 Monetary Transmission Channels

Monetary Transmission	*Subgroups*	*Examples*
Neoclassical channels	Investment	Investment demand, Tobin's q
	Consumption	Spending on durables
	International	Net export stimulus
	Expectations	Immediate market reactions
Non-neoclassical channels	Banking	Banks' portfolio adjustments
	Balance sheet	Favoring debt over equity
	Risk-based	Inviting risky marginal projects

Source: Author's classification based on literature.

produces utility by dissolving nominal rigidities. At the same time, it is well recognized that monetary policy acts through the different channels mentioned above. The output in different markets, on the one hand, and prices, on the other, change at different paces. Asset prices and capital-good prices are particularly vulnerable, as they are at the center of the monetary transmission mechanism in one way or another. The monetary impulse takes time before it fully reaches the consumer market (say, after six quarters). During this time, the process of monetary transmission is doing much more than just putting upward pressure on final prices, as we see in the prices of durables and long-term assets. The next obvious step is to recognize that huge financial imbalances may develop—even in the presence of apparent price stability. Low price inflation simply does not guarantee financial stability (Borio and Lowe 2002, p. 19). In other words, monetary policy aiming at a particular level of consumer prices may produce a significant side effect: bubbles.

ECONOMIC BUBBLES AND THE STRUCTURE OF PRODUCTION

One of the big questions addressed in the literature and central banking practice centers on choosing the right prices in direct inflation targeting. The typical goal of the central banks is to achieve specific levels of an index of final consumer goods. Other prices, outside of the consumer sector, are of no direct interest to the central banks. Yet as some other schools of thought demonstrate, movements in the other prices may actually be signs of disequilibrating tendencies in the economy. Worth particular attention are the prices of assets broadly understood: prices of financial assets, but also capital goods and durables such as housing. Bubbles are always associated with current market prices diverging from the fundamental values. The divergence is preceded by increases in bank lending (Allen and Gale 2000, p. 236)—increases that are assumed in all models of monetary policy.

Lending is inherently tied to central banks' monetary policy. Without discussing institutional details of central banks, I focused on a general description and themes present in the state of the art of monetary policy. The conclusion was that such a seemingly benign tool as a short-term nominal interest rate permeates the entire economy. Not only does it eventually reach every single market, not only does it affect all the main variables—investment, credit, consumption, output, and employment—but it even affects long-run plans, despite the shortness of the rate. Only recently (as mentioned in the previous section) have the works on the risk channel indicated that central banks can perhaps have something to do with economic bubbles. At the same time, the previously existing literature on the monetary transmission mechanism in the bank and asset markets pointed to that obvious fact. Often the traditional approach to bubbles was to treat them as somewhat endogenous to the market. Statements from central bankers are not the only proof of that. One of the most important textbooks on financial markets, Mishkin's, still treats bubbles as just being there, by asking, What should the central bank do about bubbles? Should it pop them? Should it regulate banking more? Mishkin does not even consider the influence of central banks in creating asset bubbles in the first place (Mishkin 2010, pp. 415–417). This is despite the fact that elsewhere in the same textbook Mishkin discusses channels of the monetary transmission mechanism that lead to boosting stocks, lending on assets, and even increasing moral hazard and adverse selection (2010, pp. 602–607).

Essentially any theory of bubbles is deliberating about economic errors: a divergence (over a significant amount of time) between the "real" value and perceived value of existing capital. To put it in the simplest terms, any theory of bubbles is simply a theory about investment mistakes. The same can be said about the broader category of business cycles. Theories about business fluctuations are about error and about their recurrence (Hülsmann 1998, p. 1). They try to explain in some systematic way why people should fall for the illusion of a bigger pool of available capital.

Economic bubbles have been approached by various writers. I am not inclined to analyze the works of each of them, but I plan to focus on the three most relevant theories of economic bubbles that relate in some way to interest (and monetary) policy and find their way into the production structure. Starting from the mostly monetary and ending with the mostly real sides of the bubble, I will consider Hyman Minsky's, Richardo Koo's, and Friedrich von Hayek's theories. The reason to pick those three is not only because they are the most famous ones, but because they present the mechanism of bubbles from different perspectives: psychological, financial, and macroeconomic. They differ very much on critical issues, but here I attempt to find in each of them what is best. The goal is not to create a comprehensive integrated theory but rather to show what is being missed in a typical monetary policy.

Minsky attempts to develop Fisher's debt-deflation theory, but focuses more on the inflation that precedes deflation. After emphasizing cash flows, assets, and lending, Minsky goes on to summarize a typical credit cycle that is visible in the empirical data, starting from inflationary pressure and ending with a downturn. At the heart of the process is the banking system. Here Minsky groups the borrowers and lenders according to general characteristics, which is helpful in describing economic manias: hedge, speculative, and Ponzi financing (Minsky 1980, p. 36; see also a recent general analysis: Flanders 2015). Hedge financing is the firmest one, since it is based on the notion of risk aversion that in each period the cash flow from owning an asset has to be sufficient to cover the debt and capital payments. For speculative financing, expected cash flows are based on somewhat similar thinking, but only over the long run. In the short run, more debt is financed than income is generated. In the Ponzi way of financing, the speculative element is permanent in the longer run also, so that total debt has to increase almost all the time. Both Ponzi and speculative financing are based on the concept of increasing leverage and debts outstanding. Speculative borrowers expect future flows to be high enough to cover debt payments, whereas Ponzi borrowers rely on future increases in the value of assets. Often speculative borrowers take advantage of increased mark-to-market valuation to take on more debt, without expecting a correction coming in the future (that is, without seeing the bubble). Ponzi borrowers take the approach even further: they expect values to be always higher in the future.

While analyzing some monetary systems, Minsky concludes that without fractional-reserve banking, but with a fixed money supply and stable money velocity, the accelerator-multiplier theory he discusses does not apply (Minsky 1957, p. 186). For it to apply, some way of externally financing more investments than available savings is needed. Nevertheless, he abstains from focusing on the financial architecture of the central banking system. The vital theme in describing his three types of borrowers is the "financial-instability hypothesis." While discussing the apparently inherently unstable nature of the market economy, he is focused on discussing debts, profits, and spending decisions (Minsky 1977, pp. 66–67) and in a post-Keynesian narration concludes that

> an economy with private debts is especially vulnerable to changes in the pace of investment, for investment determines both aggregate demand and the viability of debt structures. The *instability that such an economy exhibits follows from the subjective nature of expectations* about the future course of investment, as well as the subjective determination by bankers and their business clients of the appropriate liability structure for the financing of positions in different types of capital assets. In a world with capitalist financial usages, uncertainty—in the

> sense of Keynes—is a major determinant of the path of income and employment. (emphasis added; Minsky 1977, p. 68)

Relying exclusively on expectations is always tricky. After all, it is like saying that people's choices are responsible for their mistakes. Surely that is the case, yet it does not answer the fundamental question of why those mistakes are made in the first place, why those mistakes are "clustered," and more importantly why those mistakes have huge side effects. Since subjective expectations and opinions are random, under typically stable surroundings so should mistakes (White 2015, p. 109). Clearly this is not something we see in a cycle. Ponzi borrowers may appear anywhere, yet only an army of Ponzi borrowers placed within the banking system can have such disastrous effects on macroeconomic conditions. What we also lack in Minsky are considerations of why things sometimes do equilibrate in the financial system. Forgetting about this probably leads him to throw the baby out with the bathwater: recommending completely abolishing the financial markets in favor of socializing the investments in order to finance the most capital-intensive investments and expensive capital assets (Minsky 1980a, p. 83).

Minsky's description is very Mitchellian: it is generalizes some phenomena he observes in the market economy. It is a very accurate overview of wrong borrowing decisions in a cycle, which in general tells the story of the risk channel of the monetary transmission mechanism, or least a part of that story. During manias and booms speculative and Ponzi borrowers are part of the credit and business cycle. Their perception centers on the assets gaining in current market value. Surely all this is true, but what is the source of the permanent unsoundness? The story of three groups of borrowers almost becomes a historical classification truism—hence certainly correct—but not an explanatory theory (White 2015, pp. 107–109).

At the same time, Minsky's work has a problematic feature: On the one hand, he clearly sees Ponzi and speculative borrowers as the source of the problem. On the other hand, he is mostly concerned about instability following the downturns and necessary adjustments during the crises. One cannot have it both ways. Either speculative and Ponzi borrowers are the source of instability, or the instability follows directly from the crisis itself. In the second case Ponzi and speculative borrowers are actually heroes in the booming market economy, only to be stopped later on by doomsayers.[13]

Minsky is on target in describing some of the effects of the risk channel of the monetary transmission mechanism (though not really the channel itself). What he does not notice is that the risk channel is triggered by a monetary policy (Prychitko 2010, p. 209). Optimism needs leverage to thrive, expectations need money to materialize.[14] Minsky is in fact aware of this since most of his writings are about leverage, debt, cash flow, and assets. The interesting part is the accelerating effects. Speculative borrowers have to roll over their debt, whereas Ponzi borrowers need to constantly increase their debt until they are finally forced to sell their assets, which leads to fire sales and the overall bursting of the bubble (Mulligan 2013, p. 72).

Following Minsky, Steve Keen presented a basic equation in which additional debt is part of demand-creation (and increases in nominal GDP) during booms:

> Income + change in debt = gross domestic product + net asset turnover (NAT). (Keen 2011, pp. 160–162)

Income increased by new debt is the sum of spending on goods accounted for in GDP and goods not necessarily account for in GDP that are centered in the asset market. By taking the derivatives of both sides and assuming that income is almost equivalent to GDP, we reach the conclusion that net asset turnover can increase only if debt acceleration goes up. Therefore, for the prices of assets to continue to rise, debt cannot just increase. It has to increase at an increasing pace. Naturally we did not discover this by mathematical operations, since it is an almost-tautological conclusion drawn from the initially assumed equation: a fixed change in debt is a stable factor not boosting NAT or GDP. As Lavoie points out, Keen's accounting is not really correct, but the main point is to emphasize the importance of banks for the production variables (Lavoi 2014, p. 271). What matters is the empirical findings: Keen finds decent correlations between credit acceleration, unemployment change, and the stock market (Keen 2011, pp. 163–165). Of particular attention is a very strong correlation between mortgage acceleration and changes in real estate prices ($R^2 = 0.8$). Naturally the debt cannot accelerate indefinitely, so the bubble has to pop. The acceleration mechanism presumed by Keen is also present in Hayek's concept of the business cycle (see below).

Moving on to the second mentioned theorist, Richard Koo, it may be problematic to talk about the asset bubble because Koo is almost exclusively interested in the downturn and therefore he discusses bubble bursts, not bubbles per se. After all, the name of his concept is balance sheet recession. The case of 2008 seems like a perfect depiction of what has been going on in the financial markets and asset markets in general. Any firm's balance sheet consists of two sides, what is bought by the company (assets) and what it is bought with (liabilities). In a recession and bubble-bursting, companies have to struggle with parallel problems on both sides: the investments, assets, are losing their value, while liabilities are external and hence have to be paid back. Most interventions fail because the state cannot stop the meltdown of assets or creditors' willingness to retrieve at least some capital from a failing company (whose assets are losing value). Instead of searching for profits, companies are focused on improving their balance sheets: making sure to return indebtedness and leverage to the levels that are justifiable at the current market values of the assets owned. Repaying debt becomes the main goal since the traditional goal of searching for profits is frustrated by the special circumstances (Koo 2001, p. 16; Koo 2012, pp. 2–3).

Koo focuses on explaining the mechanism of a disease but not the causes preceding it. Such a method works at some level of course; however, if one is analyzing a balance sheet recession, then what do we make of the time before the recession? Perhaps it may seem worthwhile to consider a balance sheet expansion first. Why did asset prices reach such a high level? Koo does not give much of an answer—again because he focuses on one particular part of the cycle dynamics. Nevertheless, by focusing on only one part of the story, one may get incomplete answers. What causes the bubble in the first place? How did the interest rate and monetary policy affect the prices of durables and the activities of creditors and risk takers? Where does the overindebtedness come from? Rampant large-scale deleveraging on the part of the market participants requires previously rampant large-scale leveraging.

Definitely an advantage of Koo's approach is his attempt to explain why active monetary policy fails at the time of the crises. While not completely accepting his vision, the general, acceptable conclusion is that low interest rates do not work the same way under all circumstances. Active monetary policy can be broken. In the case of Koo, the reason is a balance sheet jam, where companies refuse to take more credit onto their balance sheet and decide to continue with deleveraging (Koo 2010, p. 31). The argument may in part echo the famous paradox-of-thrift argument, understandably driven by companies' self-interest. A company's quest to settle problems of debt and equity can hardly be challenged by microeconomic analysis. A company needs to survive, and getting out of debt is a coherent way to act. Yet if everyone is doing it, it looks as if we have a form of Mandevillean fallacy of composition, where everyone tries to save himself, which brings the problems to everyone at the same time (Koo 2014, p. 132).

While Koo's statement is controversial (since balance sheet reversal has its benefits), it has a certain advantage over the typical quasi neoclassical description of monetary policy. In a typical macroeconomic model, an interest rate serves a leveraging function to boost basic variables of employment, output, and inflation. With a fixed coefficient and stable function there is no reason why an interest rate should lead to opposite results at various times. Why at one point does a monetary policy of low interest rates seem to work, whereas at some later point it completely fails to expand credit? Apparently something not included in the existing basket of variables has to change the underlying mechanism. A modified approach to the monetary transmission mechanism offers a promising alternative, and Koo's direction is one such option. The credit, banking, balance sheet, and most importantly risk-based channels of the transmission mechanism can cause various forms of bottlenecks that make monetary policy ineffective.[15]

Minsky has told the story of the balance sheet expansion based on types of borrowers, yet without attributing the cause to an exact institutional setup. Koo tells the story of the balance sheet recession without any previous setup at all as if only meltdown matters, and not arrangements before the meltdown. Minsky and Koo can be seen as a part of the same tradition stemming from the late Irving Fisher, who described debt-deflation theory. His deflationary circle is based on nine interrelated factors: (1) debt liquidation leading to distress selling, (2) contraction of deposit currency, (3) a fall in the level of prices, (4) a fall in the net worth of businesses, (5) a fall in profits, (6) a reduction in output, trade, and employment, (7) pessimism and loss of confidence, (8) hoarding and increased demand for cash balances, and (9) disturbances in the interest rate levels (Fisher 1933, pp. 341–342). All those factors play their role during the downturn and lead to a sort of debt-deflation story (though because monetary systems differ they do not necessarily appear in all crises). Nonetheless, Fisher's story has a certain advantage over Koo's and Minsky's despite being decades older. The old debt-deflation story recognizes the institutional factors that play a role in the meltdown. The crisis does not appear because of sudden pessimism, and the bubble is not caused by sudden optimism, even though such sentiments do in fact play a role during the cycle (as in seven of the nine points above). The primary target is the banking system with its fractional-reserve nature that allows the bubbles to emerge. Hence, one of the reasons Fisher moved away from a government-manipulated gold standard system in favor of pure fiat money with 100 percent reserves. I am not assessing here the proposal, except to say that at least Fisher realized that an explanation needs to do more than just reference something that already exists during the cycle (expectations).

All in all, both balance sheet disintegration and seeding of speculative-Ponzi groups are financial phenomena. Financing is an initial investment step—vital at every stage of the investment process for sure. However, it is not the only element. Credit, leverage, and various forms of financing allow the monetary flows to create durables in a real-world production structure. A much more promising effort to explain those bottlenecks has been made by Friedrich von Hayek. His contribution was to try to demonstrate how such nominal flows and shuffles shape real variables.[16] The point directly relates to our inquires about the production structure.

When formulating his theory, Hayek was trying to distance himself from "real" theories of the business cycle. The name of his important macroeconomic treatise is, after all, *Monetary Theory and the Trade Cycle* (1933), where he devotes most of his time to explaining the monetary and banking mechanism of lowered interest rates. What is missing, however, are step-by-step inquiries into how new money affects the financial market and eventually lands in the realm of real production. Especially in this field, balance sheet and stock market considerations may be helpful, though at the same time they are often institutional and historical. One can hardly construct a universal theory of exact organizational preconditions for the cycles. Despite this inconvenience Hayek discusses how the bank credit affects overall economic expansions and bidding for factors in consumer- and producer-goods industries. A lowered interest rate—a tool used to enhance consumer prices—conflicts with the "natural" rate of interest, which balances the available savings with investment demand. The endogenous response of the market to such exogenous change is to reshuffle the existing capital structure (Garrison 1989, p. 7).[17]

Minsky and Koo in the end argue that the bust is a result of rigidities based on debt contracts and credit arrangements. Hayek's story need not be seen as opposed to this, but it does add a strong insight: there are real rigidities in the capital structure. The argument stems from a distinction between circulating and fixed capital, already presented in the second chapter of this book. The intermediate goods may be divided into two extremes: universal capital goods, which may be used in many stages of production, and more specific capital goods, which may only be used in a few stages of production (Hayek 1931, p. 255). Between those two extremes there are of course varying degrees of specificity. Some of the intermediate goods are closer to being very nonspecific and usable in many different production processes. Such is the case with iron and oil. Other intermediate goods may be more specific and usable only in a restricted amount of projects. Such is the case with a robot designed to produce cars. In the collapse in this sector, the aluminum and iron used to produce the car may be re-employed in other places relatively quickly. The same cannot be said of a specific robot. During production, the machine could have been highly valued. Once market conditions worsen, the possibilities for re-employment are limited. The tool may become inconvertible capital and a sunk cost.

Hayek's story of the business cycle often speaks of an increased length of production because interest falls and the pool of funding increases (Hayek 1931, p. 259). At the same time, he also talks about "more or less capitalist" methods of production and "attracting producers' goods to the earlier stages" (ibid., pp. 253, 259).[18] In fact, the former effect does not need to imply the latter effect. As we have seen in chapter 2, in extending the reswitching debate, lowered interest need not lead to longer processes of production: the processes may become shorter or stay the same. At the same time, lowered interest along with a greater pool of funding for production leads to more "capitalist" processes of production and attract factors of production for uses with higher capital intensity. Therefore, even if we set aside the whole issue of "lengthening," Hayek's insights about the specificity of capital goods in the cycle stay firmly in place.

How does heterogeneity of capital goods create potential bottlenecks in the boom phase not so easily resolved when the bubble bursts? Compare to a case of bursting a purely financial bubble: speculating in a hypothetical currency Z. Currencies are perfectly homogenous, as is the case with Z. When the market sees the currency as overvalued, it reacts by quickly correcting the prices of all Zs. Losses on various positions are almost immediately capitalized, and the new conditions after the storm lead to more accurate valuations of financial instruments. Obviously such an effect does not occur in asset bubbles in the real production structure involving various intermediate goods used up in competing investment projects. Here is how Hayek's theory strongly supplements, if not supplants, any financial theories lacking a theory of the capital structure. Currency units are homogeneous and perfectly interchangeable: there is nothing specific about each of them. Producers' goods, on the other hand, have a more specific character. When the bubble bursts they will be withdrawn from specific lines of production. Because of the market correction some of the lines will be discontinued. Nonspecific goods (or goods more nonspecific than others) will be gradually absorbed by other production projects (Hayek 1931, pp. 270–271). Because capital structure is heterogeneous, the values of neither more specific nor less specific goods are recognized, but more so with specific goods. Reallocation of factors becomes a matter for entrepreneurial judgment—that is why it is not done instantaneously as in the case of currency. Moreover, the case proves why the cycle is not purely financial and why we need to refer to real variables. Additionally more specific capital goods become a real rigidity tied to a company's pitiful financial situation, in which the fundamental values of assets cannot boost market prices back to their wrongly valued levels. Discounted revenues generated by factors' productive employment are corrected downward from previous overvaluations enhanced by debt creation and monetary increases. The pinch in financial assets can be well explained also by the pinch on the real side of production. Here is exactly how including production stages in a Jevonsian manner can greatly enrich business cycle theory.

Hayek's theory resembles Minsky's theory, or actually Keen's development of Minsky, in one more way. As we described above, Keen based his model on the idea that an increase in debt contributes to the asset boom and general stimulation of spending. Therefore, to maintain Ponzi projects based on increasing valuation, not only debt is needed, but constantly increasing debt. A similar argument is given by Hayek, though not specifically with debt, but monetary expansion, which allows for industries to constantly add necessary complementary factors of production. Since the already-extended capital structure requires more factors than previously, and also the factors are not to be bid away by the consumer industries (also experiencing the boom), their prices will be increasing. Therefore, additions of capital funding at the same pace (say, as in the Friedman rule) will not be sufficient to bid away those factors for a deepened capital structure. What is needed is the accelerating rate (Hayek 1934, pp. 160–161). For the production to be more capitalized real factors have to outdo nominal factors. That is to say, real credit expansion has to be higher than nominal expansion; therefore, the pace must be faster than already-existing price increases (Hayek 1969, pp. 280–281).

Perhaps an analogy to skyscrapers could be made with the real estate boom. Skyscrapers are very often built at the end of the boom, when prices of production factors are already high (Thornton 2005). Therefore, to complete a profitable project, aside from mistaken expectations about future apartment prices something else is needed. Credit expansion must be enough to finish the projects—much more than the expansion that was needed before the real estate boom started, when construction materials were cheaper. A bigger pool of funding is necessary for the investment to be initially justified. Hence, skyscrapers exemplify how additions to debt and money have to be progressively larger. Additionally, even though Minsky's and Hayek's frameworks mention debts and money, respectively, in banking practice they amount to almost the same thing. One of the most important followers of Hayek's macroeconomics, Joseph Salerno, defines money supply in a very broad manner that includes many debt instruments, which taken together he calls "true money supply" (Salerno 1987, pp. 115–116).

The emphasis on the real variables in the capital structure should not be too Walrasian (nonmonetary), however. Take the example of arguing that there are not enough resources to complete started investment projects. As Hayek's followers well know, thanks to the debate on socialism, entrepreneurship is organized in the realms of monetary calculation and capital constraints. Just as there is no theory of money without monetary prices, so there is no theory of pricing without monetary prices (Salerno 2006, p. 132). Capitalism is not a resource-based system, to use Kornai's classification—it is a demand- and capital-constrained system (Kornai 1979, p. 803). Limitations are set by monetary factors and contractual conditions. When we say that "not enough resources are available" it would be safer to say that a reshaped capital structure has been made so specific that it is not profitable to re-employ complementary factors to make to rational employments.

SUMMING UP: DIRECT INFLATION TARGETING VS. MACROECONOMIC STABILITY

Years ago Friedrich von Hayek presented a Wicksellian vice in a nutshell:

> But by a curious irony of fate, Wicksell has become famous, not for his real improvements on the old doctrine, but for the one point in his exposition in which he definitely erred: namely, for his attempt to establish a rigid connection between the rate of interest and the changes in the general price level. . . . When the banks, however, lower the money rate of interest below the equilibrium rate, which they can do by lending more than has been entrusted to them, i.e., by adding to the circulation, this must tend to raise prices; if they raise the money rate above the equilibrium rate—a case of less practical importance—they exert a depressing influence on prices. From this correct statement, however, which does not imply that the price level would remain unchanged if the money rate corresponds to the equilibrium rate, but only that, in such conditions, there are no monetary causes tending to produce a change in the price level, Wicksell jumps to the conclusion that, so long as the two rates agree, the price level must always remain steady. (Hayek 1931, pp. 214–215)

The argument was that there is no reason to assume that the rate of interest equilibrating the capital market has to in some way coincide with stable consumer prices. The capital market can be in balance even with falling consumer prices. Actually by amounting to a policy of lower interest rates adopted in order to achieve targets for a basket of consumer goods, monetary policy may start a credit expansion leading to an unsustainable capital-goods boom. Since the works of Hayek, not much has changed in this aspect, apart from an important fact that a lot of research about the monetary transmission mechanism (mentioned in this chapter) has confirmed that short-term nominal interest rate manipulation by the central banks may lead to asset bubbles and misdirection of production. The price of stable consumer prices may be very high. Achieving particular price stability does not guarantee other macroeconomic stabilities (Bean 2003, p. 28).

The fundamental problem with direct inflation targeting is an almost complete focus on final consumer prices expressed as an average. The goal of reaching a particular CPI (or similar index) is achieved using the tools of monetary transmission, the status of which is not settled and universally agreed upon by macroeconomists. It is safe to say we are very far away from any possible agreement. The monetary process takes time: it extends over long periods, through different markets, and through different prices. Monetary expansion changes everything: prices, output, employment, risk, and capital markets. To use it just to focus on the average of consumer prices is highly misleading since on its way monetary expansion may cause a lot of damage in asset markets, and consequently in the capital structure.

To some extent there seems to be some revival in the theory of monetary policy as more discussion is devoted to considering asset prices when stating macroeconomic goals (see for example Tymoigne 2009, pp. 21–23). There are important challenges in having the central bank include asset prices in its tracking, and the whole idea has been generally rejected for a long time. Counterarguments to such an approach are still quite strong since financial markets are the most dynamic markets in terms of pricing and therefore it is hard to imagine how the central bank with its much slower approach could fine-tune such a market. Alongside the argument in favor of such an approach we have a traditional approach of supporters of direct inflation targeting: support for manipulating the interest rate in order to manage a price index (and perhaps to some extent an "output gap"). Nevertheless, a lot of research suggests that the Wicksellian connection between stable prices and macroeconomic stability does not hold. The other approach could be that instead of final consumer prices, the goal of monetary policy should be focused on the asset market. Yet the side defending consumer price targets also has a good response: financial markets, assets, and stocks are very difficult to manage. From those two conflicting sides—targeting consumer prices versus targeting asset prices—one could form a unified approach critical of each of them. If the central bank cannot achieve macroeconomic stability by targeting consumer-goods baskets, and if it cannot do so by effectively managing asset prices, then perhaps a third answer is possible. It should not do either, and it should consider Chomsky's advice of world domination: resign.

NOTES

1. As was brilliantly demonstrated by Selgin et al. there is a complete absence of purely historical and empirical justification for the existence of the Federal Reserve System, as there seems to be no important macroeconomic variable that actually improved after 1913 (the establishing of the federal reserve) (Selgin et al. 2012).

2. Again Blanchard notes, "Once the price level has fully adjusted to the increase in money, and demand and output are back to their original level, desired relative prices end up the same as they were before the increase in money; but this is true only in the end. . . . Research suggests that, to generate the slow adjustment of the price level one observes in the data, this elasticity must indeed be small, smaller than one would expect if, for example, the price set by firms reflected the increase in marginal cost for firms, and the wage reflected the increase in the marginal disutility of work for workers" (Blanchard 1999, pp. 1390–1391).

3. The monetary-policy approach is framed as a way to allow for utility of the representative individual in the economy to be maximized (King and Wolman 1999, p. 350).

4. An analogous famous model was developed by Taylor in the case of staggered wage contracts. With a uniform distribution, all wage contracts are made for a certain amount of periods and a constant fraction of all firms determines their wages at a particular point in time (Taylor 1980, p. 4). Khan et al. attempts to combine both elements of Calvo and Taylor (Khan et al. 2003, p. 828). The private sector is divided into three groups: households paying for consumer goods, retailers selling them, and producers creating intermediate goods sold on to retailers (additionally households are the suppliers of factors).

5. Additionally, there are various differences between prices. Consumer prices are not production prices, and prices of wage goods are not wages themselves. Erceg et al. note that once we distinguish between wages and prices (and output gap also) monetary policy simply cannot pursue Pareto efficiency (Erceg et al. 2000, p. 283). It is simply impossible even under the chosen assumptions about nominal rigidity.

6. Another paradoxical example could be analyzing the effects of random injections. Dupor observes in his modeling that the Federal Open Market Committee could at times run a roulette wheel in its decisions. In the end, his answer is that it "probably should not." (Dupor 2003, p. 77). Yet, it may be the consequence of presumptions about rigidities and fixed expectations of market participants.

7. Jeanne suggests the labor market, but there are some other rigidities to be studied—for example, in the capital-goods markets, where intermediate products adapt much less to changing conditions than workers do. See below.

8. For more on how globalization affects the international transmission through the banking sector, see Cetorelli and Goldberg (2012, p. 1818).

9. The basic new Keynesian model consists of equations based on broad aggregates of output, inflation, and the short-term nominal interest rate (Ireland 2005, pp. 6–8). The role of financial intermediaries is not captured by the dynamic-stochastic-general-equilibrium models (Gambacorta and Marques-Ibanez 2011, p. 1). Although there have been attempts to do this, as with other DSGE models they again mostly mimic reality and are calibrated to already-existing (past) data (see for example Gerali et al. 2010; see also the DSGE model where balance sheets of banks may affect propagation of shocks: Meh and Moran 2008).

10. On how securitization affects fractional-reserve banking, see Gertchev (2009). On the example of how securitization helped to significantly increase credit expansion after 2001, see Jabłecki and Machaj (2009). See also Sieroń (2015) on how banks' asset structure may affect the business cycle.

11. Another study was conducted by Ioannidou at al. (2015) on the Bolivian banks under a practically dollarized economy (the business cycles of the United States and Bolivia are not synchronized despite the same currency). Lowered interest rates by the Fed increased the appetite for less safe loans and deteriorated banks' balance sheets by decreasing risk aversion.

12. Credit default swaps (CDS), which are often used to insure against possible losses on assets, are a good indicator of how big the perceived risk is. Amato finds a very strong relationship between the real interest rate gap and risk aversion (the real interest gap is based on some estimations of active monetary policy leading to lowering of interest rates) (Amato 2005, p. 65). As monetary policy becomes more

accommodative, default-risk aversion declines. The CDS market is then another good demonstration of how the central bank can change risk perception. A similar case is government bonds (e.g., the euro crisis): there is a strong correlation between spreads on government bonds and short-term interest rates set by the central bank (Manganelli and Wolswijk 2007, p. 6).

13. Elsewhere, he praises the central banking policy of contributing to booms: "In particular during a euphoric expansion the central bank should resist the temptation to introduce constraining direct controls on that part of the financial system most completely under its control—the commercial banks. The central bank should recognize that a euphoric expansion will be a period of innovation and experimentation by both bank and nonbank financial institutions. From the perspective of picking up the pieces, restoring confidence, and sustaining the economy, the portion of the financial system that the central bank most clearly protects should be as large as possible. Instead of constraining commercial banks by direct controls, the central bank should aim at sustaining the relative importance of commercial banks even during a period of euphoric expansion" (Minsky 1970, pp. 120–121). He does not see an obvious circular danger in such approach (Van Den Hauwe 2014, p. 19). At the same time, he hinted that perhaps it is not that bad to allow "crises to develop," but it is necessary to "act before severe losses" (Minsky 1970, pp. 126–127).

14. In his development of the Minskyan model, Steve Keen is also focused on the expectation side of the problem, arguing that at one point "managers and bankers come to regard the previously accepted risk premium as excessive," and then "with these rising expectations go rising investment and asset prices"; therefore, "external funds are forthcoming because the banking sector shares the increased optimism of investors" (Keen 2013, p. 223). What is missing in the description is the same thing lacking in Minsky's own work: the monetary transmission mechanism, especially the risk channel discussed above. Where do those "external funds" come from? Part of the answer may be that money is created endogenously by the banking system (Keen 2013, p. 227). Yet, even assuming this is so, money needs a specific financial architecture to be endogenous. Perhaps it is, then, the architecture that deserves at least as much emphasis as expectations (if not more).

15. Hence, Eggertsson and Krugman suggest to incorporate the issues of deleveraging into the DSGE models (Eggertsson and Krugman 2012, p. 1506). They also argue that models of the interest rate that do not differentiate between debtors and creditors are problematic (p. 1471).

16. That is not to say that the deleveraging model cannot in some form relate to the real variables. An example of the case could be Goldberg, who assumes given total-productivity levels dependent on the amount of capital, which is not constrained by the form of liquid (financial) capital, and with the natural rate of interest corresponding to the market levels (Goldber 2011, pp. 17, 22). With interest going below such a point, safe liquid capital is made less profitable: the "moral hazard parameters" are getting higher and induce the companies to undertake riskier projects.

17. The decision on the part of the market participants is to invest relatively more resources in projects that in the end appear as malinvestments (Sechrest 2006, p. 35).

18. That is not to say that Hayek's theory denies the consumer boom. Actually Hayek's take on the monetary transmission mechanism concerns both the investment sector and consumer sector. Changes in the interest rate and asset creation change the behavior of both investors and households in ways that become part of "wealth effects" (Salerno 2012, p. 15). See also Garrison (2004).

Conclusion

The notion of the production structure has had its ups and downs in the history of economic thought. It arose as a strong theoretical tool explaining the pricing process in an advanced economy. The sophisticated production and other essential aspects of the capitalist system seemed to perfectly fit the theoretical concept. At the same time, even while growing in eminence, it came under strong attack mostly because of its equilibrium nature. The ordering of stages of production surely makes sense in an equilibrated and regenerating structure. In reality, capitalism never works with such a structure. Hence, there were well-thought-out reasons for the attacks. If the real-world economy is constantly reshuffling the stages, then studying the production structure may seem like an unnecessary a priori exercise.

Nevertheless, the closer we look into the reasons for the attacks, the more we see their narrow nature: they are a call for economists to be more precise and to care more about the underlying assumptions of their models. That is why the critiques can be accepted without throwing away the whole concept. The structure is constantly reshuffled in empirical reality; the stages are always being readjusted. The same, however, can be said about any possible economic category that one may accept as real: supply, demand, costs, prices, or marginal utility, whichever you may pick. With real-world changes, it may be hard to employ such pure constructs, yet the underlying causal relationships cannot be rejected because of that.

The present volume does not answer all the questions surrounding the production-structure concept. The plan has been to prove that it can enrich vital microeconomic and macroeconomic ideas. The benefits of bringing the concept of production stages back into economic theorizing were demonstrated in the six fields in general economic theory discussed here: (1) the interest rate, (2) the length of production and return on capital, (3) aggregate demand, (4) potential output, (5) the money market, and (6) monetary policy. In each of those fields, the production structure has its place—even if empirically the structure is always being reshaped by the creative destruction, pure uncertainty, or whatever the disrupting causes may be.

In the case of interest rates, interest payments have a function in financing and therefore sustaining the extended structure. Regarding the amount of stages, although interest cannot be monotonically tied to the length of production, it can be tied to another variable—intertemporal labor intensity—that has its place in the length of production. As for aggregate demand, overall economic activity consists of all the earnings and all the spending in the structure—including the portfolios of capitalists—a view neglected in some macroeconomic theories. About potential output, we have seen that without the notion of production stages, potential production is a superficial variable because it does not apply to balanced macroeconomic conditions. In the case of the money market, the reshuffling of money—held and supplied—adds significantly to fluctuations in spending and earning patterns between the stages of production. The concept relates to the last discussed case, monetary policy, where research on the monetary transmission mechanism has neglected some of the channels leading to economic bubbles in the productive structure.

Overall, there is much to be gained by employing the production-structure concept in economic research in many fields. I hope for theoretical explorations in this direction and therefore in the direction of a more proper understanding of the capitalist process.

References

Abraham, David S. 2015. *The Elements of Power: Gadgets, Guns, and the Struggle for a Sustainable Future in the Rare Metal Age*. New Haven and London: Yale University Press.

Ahiakpor, James. C. 2001. "On the Mythology of the Keynesian Multiplier: Unmasking the Myth and the Inadequacies of Some Earlier Criticisms" *The American Journal of Economics and Sociology*, Vol. 60, No. 4.

Adrian, Tobias; and Hyun Song Shin. 2009. "Money, Liquidity, and Monetary Policy" *The American Economic Review*, Vol. 99, No. 2, Papers and Proceedings of the One Hundred Twenty-First Meeting of the American Economic Association.

Adrian, Tobias; and Hyun Song Shin. 2010. "Liquidity and leverage" *Journal of Financial Intermediation*, Vol. 19.

Albanesi, Stefania; and Roc Armenter. 2012. "Intertemporal Distortions in the Second Best" *The Review of Economic Studies*, Vol. 79, No. 4.

Alichi, Ali. 2015. "A New Methodology for Estimating the Output Gap in the United States" IMF Working paper, WP/15/144, available at (09–19–2016): https://www.imf.org/external/pubs/ft/wp/2015/wp15144.pdf

Allais, Maurice. 1987. "The Credit Mechanism and Its Implications" (in:) G. R. Feiwel (ed.) *Arrow and the Foundation of the Theory of Economic Policy*. New York: New York University Press.

Allen, Franklin; Douglas Gale. 2000. "Bubbles and Crises" *The Economic Journal*, Vol. 110, No. 460.

Altuğ, Sumru. 1993. "Time-to-Build, Delivery Lags, and the Equilibrium Pricing of Capital Goods" *Journal of Money, Credit and Banking*, Vol. 25, No. 3, Part 1.

Altunbas, Yener; Leonardo Gambacorta; and David Marqués-Ibáñez. 2010. "Does Monetary Policy Affect Bank Risk Taking?" ECB Working Paper Series, No. 1166/March.

Amato, Jeffery D. 2005. "Risk Aversion and Risk Premia in the CDS Market" *BIS Quarterly Review*, December.

Araujo, Aloiso P.; and Wilfredo L. Maldonado. 2003. "Learning in Intertemporal Equilibrium Models and the Sunspot Case" (in:) Fabio Petri and Frank Hahn (ed.). 2003. *General Equilibrium. Problems and Prospects.* New York and London: Routledge.

Arnold, Robert W. 2009. "Challenges of Estimating Potential Output in Real Time" *Federal Reserve Bank of St. Louis Review*, Vo. 94, No. 1.

Balassa, Bela. A. 1959. "John Stuart Mill and the Law of Markets" *The Quarterly Journal of Economics,* Vol. 73, No. 2.

Bałtowski, Maciej. 2009. *Gospodarka socjalistyczna w Polsce.* Warszawa: PWN.

Bar-Ilan, Avner; and William C. Strange. 1996. "Investment Lags" *The American Economic Review*, Vol. 86, No. 3.

Barnett, Russel; Sharon Kozicki; and Christopher Petrinec. 2009. "Parsing Shocks:Real-Time Revisions to Gap and Growth Projections for Canada" *Federal Reserve Bank of St. Louis Review*, Vo. 94, No. 1.

Bastiat, Frederic. 2007. *The Bastiat Collection, Vol. 2.* Auburn, Al: Ludwig von Mises Institute.

Basu, Susanto; and John G. Fernald. 2009. "What Do We Know (And Not Know) About Potential Output?" *Federal Reserve Bank of St. Louis Review*, Vo. 94, No. 1.

Baumol, William J. 1977. "Say's (at Least) Eight Laws, or What Say and James Mill May Really Have Meant" *Economica*, New Series, Vol. 44, No. 174.

Baumol, William J. 1999. "Retrospectives: Say's Law" *The Journal of Economic Perspectives*, Vol. 13, No. 1.

Baxter, Marianne; and Robert G. King. 1999. "Measuring Business Cycles: Approximate Band-Pass Filters for Economic Time Series" *The Review of Economics and Statistics,* Vol. 81, No. 4.

Bean, Charles. 2003. "Asset Prices, Financial Imbalances and Monetary Policy: Are Inflation Targets Enough?" available at: (09–11–2016): https://www.bis.org/events/conf0303/chrlsbean.pdf

Beck, Guenter W.; Volker Wieland. 2007. "Money in Monetary Policy Design: A Formal Characterization of ECB-Style Cross-Checking" *Journal of the European Economic Association*, Vol. 5, No. 2/3, Proceedings of the Twenty-First Annual Congress of the European Economic Association.

Becker, Gary; and Casey B. Mulligan. 1997. "The Endogenous Determination of Time Preference" *The Quarterly Journal of Economics*, Vol. 112, No. 3.

Belotti, Mario. 1960. "Economic Structure and Economic Development" *The American Journal of Economics and Sociology*, Vol. 20, No. 1.

Berczi, Andrew. 1981. "Information as a Factor of Production" *Business Economics*, Vol. 16, No. 1.

Bernanke, Ben S.; Mark Gertler. 1995. "Inside the Black Box: The Credit Channel of Monetary Policy Transmission" *Journal of Economic Perspectives*, Vol. 9, No. 4.

Bernholtz, Peter. 1993. "The Important of Böhm-Bawerk's Theory of Capital and Interest from a Historical Perspective" *History of Economic Ideas*, Vol. 1, No. 2.

Bernholtz, Peter; and Malte Faber. 1973. "Technical Productivity of Roundabout Processes and Positive Rate of Interest. A Capital Model with Depreciation and n-Period Horizon" *Zeitschrift für die gesamte Staatswissenschaft / Journal of Institutional and Theoretical Economics*, Bd. 129, H. 1.

Beveridge, Stephen; and Charles R. Nelson. 1981. "A New Approach to Decomposition of Economic Time Series into Permanent and Transitory Components with Particular Attention to Measurement of the 'business cycle'" *Journal of Monetary Economics,* Vol. 7, Issue 2.

Bhaduri, Amit. 1969. "On the Significance of Recent Controversies on Capital Theory: A Marxian View" *The Economic Journal,* Vol. 79, No. 315.

Blanchard, Oliver. 1997. "[The New Neoclassical Synthesis and the Role of Monetary Policy]: Comment" *NBER Macroeconomics Annual*, Vol. 12.

Blanchard, Oliver. 2000. "What Do We Know about Macroeconomics that Fisher and Wicksell Did Not?" *The Quarterly Journal of Economics*, Vol. 115, No. 4.

Blanchard, Oliver Jean; and Danny Quah. 1989. "The Dynamic Effects of Aggregate Demand and Supply Disturbances" *The American Economic Review*, Vol. 79, No. 4.

Blank, Steven. 2013. "Why the Lean Start-Up Changes Everything" *Harvard Business Review,* May 2013 Issue.

Blaug, Mark. 1997. *Economic Theory in Retrospect.* Cambridge: Cambridge University Press.

Blaug, Mark. 1997a. "Say's Law of Markets: What Did It Mean and Why Should We Care?" *Eastern Economic Journal*, Vol. 23, No. 2.

Boehm-Bawerk, Eugen. 1959. Capital and Interest. South Holland, Illinois; Libertarian Press, three volumes.

Boivin, Jean; Michael T. Kiley; and Frederic S. Mishkin. 2010. "How Has the Monetary Transmission Mechanism Evolved Over Time?" Finance and Economics Discussion Series, Federal Reserve, available at (09–30–2016):
https://www.federalreserve.gov/pubs/feds/2010/201026/201026pap.pdf

Boland, LA. 1978. "Time in Economics vs Economics in Time: The 'Hayek Problem'" *The Canadian Journal of Economics / Revue canadienne d'Economique*, Vol. 11, No. 2.

Boot, Arnoud W. 2000. "Relationship Banking: What Do We Know?" *Journal of Financial Intermediation*, Vol. 9.

Borio, Claudio; and Haibin Zhub. 2012. "Capital regulation, risk-taking and monetary policy: A missing link in the transmission mechanism?" *Journal of Financial Stability,* Vol. 8, Issue 4.

Borio, Claudio; and Phillip Lowe. 2002. "Asset prices, financial and monetary stability: exploring the nexus" BIS Working Papers, No 114.

Boulding, Kenneth E. 1977. "Noted on Goods, Services, and Cultural Economics" *Journal of Cultural Economics*, Vol. 1, No. 1.

Bresciani-Turroni, C. 1936. "The Theory of Saving. I The Forms of the Saving Process" *Economica*, New Series, Vol. 3, No. 9.

Brinkmeyer, Hartmut. 2015. *Drivers of Bank Lending.* Schriften zum europäischen Management. Springer Fachmedien Wiesbaden.

Bruno, Valentina; Hyun Song Shin. 2013. "Capital Flows and the Risk-Taking Channel of Monetary Policy" NBER Working Paper 18942, available at (04–10–2016): http://www.nber.org/papers/w18942.pdf

Buechner, Northrup M. 1976. "Frank Knight on Capital as the Only Factor of Production" *Journal of Economic Issues*, Vol. 10, No. 3.

Buechner, Northrup M. 1989. "Roundaboutness and Productivity in Böhm-Bawerk" *Southern Economic Journal*, Vol. 56, No. 2.

Bullard, James. 2012. "Inflation Targeting in the USA" lecture at Union League Club of Chicago. Federal Reserve Bank of St. Louis.

Burdett Kenneth; Alberto Trejos; Randall Wright. 2001. "Cigarette Money" *Journal of Economic Theory*, Vol. 99, Issues 1–2.

Cahn, Christophe; Arthur Saint-Guilhem. 2009. "Issues on Potential Growth Measurement and Comparision: How Structural Is the Production Function Approach?" *Federal Reserve Bank of St. Louis Review*, Vol. 91, no. 4.

Calvo, Guillermo A. 1983. "Staggered prices in a utility-maximizing framework" *Journal of Monetary Economics*, Vol. 12.

Cantillon, Richard. 2010. *An Essay on Economic Theory*. Auburn, Al: Ludwig von Mises Institute.

Case, Karl. E. 2002. "Reconsidering Crucial Concepts in Micro Principles" *The American Economic Review*, Vol. 92, No. 2, Papers and Proceedings of the One Hundred Fourteenth Annual Meeting of the American Economic Association.

CBO. 2001. "CBO's Method for Estimating Potential Output: An Update". Congressional Budget Office, August 2001.

CBO. 2014. "Revisions to CBO's Projection of Potential Output Since 2007". Congressional Budget Office, February 2014.

CBO. 2015. "Why CBO Projects That Actual Output Will Be Below Potential Output on Average". Congressional Budget Office. February 2015.

Cetorelli, Nicola; and Linda S. Goldberg. 2012. "Banking Globalization and Monetary Transmission" *The Journal of Finance*, Vol. LXVII, No. 5.

Champernowne, D. G. 1953–54. "The Production Function and the Theory of Capital: A Comment" *The Review of Economic Studies*, Vol. 21, No. 2.

Chari, V.V.; Patrick J. Kehoe; Ellen R. McGrattan. 1999. "Sticky Price Models of the Business Cycle: Can the Contract Multiplier Solve the Persistence Problem?" NBER Working Paper No. 5809, available at (09–27–2016): http://www.nber.org/papers/w5809

Christiano, Lawrence J.; Martin Eichenbaum, and Charles L. Evans. 2005. "Nominal Rigidities and the Dynamic Effects of a Shock to Monetary Policy" *Journal of Political Economy*, Vol. 113.

Clarida, Richard; Jordi Galí; and Mark Gertler. 1999. "The Science of Monetary Policy: A New Keynesian Perspective" *Journal of Economic Literature*, Vol. XXXVII.

Clark, John Bates. 1888. "Capital and Its Earnings" *Publications of the American Economic Association*, Vol. 3, No. 2.

Clark, John Bates. 1894. "The Genesis of Capital" *Publications of the American Economic Association*, Vol. 9, No. 1, Hand Book of the American Economic Association.

Clark, John Bates. 1895. "Real Issues Concerning Interest" *The Quarterly Journal of Economics*, Vol. 10, No. 1.

Clark, John Bates. 1895a. "The Origin of Interest" *The Quarterly Journal of Economics*, Vol. 9, No. 3.

Clark, John Bates. 1907. "Concerning the Nature of Capital: A Reply" *The Quarterly Journal of Economics*, Vol. 21, No. 3.

Clark, John Bates. 1908. *The Distribution of Wealth: A Theory of Wages, Interest and Profits*. London: Macmillan Co.

Clower, Robert W.; and Leijonhufvud, Axel. 1973. "Say's Principle: What It Means and Doesn't Mean" (in:) Donald A. Walker (ed.). 1986. *Money and Markets: Essays by Robert W. Clower*. Cambridge: Cambridge University Press.

Cochrane, James L.; and B. F. Kiker. 1970. "An 'Austrian' Approach to the Theory of Investment in Human Beings" *Southern Economic Journal*, Vol. 36, No. 4.

Cotis, Jean-Philippe; Jørgen Elmeskov; Annabelle Mourougane. 2004. "Estimates of potential output: benefits and pitfalls from a policy perspective", OECD Economics Department.

Cuhel, Franz. 1907. Zur Lehre von den Bedurfnissen. Innsbruck.

Dean, Alison; and Martin Kretschmer. 2007. "Can Ideas Be Capital? Factors of Production in the Postindustrial Economy: A Review and Critique" *The Academy of Management Review*, Vol. 32, No. 2.

Delle Chiaie, Simona. 2009. "Monetary Policy and Potential Output Uncertainty: A Quantitative Assessment" ECB Working Paper No. 1130, December, available at (09–20–2016): https://www.ecb.europa.eu/pub/pdf/scpwps/ecbwp1130.pdf?d143db7800821953f007b4956f65029d

Dickens William T.; Lorenz Goette; Erica L. Groshen; Steinar Holden; Julian Messina; Mark E. Schweitzer; Jarkko Turunen; Melanie E. Ward. 2006. "How Wages Change: Micro Evidence from the International Wage Flexibility Project" ECB Working Series, November No. 697.

Disyatat, Piti. 2011. "The Bank Lending Channel Revisited" *Journal of Money, Credit and Banking*, Vol. 43, No. 4.

Dillard, Dudley. 1988. "The Barter Illusion in Classical and Neoclassical Economics" *Eastern Economic Journal*, Vol. 14, No. 4.

Dimand, Robert W; John Geanakoplos. 2005. "Celebrating Irving Fisher: The Legacy of a Great Economist" *American Journal of Economics and Sociology*, Vol. 64, No. 1.

Dixon, Huw David. 2001. "The Role of Imperfect Competition in New Keynesian Economics" (in:) idem. 2001. *Surfing Economics*. Chapter available at (09–27–2016): http://huwdixon.org/surfing-economics/index.html

Dixon, Huw David. 2001a. "New Keynesian Economics, Nominal Rigidities and Involuntary Unemployment" (in:) idem. 2001. *Surfing Economics*. Chapter available at (09–27–2016): http://huwdixon.org/SurfingEconomics/chapter5.pdf

Dorfman. R. 1959. "A Graphical Exposition of Böhm-Bawerk's Interest Theory" *The Review of Economic Studies*, Vol. 26, No. 2.

Dorfman, Robert. 1959a. "Waiting and the Period of Production" *The Quarterly Journal of Economics*, Vol. 73, No. 3.

Dupor, Bill. 2003. "Optimal Random Monetary Policy with Nominal Rigidity" *Journal of Economic Theory*, Vol. 112.

ECB. 2008. "The Role of Banks in the Monetary Policy Transmission Mechanism" *European Central Bank Monthly Bulletin*, August.

Ewards, James Rolph. 1980. "Monopoly and Competition in Money" *Journal of Libertarian Studies*, Vol. 4, No. 1.
Eggertsson, Gauti B.; and Paul Krugman. 2012. "Debt, Deleveraging, and the Liquidity Trap: A Fisher-Minsky-Koo Approach" *Quarterly Journal of Economics*, Vol. 127, Issue 3.
Ehrmann, Michael; and Frank Smets. 2001. "Uncertain Potential Output: Implications for Monetary Policy" ECB Working Paper No. 59, April 2001, available at:
https://www.ecb.europa.eu/pub/pdf/scpwps/ecbwp059.pdf?21da80eb4acae68dca1e03f57c47b4b5
Erceg, Christopher J.; Dale W. Henderson; and Andrew T. Levin. 2000. "Optimal Monetary Policy with Staggered Wage and Price Contracts" *Journal of Monetary Economics,* vol. 46.
Faber, Malte; and Ralph Winkler. 2006. "Heterogeneity and Time: From Austrian Capital Theory to Ecological Economics" *The American Journal of Economics and Sociology*, Vol. 65, No. 3, Natural Resources, Taxation, and Regulation: Unusual Perspectives on a Classic Topic.
Farhi, Emmanuel; and Jean Tirole. 2009. "Leverage and the Central Bank's Put" *American Economic Review*, Vol. 99, No. 2.
Fernald, John G. 2014. "Productivity and Potential Output before, during, and after the Great Recession" *NBER Macroeconomics Annual*, Vol. 29, No. 1.
Fernández-Villaverde, Jesús. 2010. "The Econometrics of DSGE Models" *Series*, Vol. 1, Issue 1.
Ferris, J. Stephen. 2003. "Competitive Bank Monies: Reconsidering Hayek and Klein from a Transactions Perspective" Carleton Economic Paper CEP 03–02; available at (10–16–2016):
http://carleton.ca/economics/wp-content/uploads/cep03–02.pdf
Fetter, Frank. 1900. "Recent Discussion of the Capital Concept" *The Quarterly Journal of Economics,* Vol. 15, No. 1.
Fetter, Frank A. 1902. "The 'Roundabout Process' in the Interest Theory" *The Quarterly Journal of Economics*, Vol. 17, No. 1.
Fetter, Frank. 1914. "Capitalization versus Productivity: Rejoinder" (in:) Murray Rothbard (ed.). 1977. *Capital, Interest, and Rent. Essays in the Theory of Distribution by Frank Fetter.* Menlo Park: Institute for Humane Studies.
Fetter, Frank. 1914a. "Interest Theories, Old and New" (in:) Murray Rothbard 1997.
Filipe, Jesus; F. Gerard Adams. 2005. "'A Theory of Production' The Estimation of the Cobb-Douglas Function: A Retrospective View" *Eastern Economic Journal*, Vol. 31, No. 3.
Filipe, Jesus; J.S.L. McCombie. 2005. "How Sound Are the Foundations of the Aggregate Production Function?" *Eastern Economic Journal*, Vol. 31, No. 3.
Fillieule, Renaud. 2007. "A Formal Model in Hayekian Macroeconomics: The Proportional Goods-in-Process Structure of Production" *Quarterly Journal of Austrian Economics,* vol. 10, no. 3.
Fisher, Irving. 1912. *The Purchasing Power of Money, its Determination and Relation to Credit, Interest and Crises.* New York: Macmillan.
Fisher, Irving. 1930. *The Theory of Interest, as Determined by Impatience to Spend Income and Opportunity to Invest it.* New York: Macmillan Company.

Fisher, Irving. 1933. "The Debt-Deflation Theory of Great Depressions" *Econometrica*, Vol. 1.

Fisher, Irving. 1936. "100% Money and Public Debt" (in:) *Economic Forum*, April-June.

Fisher, Franklin M. 2005. "Aggregate Production Functions - A Pervasive, but Unpersuasive, Fairytale" *Eastern Economic Journal*, Vol. 31, No. 3.

Flanders, M. June. 2015. "It's Not a Minsky Moment, It's a Minsky Era, Or: Inevitable Instability" *Econ Journal Watch*, Vol. 12, No. 1.

Foldvary, Fred. E. 2008. "The Marginalists Who Confronted Land" *The American Journal of Economics and Sociology*, Vol. 67, No. 1, Henry George: Political Ideologue, Social Philosopher and Economic Theorist.

Foster, Gladys Parker. 1987. "Financing Investment" *Journal of Economic Issues*, Vol. 21, No. 1.

Friedman, Milton. 1956. "The Quantity Theory of Money: A Restatement" (in:) Friedman 1969a.

Friedman, Milton. 1960. *A Program for Monetary Stability*. New York: Fordham University Press.

Friedman, Milton. 1963. "Money and Business Cycles" (in:) Friedman 1969a.

Friedman, Milton. 1964. "Monetary Studies of the National Bureau" (in:) Friedman 1969a

Friedman, Milton. 1968. "The Role of Monetary Policy" (in:) M. Friedman. 1969a.

Friedman, Milton. 1969. "The Optimum Quantity of Money" (in:) M. Friedman (ed.). 1969a. *The Optimum Quantity of Money and other essays*. Chicago: Aldine Publishing Company.

Gambacorta, Leonardo; and David Marques-Ibanez. 2011. "The Bank Lending Channel: Lessons from the Crisis" BIS Working Papers No. 345.

Gerali, Andrea; Stefano Neri; Luca Sessa; and Federico M. Signoretti. 2010. "Credit and Banking in a DSGE Model of the Euro Area" *Journal of Money, Credit and Banking*, Vol. 42.

Garegnani, P. 1966. "Switching of Techniques" *The Quarterly Journal of Economics*, Vol. 80, No. 4.

Garegnani, P. 1970. "Heterogeneous Capital, the Production Function and the Theory of Distribution" *The Review of Economic Studies*, Vol. 37, No. 3.

Garrison, Roger. 1979. "In Defence of the Misesian Theory of Interest" in Herbener, Jeffrey (ed.). 2011. *The Pure Time Preference Theory of Interest*. Auburn: Ludwig von Mises Institute.

Garrison, Roger. 1979a. "Waiting in Vienna. Comment on Leland B. Yeager's "Capital Paradoxes and the Concept of Waiting'" in *Time, Uncertainty, and Disequilibrium*. (ed. by Mario Rizzo). Lexington, Massachusetts: Lexington Books.

Garrison, Roger. 1988. "Professor Rothbard and the Theory of Interest" (in:) Herbener, Jeffrey (ed.). 2011. The Pure Time-Preference Theory of Interest. Auburn: Ludwig von Mises Institute.

Garrison, Roger. 1989. "The Austrian Theory of the Business Cycle in the Light of Modern Macroeconomics" *Review of Austrian Economics*, Vol. 3.

Garrison, Roger. 1997. "Equilibrium and Entrepreneurship" *Advances in Austrian Economics,* Vol. 2, Part A. available at (09–22–2016): http://www.auburn.edu/~garriro/j1scham.htm

Garrison, Roger. 2001. *Time and Money. The Macroeconomics of Capital Structure.* London: Routledge.

Garrison, Roger W. 2004. "A Roundabout Approach to Macroeconomics: Some Autobiographical Reflections" *The American Economist*, Vol. 48, No. 2.

Garrison, Roger W. 2004a. "Overconsumption and Forced Saving in the Mises-Hayek Theory of the Business Cycle" *History of Political Economy*, Vol. 36, no. 2.

Garrison, Roger. 2006. "Reflections on Reswitching and Roundaboutness" in (ed. Roger Koppl). *Money and Markets. Essays in honor of Leland B. Yeager*. Routledge: New York.

Gavin, William T. 2012. "What Is Potential GDP and Why Does It Matter?" *Economic Synopses*. Short essays and reports on the economic issues of the day. Federal Reserve Bank of St. Louis.

Georgescu-Rogen, Nicholas. 1975. "Energy and Economic Myths" *Southern Economic Journal*, Vol. 41, No. 3.

Gehrke, Christian. 2003. "The Ricardo Effect: Its Meaning and Validity" *Economica*, Vol. 70, No. 277.

Gerrard, Bill. 1995. "Keynes, The Keynesians and the Classics: A Suggested Interpretation" *The Economic Journal*, Vol. 105, No. 429.

Giorno, Claude; Pete Richardson; Deborah Roseveare; and Paul van den Noord. 1995. "Potential Output, Output Gaps, and Structural Budget Balances" *OECD Economic Studies* Np. 24, 1995/1.

Goldber, Jonathan. 2011. "A Model of Deleveraging" Massachusetts Institute of Technology Job Market Paper; available at (09–10–2016): http://economics.mit.edu/files/6230

Goodfriend, Marvin; and Robert G. King. 1997 "The New Neoclassical Synthesis and the Role of Monetary Policy" *NBER Macroeconomics Annual*, Vol. 12.

Gordon, B. J. 1965. "Say's Law, Effective Demand, and the Contemporary British Periodicals, 1820–1850" *Economica*, New Series, Vol. 32, No. 128.

Gordon, David. 1997. "Review of *Essays on Capital and Interest: An Austrian Perspective*, by Israel Kirzner" *Mises Review* Vol. 3, No. 2.

Gordon, Robert J.; Peter K. Clark. 1984. "Unemployment and Potential Output in the 1980s" *Brookings Papers on Economic Activity*, Vol. 1984, No. 2.

Gorton, Gary; Andrew Metrick. 2012. "Securitized Banking and the Run on Repo" *Journal of Financial Economics*, Vol. 104, No. 3.

Green, David I. 1981. "The Cause of Interest" *The Quarterly Journal of Economics*, Vol. 5, No. 3.

Grenville, S. A. 1995. "The Monetary Policy Transmission Process: What Do We Know? (And What Don't We Know?)" *Reserve Bank of Australia Bulletin*, September 1995.

Grigoli, Francesco; Alexander Herman; Andrew Swiston; and Gabriel Di Bella. 2015. "Output Gap Uncertainty and Real-Time Monetary Policy" IMF Working Paper, WP/15/14, available at (09–20–2016):
https://www.imf.org/external/pubs/ft/wp/2015/wp1514.pdf

Gunning, J. Patrick. 2005. "Praxeological vs. Positive Time Preference: Ludwig von Mises's Contribution to Interest Theory" *History of Economic Ideas*, Vol. 13, No. 1.

Gunter, Coenena; Andrew T. Levin; Kai Christoffel. 2007. "Identifying the Influences of Real and Nominal Rigidities in Aggregate Price-Setting Behavior" *Journal of Monetary Economics*, Vol. 54, No. 8.

Hamilton, David. 1955. "A Theory of the Social Origin of Factors of Production" *The American Journal of Economics and Sociology,* Vol. 15, No. 1.

Han, Zonghie; and Bertram Schefold. 2006. "An Empirical Investigation of Paradoxes: Reswitching and Reverse Capital Deepening in Capital Theory" *Cambridge Journal of Economics,* Vol. 30, No. 5.

Hanes, Christopher; and John A. James. 2003. "Wage Adjustment under Low Inflation: Evidence from U.S. History" *The American Economic Review*, Vol. 93, No. 4.

Hansen, Richard B.; Ken McCormick and Janet M. Rives. 1985. "The Aggregate Demand Curve and Its Proper Interpretation" *The Journal of Economic Education*, Vol. 16, No. 4.

Harcourt, G. C.; Avi J. Cohen. 2003. "Retrospectives: Whatever Happened to the Cambridge Capital Theory Controversies?" *Journal of Economic Perspectives*, Vol. 17. No. 1.

Harris, Donald J. 1973. "Capital, Distribution, and the Aggregate Production Function" *The American Economic Review*, Vol. 63, No. 1.

Hawley, Frederick B. 1892. "The Fundamental Error of 'Kapital und Kapitalzins'" *The Quarterly Journal of Economics*, Vol. 6, No. 3.

Hayek, Friedrich August von. 1931. "Prices and Production" (in:) idem. 2008. *Prices and Production and Other Essays*, Auburn, Al: Ludwig von Mises Institute.

Hayek, Friedrich August von. 1933. "Monetary Theory and the Trade Cycle" in idem. 2008.

Hayek, Friedrich August von. 1934. "Capital and Industrial Fluctuations" *Econometrica*, Vol. 2, No. 2.

Hayek, Friedrich August von. 1937. "Economics and Knowledge" (in:) idem. 1948. *Individualism and Economic Order*. Chicago: The University of Chicago Press.

Hayek, Friedrich August von. 1941. *The Pure Theory of Capital.* Chicago: The University of Chicago Press.

Hayek, Friedrich August von. 1945. "Time-Preference and Productivity: A Reconsideration" *Economica*, New Series, Vol. 12, No. 45.

Hayek, Friedrich August von. 1969. "Three Elucidations of the Ricardo Effect" *Journal of Political Economy*, Vol. 77, No. 2.

Hayek, Friedrich A. 1976. *Denationalisation of Money*. London: The Institute of Economic Affairs.

Hazlitt, Henry. 1959. *The Failure of the 'New Economics'. An Analysis of the Keynesian Fallacies.* New York: Van Nostrand Company Inc.

Heilperin, Michael. 1939. *International Monetary Economics*. New York: Longmans, Green and Co.

Hippe, Ralph. 2013. "Are You NUTS? The Factors of Production and their Long-Run Evolution in Europe from a Regional Perspective" *Historical Social Research / Historische Sozialforschung*, Vol. 38, No. 2.

Hirshleifer, J. 1967. "A Note on the Bohm-Bawerk/Wicksell Theory of Interest" *The Review of Economic Studies*, Vol. 34, No. 2.

Hodrick, Robert J.; and Edward C. Prescott. 1997. "Postwar U.S. Business Cycles: An Empirical Investigation" *Journal of Money, Credit and Banking*, Vol. 29, No. 1.

Hoppe, Hans Hermann. 1994. "How Is Fiat Money Possible?—or, the Devolution of Money and Credit" *The Review of Austrian Economics*, Vol. 7, No. 2.

Hoppe, Hans Hermann; Joerg G. Hülsmann; and Walter Block. 1998. "Against Fiduciary Media" *Quarterly Journal of Austrian Economics*, Vol. 1, No. 1.

Horwitz, Steven. 2000. *Microfoundations and Macroeconomics*. London: Routledge.

Huerta de Soto, Jesús. 1998. "A Critical Note on Fractional-Reserve Free Banking" *Quarterly Journal of Austrian Economics*, Vol. 1, No. 4.

Huerta de Soto, Jesús. 2006. *Money, Bank Credit, and Economic Cycles*, Auburn, Al: Ludwig von Mises.

Hume, David. 1742. *Of Money*. Available at (10–11–2016): http://www.econlib.org/library/LFBooks/Hume/hmMPL26.html

Hutt, William H. 1956. "The Yield from Money Held" (in:) M. Sennholz. 1956. *Freedom and Free Enterprise: Essays in Honor of Ludwig von Mises*. Chicago: Van Nostrand.

Hutt, William H. 1963. *Keynesianism—Retrospect And prospect: A Critical Restatement of Basic Economic Principles*. Chicago: H. Regnery Co.

Hutt, William Harold. 1974. *A Rehabilitation of Say's Law*. Athens: Ohio University Press.

Hutt, William Harold. 1979. *The Keynesian Episode: A Reassessment*. Indianapolis: Liberty Press.

Hülsmann, Jörg Guido. 1996. "Free Banking and Free Bankers" *Review of Austrian Economics*, Vol. 9, No. 1.

Hülsmann, Jörg Guido. 1998. "Toward a General Theory of Error Cycles" *The Quarterly Journal of Austrian Economics*, Vol. 1, No. 4.

Hülsmann, Jörg Guido. 2000. "A Realistic Approach to Equilibrium" *The Quarterly Journal of Austrian Economics*, Vol. 3, No. 4.

Hülsmann, Jörg Guido. 2000a. "Banks Cannot Creat Money" *The Independent Review*, Vol. 5, No. 1.

Hülsmann, Joerg Guido. 2001. "Garrisonian Macroeconomics" *Quarterly Journal of Austrian Economics*, Vol. 4, No. 3.

Hülsmann, Jörg Guido. 2002. "Theory of Interest" *The Quarterly Journal of Austrian Economics*, Vol. 5, No. 4.

Hülsmann, Jörg Guido. 2003. "New Keynesian Monetary Views: A Comment" *The Quarterly Journal of Austrian Economics*, Vol. 6, No. 4.

Hülsmann, Jörg Guido. 2004. "Legal Tender Laws and Fractional-Reserve Banking" *Journal of Libertarian Studies*, Vol. 18, No. 3.

Hülsmann, Jörg Guido. 2008. *Ethics of Money Production*. Auburn, Al: Ludwig von Mises Institute.

Hülsmann, Jörg Guido. 2010. "The Structure of Production" working paper. http://www.guidohulsmann.com/pdf/Structure_Production_Reconsidered.pdf

Ingrao, Bruna. 1998. "Free Market" (in:) Richard Arena and Christian Longhi (ed.). 1998. *Markets and Organization*. New York: Springer.

Innocenti, Alessandro; and Carlo Zappia. 2005. "Thought- and Performed Experiments in Hayek and Morgenstern" (in:) Philippe Fontaine and Robert Leonard (ed.). 2005. *The Experiment in the History of Economics*. London and New York: Routledge.

Ioannidou, Vasso; Steven Ongena; and José-Luis Peydró. 2015. "Monetary Policy, Risk-Taking, and Pricing: Evidence from a Quasi-Natural Experiment" *Review of Finance*, Vol. 19, No. 1.

Ireland, Peter N. 2005. "The Monetary Transmission Mechanism". FRB of Boston Working Paper No. 06–1.

Jabłecki, Juliusz; and Mateusz Machaj. 2009. "The Regulated Meltdown of 2008" *Critical Review. A Journal of Politics and Society*, Vol. 21, Issue 2–3.

Jeanne, Olivier. 1997. "Generating Real Persistent Effects of Monetary Shocks: How Much Nominal Rigidity Do We Really Need?" NBER Working Paper No. 6258, available at (09–28–2016): http://www.nber.org/papers/w6258

Jevons, William Stanley. 1957. *The Theory of Political Economy*. New York: Sentry Press.

Jiménez, Gabriel; Steven Ongena; José-Luis Peydró; Jesús Saurina. 2014. "Hazardous Times for Monetary Policy: What Do Twenty-Three Million Bank Loans Say About the Effects of Monetary Policy on Credit Risk-Taking?" *Econometrica*, Vol. 82, No. 2.

Johnson, Harry G. 1949. "Demand for Commodities is Not Demand for Labour" *The Economic Journal*, Vol. 59, No. 236.

Johnson, Ivan C. 2001. "A reappraisal of the say's law controversy" *The Quarterly Journal of Austrian* Economics Vol. 4, Issue 4.

Johnson, Jerah 1966. "The Role of Spending in Physiocratic Theory" *The Quarterly Journal of Economics*, Vol. 80, No. 4.

Jonsson, Petur O. 1995. "On the Economics of Say and Keynes' Interpretation of Say's Law" *Eastern Economic Journal*, Vol. 21, No. 2.

Kahn, Richard. 1931. "The Relation of Home Investment to Unemployment" *The Economic Journal*, Vol. 41, No. 162.

Kalecki, Michał. 1935. "A Macrodynamic Theory of Business Cycles" *Econometrica*, Vol. 3, No. 3.

Kalecki, Michał. 1937. "A Theory of Commodity, Income, and Capital Taxation" *The Economic Journal*, Vol. 47, No. 187.

Kalecki, Michał. 1937a. "A Theory of the Business Cycle" *The Review of Economic Studies*, Vol. 4, No. 2.

Kalecki, Michał. 1941. "A Theorem on Technical Progress" *The Review of Economic Studies*, Vol. 8, No. 3.

Kalecki, Michał. 1942. "A Theory of Profits" *The Economic Journal*, Vol. 52, No. 206/207.

Kalecki, Michał. 1945. "Full Employment by Stimulating Private Investment?" *Oxford Economic Papers*, No. 7.

Kalecki, Michał. 1949. "A New Approach to the Problem of Business Cycles" *The Review of Economic Studies*, Vol. 16, No. 2.

Kates, Steven. 1995. "Crucial Influences on Keynes' Understanding of Say's Law" *History of Economics Review*, No. 23, Winter.

Kates, Steven. 1997. "On the True Meaning of Say's Law" *Eastern Economic Journal*, Vol. 23, No. 2.

Kates, Steven. 2007. "Mill, McCracken and the Modern Interpretation of Say's Law" *History of Economics Review*, Vol. 46, No. 1.

Kates, Steven. 2008. "A Letter from Keynes to Harlan McCracken dated 31st August 1933: Why the Standard Story on the Origins of the General Theory Needs to be Rewritten" *History of Economics Review*, Vol. 47, No. 1.

Kates, Steven. 2010. "Why Your Grandfather's Economics Was Better than Yours: On the Catastrophic Disappearance of Say's Law" *The Quarterly Journal of Austrian Economics*, Vol. 13, No. 4.

Keen, Steven. 2011. "Debunking Macroeconomics" *Economic Analysis and Policy*, Vol. 41, No. 3, December.

Keen, Steve. 2013. "A monetary Minsky Model of the Great Moderation and the Great Recession" *Journal of Economic Behavior & Organization*, Volume 86, February.

Kent, Richard J. 2005. "Keynes and Say's Law" *History of Economics Review*, Vol. 41, No. 1.

Khan, Aubhik; Robert G. King; Alexander L. Wolman. 2003. "Optimal Monetary Policy" *Review of Economic Studies*, Vol. 70, Issue 4.

King, Robert G., and Alexander Wolman. 1999. "What Should the Monetary Authority do when Prices are Sticky?" (in:) John Taylor (ed.). 1999. *Monetary Policy Rules.* NBER by the University of Chicago Press.

Kirzner, Israel. 1993. "The Pure Time-Preference Theory of Interest: An Attempt At Clarification" in Herbener, Jeffrey (ed.). 1993. *The Meaning of Ludwig von Mises. Contributions in Economics, Sociology, Epistemology, and Political Philosophy.* Norwell, MA: Kluwer Academic Publishers.

Kirzner, Israel. 1996. *Essays on Capital and Interest: An Austrian Perspective.* Brookfield, MA: Edward Elgar.

Klein, Benjamin. 1974. "The Competitive Supply of Money" *Journal of Money, Credit and Banking*, Vol. 6, Issue 4.

Klein, Philip A. 1988. "Changing Perspectives on the Factors of Production" *Journal of Economic Issues*, Vol. 22, No. 3.

Kleinman, E; and T. Ophir. 1966. "The Durability of Durable Goods" *The Review of Economic Studies*, Vol. 33, No. 2.

Kliesen, Kevin L. 2004. "Mind the Gap: Measuring Actual vs. Potential Output" Economic SYNOPSES. Short essays and reports on the economic issues of the day, Number 2, Federal Reserve St. Louis.

Knight, Frank. 1916. "Neglected Factors in the Problem of Normal Interest" *The Quarterly Journal of Economics*, Vol. 30, No. 2.

Knight, Frank H. 1931. "Professor Fisher's Interest Theory: A Case in Point" *Journal of Political Economy*, Vol. 39, No. 2.

Knight. Frank. 1934. "Capital, Time, and the Interest Rate" *Economica*, New Series, Vol. 1, No. 3.

Knight, Frank. 1935. "Professor Knight and the 'Period of Production': Comment" *Journal of Political Economy*, Vol. 43, No. 5.

Knight, Frank. 1935a. "The 'Period of Production': A Final Word" *Journal of Political Economy*, Vol. 43, No. 6.

Knight, Frank. 1935b. "The Theory of Investment Once More: Mr. Boulding and the Austrians" *The Quarterly Journal of Economics*, Vol. 50, No. 1.

Knight, Frank. 1935c. "Professor Hayek and the Theory of Investment" *The Economic Journal*, Vol. 45, No. 177.

Knight, Frank. 1935d. "The Ricardian Theory of Production and Distribution" *The Canadian Journal of Economics and Political Science / Revue canadienned'Economique et de Science Politique*, Vol. 1, No. 1.

Knight, Frank. 1936. "The Quantity of Capital and the Rate of Interest: I" *Journal of Political Economy*, Vol. 44, No. 4.

Knight, Frank. 1936a. "The Quantity of Capital and the Rate of Interest: II" *Journal of Political Economy*, Vol. 44, No. 5.

Knight, Frank. 1944. "Diminishing Returns from Investment" *Journal of Political Economy*, Vol. 52, No. 1.

Koo, Richard C. 2001. "The Japanese Economy in Balance Sheet Recession: THE REAL CULPRIT IS FALLACY OF COMPOSITION, NOT COMPLACENCY" *Business Economics*, Vol. 36, No. 2.

Koo, Richard C. 2010. "Lessons from Japan: Fighting a Balance Sheet Recession" lecture at CFA Institute Annual Conference; available at (09–10–2016): http://www.cfapubs.org/doi/pdf/10.2469/cp.v27.n4.4

Koo, Richard C. 2012. "Balance Sheet Recession as the Other-Half of Macroeconomics" Nomura Research Institute; available at (09–10–2016): http://www.boeckler.de/pdf/v_2012_10_25_koo.pdf

Koo, Richard C. 2014. "Balance Sheet Recession Is the Reason for Secular Stagnation" (in:) Coen Teulings and Richard Baldwin (ed.). 2014. *Secular Stagnation: Facts, Causes, and Cures*. London: Center for Economic Policy Research.

Koopmans, Tjalling C. 1960. "Stationary Ordinal Utility and Impatience" *Econometrica*, Vol. 28, No. 2.

Kornai, János. 1979. "Resource-Constrained versus Demand-Constrained Systems" *Econometrica*, Vol. 47, No. 4.

Krugman, Paul. 2012. "Bubbles and Economic Potential" (2016–09–16) blog post http://krugman.blogs.nytimes.com/2012/02/11/bubbles-and-economic-potential/

Kuenne, Robert. E. 1958. "On the Existence and Role of Money in a Stationary System" *Southern Economic Journal,* Vol. 25, No. 1.

Kurtz, Heinz D.; and Neri Salvadori. 2003. "'Classical' versus 'neoclassical' Theories of Value and Distribution and the Long-Period Method. (in:) Fabio Petri and Frank Hahn (ed.). 2003. *General Equilibrium. Problems and Prospects*. New York and London: Routledge.

Kuttner, Kenneth. 1992. "Monetary Policy with Uncertain Estimates of Potential Output" *Economic Perspectives*, Vol. 16, No. 1. Federal Reserve Bank of Chicago.

Kydland, Finn E.; Edward C. Prescott. 1982. "Time to Build and Aggregate Fluctuations" *Econometrica*, Vol. 50, No. 6.

Lachmann, Ludwig. 1947. "Complementarity and Substitution in the Theory of Capital" (in:) idem. 1977. *Capital, Expectations, and the Market Process. Essays on the Theory of the Market Economy*. Menlo Park: Institute for Humane Studies.

Lachmann, Ludwig. 1948. "Investment Repercussions" (in:) idem (edited by Don Lavoi). 1997. *Expectations and the Meaning of Institutions. Essays in economics by Ludwig Lachmann*. London and New York: Routledge.

Laffer, Arthur. 1980. *Reinstatement of the Dollar: The Blueprint*. Rolling Hill Estates, Cal.: A. B. Laffer Associates.

Lagos, Ricardo. 2006. "Inside and Outside Money" Federal Reserve Bank of Minneapolis, Research Department Staff Report 374.

Laibman, David; and Eward J. Nell. 1977. "Reswitching, Wicksell Effects, and the Neoclassical Production Function" *The American Economic Review*, Vol. 67, No. 5.

Lange, Oscar. 1942. "Say's Law: A Restatement and Criticism" (in:) John Cunningham Wood and Steven Kates (ed.). 2000. *Jean Baptiste Say. A Critical Assessment of Leading Economists*. London: Routledge.

Lavoie, Marc. 2014. *Post-Keynesian Economics: New Foundations*. Cheltenham: Edward Elgar.

Leijonhufvud, Axel. 1988. "Did Keynes Mean Anything? A Rejoiinder to Yeager" *Cato Journal*, Vol. 8, No. 1.

Levhari, David. 1965. "A Nonsubstitution Theorem and Switching of Techniques" *The Quarterly Journal of Economics*, Vol. 79, No. 1.

Lewin, Peter. 1997. "Murray Rothbard on Interest and Capital: An Exercise in Theoretical Purity" http://www.utdallas.edu/~plewin/ptpt.pdf (also printed in *Journal of the History of Economic Thought*).

Loutskina, Elena. 2011. "The Role of Securitization in Bank Liquidity and Funding Management "*Journal of Financial Economics*, Vol. 100, No. 3.

Lown, Cara S.; Donald P. Morgan. 2002. "Credit Effects in the Monetary Mechanism" *FRBNY Economic Policy Review*, May.

Lucas, Robert. 1972. "Expectations and the Neutrality of Money" *Journal of Economic Theory*, Vol. 4, Issue 2.

Lucas, Robert. 1976. "An Equilibrium Model of the Business Cycle" *Journal of Political Economy*, Vol. 83, No. 6.

Lucas, Robert. 1980. "Methods and Problems in Business Cycle Theory, *Journal of Money, Credit and Banking*, Vol. 12, No. 4, Part 2: Rational Expectations.

Luther, William J.; Lawrence H. White. 2011. "Positively Valued Fiat Money after the Sovereign Disappears: The Case of Somalia" GMU Working Paper; available at (10–16–2016): https://papers.ssrn.com/sol3/papers.cfm?abstract_id=1801563

Luther, William J.; Lawrence H. White. 2014. "Can Bitcoin Become a Major Currency?" GMU Working Paper in Economics No. 14–17; available at (10–16–2016): https://papers.ssrn.com/sol3/papers.cfm?abstract_id=2446604

Lydall, H. F. 1961. "Say's Law and Anti-Say's Law: The Danger of Closed Circuits" *Oxford Economic Papers*, New Series, Vol. 13, No. 1.

Machaj, Mateusz. 2015. "The Interest Rate and the Length of Production: An Attempt at Reformulation" *Quarterly Journal of Austrian Economics*, vol. 18, no. 3.

Machaj, Mateusz. 2016. "Can the Taylor Rule be a Good Guidance for Policy? The Case of 2001–2008 Real Estate Bubble" *Prague Economic Papers*, Vol. 25, No. 4.

Machlup, Fritz. 1935. "The 'Period of Production': A Further Word" *Journal of Political Economy*, Vol. 43, No. 6.

Manganelli, Simone; Guido Wolswijk. 2007. "Market Discipline, Financial Integration and Fiscal Rules: What Drives Spreads in the Euro Area Government Bond Market?" ECB Working Paper Series No. 745, April.

Mankiw, Gregory. 2006. "The Macroeconomist as Scientist and Engineer" *The Journal of Economic Perspectives*, Vol. 20, No. 4.

Meltzer, Allan. 1995. "Monetary, Credit and (Other) Transmission Processes: A Monetarist Perspective" *Journal of Economic Perspectives*, Vol. 9, No. 4.

Merton, R. C.; and Z. Bodie. 1993. "Deposit Insurance Reform: A Functional Approach" *Carnegie Rochester Conference Series on Public Policy* 38.
McCombie, John; and Maureen Pike. 2013. "No End to the Consensus in Macroeco-nomicTheory? A Methodological Inquiry" *American Journal of Economics and Sociology* Vol. 72, No. 2.
McGrattan, Ellen. 1997 "[The New Neoclassical Synthesis and the Role of Monetary Policy]: Comment" *NBER Macroeconomics Annual*, Vol. 12.
McLaughlin, Kenneth J. 1994. "Rigid wages?" *Journal of Monetary Economics*, Vol. 34, Issue 3.
Meh, Césaire; and Kevin Moran. 2008. "The Role of Bank Capital in the Propagation of Shocks" Bank of Canada Working Paper, 2008–36.
Menger, Carl. 1976. *Principles of Economics*. Grove City, PA: Libertarian Press.
Milgate, Murray. 1979. "On the Origin of the Notion of 'Intertemporal Equilibrium' *Economica*, New Series, Vol. 46, No. 181.
Minsky, Hyman. 1957. "Monetary Systems and Accelerator Models" in Minsky 2016.
Mnsky, Hyman. 1970. "Financial Instability Revisited: The Economics of Disaster" in Minsky 2016.
Minsky, Hyman. 1977. "The Financial Instability Hypothesis: An Interpretation of Keynes and an Alternative to 'Standard' Theory" (in:) Minsky 2016.
Minsky, Hyman. 1980. "Finance and Profits: The Changing Nature of American Business Cycles" in Minsky 2016.
Minsky, Hyman. 1980a. "Capitalist Financial Processes and the. Instability of Capi-talism" in Minsky 2016.
Minsky, Hyman. 2016. *Can "It" Happen Again? Essays on Instability and Finance*, London and New York: Routledge.
Miron, Jeffrey A.; Christina D. Romer; David N. Weil. 1993. "Historical Perspectives on the Monetary Transmission Mechanism" NBER Working Paper No. 4326.
Mises, Ludwig. 1966. *Human Action*. Chicago: Contemporary Books, Inc.
Mishan, E. J. 1963. "Say's Law and Walras' Law Once More" *The Quarterly Journal of Economics*, Vol. 77, No. 4.
Mishkin, Frederic S. 1995. "Symposium on the Monetary Transmission Mechanism" *Journal of Economic Perspectives*, Vol. 9, No. 4.
Mishkin, Frederic S. 1996. "The Channels of Monetary Transmission: Lessons for Monetary Policy" NBER Working Paper No. 5464, available at (03–10–2016): http://www.nber.org/papers/w5464
Mishkin, Frederic S. 2010. *The Economics of Money, Banking, and Financial Mar-kets*. Addison-Wesley.
Mitchell, Daniel J.B. 1985. "Wage Flexibility: Then and Now" *Industrial Relations. Journal of Economy and Society*, Vol. 24, No. 2.
Morgenstern, Oskar. 1935. "Perfect Foresight and Economic Equilibrium" (in:) Andrew Schotter (ed.). 1976. *Selected Economic Writings of Oscar Morgenstern*. New York: New York University Press.
Morrow, Mc Kieran' and Werner Roeger. 2001. "Potential Output: Measurement Methods, 'New' Economy Influences and Scenarios for 2001–2010. A Comparison of the EU15 and the US". *Economic Papers*, Number 150, European Commission.
Mosley, Layna. 2005. "Dropping Zeros, Gaining Credibility? Currency Redenomina-tion in Developing Nations". Paper presented at the 2005 Annual Meetings of the

American Political Science Association; available at (10–16–2016): https://www.unc.edu/~lmosley/APSA%202005.pdf

Mulligan, Robert F. 2013. "New Evidence on the Structure of Production: Real and Austrian Business Cycle Theory and the Financial Instability Hypothesis" *Journal of Economic Behavior & Organization*, Vol. 86, Issue C.

Mundell, Robert. 1997. "The International Monetary System in the 21st Century: Could Gold Make a Comeback?" Lecture delivered at St. Vincent College, Letrobe, Pennsylvania, March 12; available at (10–16–2016): http://www.columbia.edu/~ram15/LBE.htm

Murphy Robert P. 2003. *Unanticipated Intertemporal Change in Theories of Interest. Doctoral dissertation*. New York University.

Murphy Robert P. 2011. "Multiple Interest Rates and Austrian Business Cycle Theory" Working Paper (available at http://consultingbyrpm.com/uploads/Multiple%20Interest%20Rates%20and%20ABCT.pdf)

Nelson, Charles; and Charles Plosser. 1982. "Trends and Random Walks in Macroeconomic Time Series: Some EVIDENCE and implications" *Journal of Monetary Economics*, Vol. 10, Issue 2.

Neuberger, Egon. 1960. "Waiting and the Period of Production: Comment" *The Quarterly Journal of Economics*, Vol. 74, No. 1.

O'Discroll, Gerald P., Jr; and Mario J. Rizzo. 1996. *The Economics of Time and Ignorance*. London and New York: Routledge.

Okun, Arthur M. 1962. "Potential GDP: Its Measurement and Significance" American Statistical Association. Proceedings of the Business and Economics Statistics Section.

Orphanides, Athanasios; and Simon van Norden. 2002. "The Unreliability of Output-Gap Estimates in Real Time" *The Review of Economics and Statistics*, Vol. 84, No. 4.

Pasinetti, Luigi L. 1966. "Changes in the Rate of Profit and Switches of Techniques" *The Quarterly Journal of Economics*, Vol. 80, No. 4.

Pasinetti, Luigi L. 1969. "Switches of Technique and the 'Rate of Return' in Capital Theory" *The Economic Journal*, Vol. 79, No. 315.

Pasinetti, Luigi. L. 1978. "Wicksell Effects and Reswitchings of Technique in Capital Theory" *The Scandinavian Journal of Economics*, Vol. 80, No. 2, The Arne Ryde Symposium on the Theoretical Contributions of Knut Wicksell.

Patinkin, Don. 1948. "Relative Prices, Say's Law, and the Demand for Money" *Econometrica*, Vol. 16, No. 2.

Patinkin, Don. 1973. "In Search of the 'Wheel of Wealth': On the Origins of Frank Knight's Circular-Flow Diagram" *The American Economic Review*, Vol. 63, No. 5.

Phelps Brown, E. H. 1957. "The Meaning of the Fitted Cobb-Douglas Function" *The Quarterly Journal of Economics*, Vol. 71, No. 4.

Plosser, Charles I; and William G. Schwert. 1979. "Potential GNP: Its Measurement and Significance: A Dissenting Opinion" *Journal of Monetary Economics*, Spring.

Polleit, Thornstein. 2015. "Hayek's 'Denationalization of Money' – a Praxeological Reassessment" *Journal of Prices and Markets*, vol. 5, No. 1.

Pressman, Steven. 2005. "What Is Wrong with the Aggregate Production Function?" *Eastern Economic Journal*, Vol. 31, No. 3.

Prychitko, David L. 2010. "Competing Explanations of the Minsky Moment: The Financial Instability Hypothesis in Light of Austrian Theory" *Review of Austrian Economics*, Vol. 23, Issue 3.

Rajan, Raghuram G. 2006. "Has Finance Made the World Riskier?" *European Financial Management*, Vol. 12, No. 4.

Reati, Angelo. 1986. "The Rate of Profit and the Organic Composition of Capital in the Post-1945 Long Wave: The Case of British Industry from 1959 to 1981" *Review* (Fernand Braudel Center), Vol. 9, No. 4.

Ritter, Joseph. 1995. "The Transition from Barter to Fiat Money" *The American Economic Review*, Vol. 85, No. 1.

Robinson, Joan. 1953–54. "The Production Function and the Theory of Capital" *The Review of Economic Studies*, Vol. 21, No. 2.

Robinson, Joan. 1955. "The Production Function" *The Economic Journal*, Vol. 65, No. 257.

Robinson, Joan. 1959. "Some Problems of Definition and Measurement of Capital" *Oxford Economic Papers*, New Series, Vol. 11, No. 2.

Robinson, Joan. 1964. "Solow on the Rate of Return" *The Economic Journal*, Vol. 74, No. 294.

Robinson, Joan. 1967. "Marginal Productivity" *Indian Economic Review*, New Series, Vol. 2, No. 1.

Robinson, Joan. 1971. "The Measure of Capital: The End of the Controversy" *The Economic Journal*, Vol. 81, No. 323.

Robinson, Joan. 1975. "The Unimportance of Reswitching" *The Quarterly Journal of Economics*, Vol. 89, No. 1.

Romer, Christina D.; David H. Romer. 1991. "New Evidence on the Monetary Transmission Mechanism" NBER Working Paper No. R1500.

Romer, David. 1993. "The New Keynesian Synthesis" *The Journal of Economic Perspectives*, Vol. 7, No. 1.

Rotemberg, Julio J. 2002. "Stochastic Technical Progress, Nearly Smooth Trends and Distinct Business Cycles" NBER Working Paper 8919, available at (09–20–2016): http://www.nber.org/papers/w8919.pdf

Rothbard, Murray N. 1991. *The Case for a 100 Percent Gold Dollar*. Auburn, Al: Mises Institute.

Rothbard, Murray N. 1995. *Classical Economics: An Austrian Perspective on the History of Economic Thought. Brookfield.* VT: Edward Elgar Publishing Company.

Rothbard, Murray N. 1995a. *Economic Thought before Adam Smith*. Brookfield, VT: Edward Elgar Publishing Company.

Rothbard, Murray. 2000. *America's Great Depression*. Auburn: Ludwig von Mises Institute.

Rothbard, Murray. 2004. *Man, Economy, and State with Power and Market*. Auburn: Ludwig von Mises Institute.

Rothbard, Murray. 2008. M*ystery of Banking*. Auburn, Al: Ludwig von Mises Institute.

Ryding, John. 1990. "Housing Finance and the Transmission of Monetary Policy" *Quarterly Review*, Summer.

Salerno, Joseph. 1983. "Gold Standards: True and False" *Cato Journal: An Interdisciplinary Journal of Public Policy Analysis*, Vol. 3, No. 1.

Salerno, Joseph. 1987. "The 'True' Money Supply: A Measure of the Supply of the Medium of Exchange in the U.S. Economy" (in:) Joseph Salerno. 2010. *Money, Sound and Unsound.* Auburn, Al: Ludwig von Mises Institute.

Salerno, Joseph. 1991. "The Concept of Coordination in Austrian Macroeconomics" (in:) Joseph Salerno. 2010. *Money, Sound and Unsound.* Auburn: Ludwig von Mises Institute.

Salerno, Joseph. 2001. "Does the Concept of Secular Growth Have a Place in Capital-Based Macroeconomics?" *Quarterly Journal of Austrian Economics*, Vol. 4, No. 3.

Salerno, Joseph. 2003. "An Austrian Taxonomy of Deflation – with Applications to the U.S" in Salerno 2010.

Salerno, Joseph. 2006. "A Simple Model of the Theory of Money Prices" in Salerno 2010.

Salerno, Joseph. 2012. "A Reformulation of Austrian Business Cycle Theory in Light of the Financial Crisis" *Quarterly Journal of Austrian Economics*, Vol. 17, No. 1.

Samuelson, Paul. A. 1962. "Parable and Realism in Capital Theory: The Surrogate Production Function" *The Review of Economic Studies*, Vol. 29, No. 3.

Samuelson, Paul. 1966. "A Summing Up". *Quarterly Journal of Economics*, Vol. 80, No. 4.

Samuelson, Paul. A. 1979. "Paul Douglas's Measurement of Production Functions and Marginal Productivities" *Journal of Political Economy*, Vol. 87, No. 5.

Samuelson, Paul A. 1997. "Credo of a Lucky Textbook Author" *The Journal of Economic Perspectives*, Vol. 11, No. 2.

Samuelson, Paul A; William H. Nordhaus. 2010. *Economics*. New York: McGraw-Hill.

Sanders, Frederic W. 1896. "The Natural Basis of Interest" *Journal of Political Economy,* Vol. 4, No. 4.

Say, Jean Baptiste. 1971. *A Treatise on Political Economy*. New York: Augustus M. Kelley Publishers.

Scazzieri, Roberto. 1990. "Vertical Integration in Economic Theory" *Journal of Post Keynesian Economics*, Vol. 13, No. 1.

Schachter, Gustav. 1991. "Francois Quesnay: Interpreters and Critics Revisited" *The American Journal of Economics and Sociology*, Vol. 50, No. 3.

Schmitt-Grohe, Stephanie; and Martin Uribe. 2004. "Optimal Fiscal and Monetary Policy under Sticky Prices" *Journal of Economic Theory*, Vol. 114.

Schumpeter, Joseph. 1954. *History of Economic Analysis*. Oxford: Oxford University Press.

Sechrest, Larry. 1993. "Free Banking: Theory, History, and a Laissez-Faire Model". Westport, C.T.: Greenwood Publishing Group, Inc.

Sechrest, Larry. 2006. "Explaining Malinvestment and Overinvestment" *Quarterly Journal of Austrian Economics*, Vol. 9, No. 4.

Sekine, Thomas T. 1981. "The Circular Motion of Capital" *Science & Society*, Vol. 45, No. 3.

Selgin, George A. 1987. "The Stability and Efficiency of Money Supply under Free Banking" *Journal of Institutional and Theoretical Economics*, Vol. 143, No. 3.

Selgin, George A. 1988. *The Theory of Free Banking: Money Supply under Competitive Note Issue*. Totowa, N.J.: Rowman and Littlefield.

Selgin, George. 2000. "Should We Let Banks Create Money?" *The Independent Review*, Vol. 5, No. 1.

Selgin, George. 2014. *Bitcoin: Problems and Prospects*. A lecture given at Hillsdale University; available at https://www.hillsdale.edu/wp-content/uploads/2016/02/FMF-2014-Bitcoin-Problems-and-Prospects.pdf

Selgin, George A.; Lawrence H. White. 1994. "How Would the Invisible Hand Handle Money?" *Journal of Economic Literature*, Vol. 32, No. 4.

Selgin, George; and Lawrence H. White. 1996. "In Defense of Fiduciary Media—Or, We Are Not Devo(lutionists), We Are Misesians!" *The Review of Austrian Economics*, Vol. 9, Issue 2.

Selgin, George; William D. Lastrapes; and Lawrence H. White. 2012. "Has the Fed Been a Failure?" *Journal of Macroeconomics*, Vol. 34, Issue 3.

Sen, Amartya. 1974. "On Some Debates in Capital Theory" *Economica*, New Series, Vol. 41, No. 163.

Shaikh, Anwar. 2005. "Nonlinear Dynamics and Pseudo-Production Functions" *Eastern Economic Journal*, Vol. 31, No. 3.

Shoul, Bernice. 1957. "Karl Marx and Say's Law" *The Quarterly Journal of Economics*, Vol. 71, No. 4.

Sieroń, Arkadiusz. 2015. "Disaggregating the Credit Expansion: The Role of Changes in Banks' Asset Structure in the Business Cycle". *Quarterly Journal of Austrian Economics*, Vol. 18, No. 3.

Skinner, A. S. 1967. "Say's Law: Origins and Content" *Economica*, New Series, Vol. 34, No. 134.

Skousen, Mark. 1988. *The Economics of a Pure Gold Standard*. New York: Foundation for Economic Education.

Skousen, Mark. 1990. *The Structure of Production*. New York: New York University Press.

Snowdon, Brian; and Howard R. Vave. *Modern Macroeconomics. Its Origins, Development and Current State*. Cheltenham: Edward Elgar.

Solow, Robert M. 1955–1956. "The Production Function and the Theory of Capital" *The Review of Economic Studies*, Vol. 23, No. 2.

Solow, Robert. 2010. "Building a Science of Economics for the Real World" Prepared Statement: House Committee on Science and Technology. Subcommittee on Investigations and Oversight, available at (09–21–2016): https://web.archive.org/web/20110204034313/http://democrats.science.house.gov/Media/file/Commdocs/hearings/2010/Oversight/20july/Solow_Testimony.pdf

Somers, Harold M. 1941. "Monetary Policy and the Theory of Interest" *The Quarterly Journal of Economics*, Vol. 55, No. 3.

Spengler, Joseph J. 1945. "The Physiocrats and Say's Law of Markets" *Journal of Political Economy*, Vol. 53, No. 3.

Sraffa, Piero. 1960. *Production of Commodities by Means of Commodities*. Cambridge: Cambridge University Press.

St-Amant, Pierre; and Simon van Norder. 1997. "Measurement of the Output Gap: A Discussion of Recent Research at the Bank of Canada" Technical Report No. 79 / Rapport technique no 79.

Stein, Jeremy C. 1998. "An Adverse-Selection Model of Bank Asset and Liability Management with Implications for the Transmission of Monetary Policy" *The RAND Journal of Economics*, Vol. 29, No. 3.

Stiglitz, Joseph. 1974. "The Cambridge-Cambridge Controversy in the Theory of Capital; A View from New Haven: A Review Article" *Journal of Political Economy,* Vol. 82, No. 4.

Storper, Michael. 1989. "The Transition to Flexible Specialisation in the US Film Industry: External Economies, the Division of Labour, and the Crossing of Industrial Divides" *Cambridge Journal of Economics*, Vol. 13, No. 2.

Strigl, Richard. 2000. *Capital and Production*. Auburn, Al: Ludwig von Mises Institute.

Swaney, James A. 1985. "Economics, Ecology, and Entropy" *Journal of Economic Issues*, Vol. 19, No. 4.

Swann, Trevor. 1956. "Economic Growth and Capital Accumulation" *Economic Record*, Vol. 32, No. 2.

Takáts, Előd; and Abraham Vela. 2014. "International Monetary Policy Transmission" BIS Papers No. 78: The Transmission of Unconventional Monetary Policy to the Emerging Markets.

Taub, Bart. 1985. "Private Fiat Money with Many Suppliers" *Journal of Monetary Economics*, Vol. 16, Issue 2.

Taussig, F. W. 1908. "Capital, Interest, and Diminishing Returns" *The Quarterly Journal of Economics*, Vol. 22, No. 3.

Taylor, J. B. 1980. "Aggregate Dynamics and Staggered Contracts" *Journal of Political Economy*, Vol. 88.

Taylor, J. B. 1994. "The Monetary Transmission Mechanism: An Empirical Framework" *Journal of Economic Perspectives,* Vol. 9, No. 4.

Taylor, John. B. 2000. "Teaching Modern Macroeconomics at the Principles Level" *The American Economic Review*, Vol. 90, No. 2, Papers and Proceedings of the One Hundred Twelfth Annual Meeting of the American Economic Association.

Taylor, John B. 2007. "Housing and Monetary Policy" NBER Working Paper Series 13682; available at (06–10–2016): www.nber.org/papers/w13682.pdf

Thornton, Mark. 2005. "Skyscrapers and Business Cycle" *Quarterly Journal of Austrian Economics*, Vol. 8, No. 1.

Thornton, Mark. 2006. "Cantillon on the Cause of the Business Cycle" *Quarterly Journal of Austrian Economics*, Vol. 9, No. 3.

Thweatt, William O. 1980. "Baumol and James Mill on 'Say's' Law of Markets" *Economica*, New Series, Vol. 47, No. 188.

Tobin, James. 1969. "A General Equilibrium Approach to Monetary Theory" *Journal of Money, Credit and Banking*, Vol. 1, No. 1.

Tobin, James. 1985. "Financial Innovation and Deregulation in Perspective" *Bank of Japan Monetary and Economic Studies* 3.

Tsiang, S. C. 1966. "Walras' Law, Say's Law and Liquidity Preference in General Equilibrium Analysis" *International Economic Review*, Vol. 7, No. 3.

Tymoigne, Éric. 2009. *Central Banking, Asset Prices, and Financial Fragility*. London and New York: Routledge.

Van Allen, Laurel Cameron. 2001. *Say's Law and Modern Macroeconomics.* A Senior Honors Thesis at Texas A&M University.

Van den Hauwe, Ludwig. 2014. "Understanding Financial Instability: Minsky Versus the Austrians" Working Paper; available at (06–10–2016): http://papers.ssrn.com/sol3/papers.cfm?abstract_id=2539839

Van den Heuvel, Skander J. 2002. "Does Bank Capital Matter for Monetary Transition?" *FRBNY Economic Policy Review*, May.

Walker, Francis A. 1892. "Dr. Böhm-Bawerk's Theory of Interest" *The Quarterly Journal of Economics*, Vol. 6, No. 4.

Wanniski, Jude. 1978. *The Way the World Works*. New York: Simon and Schuster.

Warburton, Clark. 1928. "Economic Terminology: Factors of Production and Distributive Shares" *The American Economic Review*, Vol. 18, No. 1.

Watkins, G.P. 1928. "Parity in the Exchange of Future Money and Future Commodities" *The Quarterly Journal of Economics,* Vol. 42, No. 3.

Weston, J. Fred. 1951. "Some Perspectives on Capital Theory" *The American Economic Review*, Vol. 41, No. 2, Papers and Proceedings of the Sixty-third Annual Meeting of the American Economic Association.

White, Lawrence H. 1984. *Free Banking in Britain: Theory, Experience and Debate, 1800–1845*. London and New York: Cambridge University Press.

White, Lawrence H. 1989. *Competition and Currency: Essays on Free Banking and Money*. New York: New York University Press.

White, Lawrence H. 2005. "The Federal Reserve System's Influence on Research in Monetary Economics" *Econ Journal Watch*, Vol. 2, No. 2.

White, Lawrence H. 2010. "Skepticism About Minsky's Financial Instability Hypothesis: A Comment on Flanders" *Econ Journal Watch*, Vol. 12, No. 1.

Wicksell, Knut. 1962. *Interest and Prices*. New York: Sentry Press.

Woodford, Michael. 2009. "Convergence in Macroeconomics: Elements of the New Synthesis" *American Economic Journal: Macroeconomics*, Vol. 1, No. 1.

Wray, Randall L. 1991. "Saving, Profits, and Speculation in Capitalist Economies" *Journal of Economic Issues*, Vol. 25, No. 4.

Wright, J. F. 1975. "The Dynamics of Reswitching" *Oxford Economic Papers*, New Series, Vol. 27, No. 1.

Xu, Bin; Sohail S. Chaudhry; and Yanfang Li. 2009. "Factors of Production: Historical Theories and New Developments" *Systems Research and Behavioral Science* 26. Research note.

Yermack, David. 2013. "Is Bitcoin a Real Currency? An Economic Appraisal" NBER Working Paper No. 19747; available (12–12–2016) at http://www.nber.org/papers/w19747

Young, Warren; Robert Leeson; William Darity Jr. 2004. *Economics, Economists and Expectations: From Microfoundations to Macroapplications*. New York and London: Routledge.

Yeager, Leland. 1976. "Towards Understanding Some Paradoxes in Capital Theory" *Economic Inquiry*, Vol. XIV, No. 3.

Yeager, Leland. 1979. "Capital Paradoxes and the Concept of Waiting" (in:) Mario Rizzo(ed.) *Time, Uncertainty, and Disequilibrium*. Lexington, Massachusetts: Lexington Books.

Zhou, Chungsheng. 2000. "Time-to-Build and Investment" *The Review of Economics and Statistics*, Vol. 82, No. 2.

Zimmerman, Guido. 2003. "Optimal Monetary Policy: A New Keynesian View" *Quarterly Journal of Austrian Economics*, Vol. 6, No. 4.

Žídek, Libor; Michal Chribik. 2015. "Impact of Currency Redenomination on Inflation Case Study Turkey". *Asian Economic and Financial Review*, Vo. 5, No. 6.

Index

About the Author

Mateusz Machaj is an assistant professor at the Institute of Economic Sciences, the University of Wroclaw and a research fellow at the Faculty of Social and Economic Studies, Jan Evangelista Purkyne University in Usti nad Labem. He defended his Ph.D. thesis in economics on the market socialism model. He has authored academic articles, which (among others) appeared in *Critical Review, American Journal of Economics and Sociology, Econ Journal Watch, Prague Economic Papers,* and *Quarterly Journal of Austrian Economics.*

www.ingramcontent.com/pod-product-compliance
Ingram Content Group UK Ltd.
Pitfield, Milton Keynes, MK11 3LW, UK
UKHW012039150926
475560UK00001B/91

9 781498 557542